A Place Apart

Contents

Frontispiece: ROZ IN BELFAST. *Photo: Stanley Matchett*

A Place Apart

DERVLA MURPHY

I have yet to see any problem,
however complicated, which when
you looked at it the right way did
not become still more complicated.
PAUL ANDERSON

The Devin-Adair Company
Old Greenwich

Printed in Great Britain

ISBN 0–8159–6516–8

*To the Northern Irish
who made me so welcome
and taught me so much*

Glossary

B SPECIALS—an armed auxiliary police force, once the paramilitary wing of the Orange Order but now disbanded by order of the British Government

CUMANN (Gaelic)—clubs

DAIL—the Irish Parliament

DAIL ULADH—an imaginary Ulster Parliament envisaged by the IRA

FENIANS—Protestant term of contempt for Republicans

IRA—Irish Republican Army

IRSP—Irish Republican Socialist Party, a breakaway group of Official IRA also known as the Irps

NICRA—Northern Ireland Civil Rights Association

NILP—Northern Ireland Labour party

NO-GO AREA—district too dangerous for the police to enter

OFFICIAL SINN FEIN—Political wing of the Official IRA

ORANGE ORDER—A Protestant semi-secret society founded in the 1790s

ORANGES—Catholic term of contempt for Protestants

PIONEER—member of a Roman Catholic total abstinence group

PROVISIONAL SINN FEIN—political wing of the Provisional IRA

PROVOS—Provisional IRA

RUC—Royal Ulster Constabulary

SDLP—Social Democratic Labour Party

STICKIES—Official (Marxist) IRA

STREEL—slut

TAIGS—Protestant term of contempt for Catholics

TD—Member of the Irish Parliament

UDA—Ulster Defence Association (legal Protestant Parliamentary organisation)

UDR—Ulster Defence Regiment (a regular regiment of the British Army recruited in Northern Ireland)

UFF—Ulster Freedom Fighters (illegal Protestant Parliamentary organisation)

UNA—United Nations Association

UVF—Ulster Volunteer Force (illegal Protestant paramilitary organisation)

WAINS—wee ones, used of children

Foreword

Before June 1976 I had spent in Northern Ireland precisely thirty-six hours out of forty-four years. My one crossing of the border, in September 1973, was to give a talk in Enniskillen; and as soon as possible I was on my way home having felt no urge to stand and stare. To me, in County Waterford, Northern Ireland was merely a squalid little briar-patch swarming with human anachronisms—who often seemed sub-human—and seething with dreary dissensions punctuated by ghastly excesses. Since there seemed to be nothing anybody could do about it, it was best forgotten. So I went to South India that winter, and to Baltistan the following winter, and wherever I went people asked me why Christians were fighting in Ireland. To which I replied impatiently that I didn't know myself. It never occurred to me that this reply, from an Irishwoman, betrayed an attitude both stupid and unkind; even, some might say, irresponsible.

In the Spring of 1976, after listening to two of the more bone-headed Northern politicians arguing on the wireless one evening, I was appalled to hear myself saying viciously, "Why don't the Brits get out and let them all slaughter each other if that's how they feel? There's nothing to choose between them. Why did we ever long for a united Ireland?" It was then that this book was conceived, by shame out of repentance. It is not a study of history, politics, theology, geography, sociology, economics or guerrilla warfare. It is simply an honest portrayal of emotions—my own and other people's—and an attempt to find the sources of those emotions. At one stage I had hoped to be able to clarify the present Northern Irish turmoil for the ordinary citizens of Britain and the Republic. But the more time I spent up North the less capable I felt of doing any such thing.

In Ireland, during recent years, many Southerners have been

voicing anti-Northern sentiments with increasing vehemence and frequency. Some such outbursts may be excused on the grounds of frustration and despair but most, I fear, are symptoms of a spreading infection. To me it seems unlikely that the North's physical violence will ever overflow seriously into the South, yet this is a tiny island and gradually the emotional violence 'up there' has affected the atmosphere 'down here'. Moreover, because the Provisional IRA hope one day to be free to transfer their attentions to the Republic, many—less optimistic than myself—feel threatened by the Northern chaos. And the maggots of bigotry breed so fast on fear that we may soon see a new form of intolerance in Ireland, between Southern and Northern Catholics.

It is ironical (or do I mean comical?) that so many in the Republic are so thankful now that Westminster rather than Dublin is responsible for Northern Ireland. And it seems odd that, despite decades of political bombast and emotional white-heats about a united Ireland, so few of us have ever crossed the border or taken a normal neighbourly interest in our Northern fellow-countrymen. It is true, sadly, that there is nothing tangible we in the South can do. But the intangible also counts. Why should we not travel in the North to express a concerned interest in the people there and to see for ourselves what really goes on, as distinct from what the media choose to tell us? When I urge my friends to holiday in Northern Ireland they look at me as though I were delirious. Yet it is an entirely sensible suggestion, from every point of view. Visitors from the South would find books, beer and butter cheaper than at home. And they would find the people as welcoming, the scenery as good, the roads better and the weather no worse.

Having cycled hundreds of miles through superb countryside, and into (and safely out of) dozens of small towns and villages, I feel no hesitation about recommending the rural North of Ireland as a holiday area for families of any nationality. During July and August I was accompanied by my seven-year-old daughter, Rachel, who rode her pony, Scamp, for more than 300 miles while I cycled ahead and her elkhound, Olaf, trotted along behind. We camped out in a tiny tent in the counties of Fermanagh, Tyrone, Londonderry and Donegal and spent one night in a field bisected by the border. While we slept in Northern Ireland Scamp grazed in the Republic. It was not a bit like what you read in the papers.

However, these were not my sentiments as I cycled North in early June from my tranquil home in the far South. I then experienced, at intervals, sick little spasms of fear. Even those of us who cherish our independence of thought can no longer protect our emotions from the influence of the media; though we may continue to think for ourselves, our feelings are all the time being manipulated. Also, for weeks my local friends (perfectly sensible people, most of them) had been begging me to 'forget Ulster'—which naturally increased both my determination to go and my nervousness. Never before had I embarked on a journey that required courage.

* * *

The difficulties involved in writing about Northern Ireland at this time will be apparent to every reader. In a situation that has developed out of centuries of fear, distrust, resentment and contempt, the enquiring outsider is given an enormous amount of biassed misinformation. I discarded as 'likely to be inaccurate' at least 75 per cent of the 'facts' I collected. But this does not mean that my collection was worthless; the manner in which facts are consciously or unconsciously distorted, and the reasons why they are distorted, can be very illuminating.

Another difficulty concerns the identification of individuals: I have felt bound to disguise the identity of all those to whom I talked. Several people have been killed in Northern Ireland because of journalistic indiscretions. In one case a New York newspaper named a certain pub as the area headquarters of a paramilitary group and as a direct result that pub was blown up and three lives were lost.

Again for security reasons, I cannot acknowledge in the usual way the generous help and hospitality I received from so many people in Northern Ireland—of every sort and condition. Without their guidance I could never have begun to understand Northern society. But to mention names would be tactless as well as dangerous since *all* my Northern friends would wish not to be associated with *some* of my views. However, I can at least acknowledge the support of a Southern friend, Joyce Green, without whose faith in this book it might never have been begun and would certainly not have been finished.

I

Jottings on the Way

Fethard. 6 June

This morning I felt a mild pang as I said good-bye to Rachel. But it was soon counteracted by the joy of being again wheel-loose on Roz,* free and alone. We crossed the Knockmealdown Mountains on a narrow road with a spine of grass—no traffic for two hours. There was a stiff southerly breeze, a hot sun and a few wispy clouds high in the blue. New, through-the-looking-glass signposts made my destination seem more distant the farther I cycled. Perhaps some poetical County Council worker was so overcome by the glorious landscape that he got them muddled. The countryside was laden with June riches: fox-gloves, forget-me-nots, loosestrife, Queen Anne's Lace, honey-suckle, dog-roses, cow-parsley, mustard, may-blossom. Tall white bells and tiny white stars shone in the deep grass of the verges; bluebells were still thick in mixed woods of beech, pine, hazel and ash; boulder-strewn expanses of brilliant turf were scattered with minute pink flowers. One solitary rounded hil-lock was all covered in gorse, violently yellow against the blue, its nutty scent heavy on the warm air. Why do people *leave* Ire-land for their holidays?

Then steeply down to the wide lushness of Tipperary. For miles, as I free-wheeled, dense seven-foot fuchsia hedges rose on either side like walls draped in red velvet. On the plain I passed groups of venerable chestnut trees pinkly in flower, and an old grey handsome house with valerian bursting from every crack in its rough surrounding wall. The narrow road meandered between tangled hedges fifteen feet high—and long may they remain so! One can always stop by a gateway to look at the view.

* My bicycle, on which I cycled to India in 1963. Since being flown back to Europe in 1964 she has covered many thousands of miles but has needed only a new saddle and a new chain.

I paused for a pint in Clonmel. The sleazy plastic Lounge
Bar had a vomit-green carpet and purple curtains with canary
blotches. How is it that the race bred in this lovely country has
never developed a sense of visual beauty? Or aural, for that
matter. Everywhere one has to endure the vile piped music of
RTE sponsored programmes. At present pseudo-risqué songs
seem very popular. No witty lewdness—just awful sniggering
vulgarity. This is sexual liberation in Ireland.

The next pint-pause was better. A dark little village pub with
hard wooden seats, a dirty tiled floor and no plastic nonsense.
Three men were drinking slowly at 3.30, looking as if they grew
there and sounding preternaturally knowledgeable about
horses and cynical about politicians. Referring to the death of
a local TD one said—"They'll put the wida back in because
of he dyin' on her".

The publican remarked casually that his sister left for
Lourdes yesterday. A lanky middle-aged man with a thin red
face and small, very blue eyes looked impressed, as he was
meant to do. "You'd want a fierce amounta cash goin' out to
them places these times. Th'oul pound's worth nathin' no
more." English writers who report such turns of speech are
sometimes wrongly accused of stage Irishry.

I steered the talk towards the Northern problem and the
lanky man said vehemently, "God forbid 'twill ever come our
way! 'Twould be a shame to lay a finger on a Protestant an'
they such decent people—the best we have. And the most o'
them is leadin' wicked lonely lives these times, with not the half
of what they were used to. And all the same they're the ones
that pays their bills and gives the employment. Terrible honest,
so they are."

The publican agreed, adding, "Sure we'd never have a civil
war down here anyway. For who'd be fightin' over what?" But
a sallow little man—standing in his socks beside sweaty Well-
ingtons—looked up from *The Irish Press* to say, "Have sinse,
Larry! You could always raise a gang for fightin' an' burnin'—
even here an' now." True, no doubt. Almost anywhere
in the world a gang could be raised to do almost anything.

I am interested in this new mixture of shrewdness and faint
condescension in rural Irish attitudes towards the remnants of

the Ascendency. No more forelock pulling and no more resentment. People feel very secure when their community forms 95 per cent of the population. The average Protestant still has a far bigger farm than the average Catholic but it doesn't matter now. Most Irish countrymen are not envious by nature if they have enough to keep going and they are not yet much troubled by socialism. It seems natural to them that the gentry, whatever their religion, should have bigger farms and better houses.

Ballymackey. 7 June

This evening I am asking myself why I have been so determined to go North? Partly, I suppose, because of the challenge to my philosophy of travel. (Only discovered I had one lately, when being interviewed by a fatuous television 'personality'.) I've always found people trustworthy if you trust them and why shouldn't this apply in the North? As well, there is the opportunity for once to do something genuinely brave. It's quite a relief to be what I'm supposed to be, after years of feeling a phoney. Odd to fear the known rather than the unknown. Though in a way it's more the unknown *here*, or at least the unpredictable and incomprehensible. One can accept fanaticism as part of the Meshed way of life, or murderous *shifta* as part of the Ethiopian way of life—but not sectarian assassinations as part of one's own way of life. Of course there must still be many aspects of Northern Ireland to be enjoyed, apart from the horrors—or maybe they can't be 'apart from' but anyway *as well as*. And I want to find them. We like now to take the attitude 'They're impossible'. But are they any more so than ourselves? Or are we just more subtle in our manifestations of intolerance? Yesterday as I crossed the mountains I remembered my patriotic ecstasy when I made a pilgrimage along that road, at the age of seventeen, to the Liam Lynch* memorial. I seem a different person now. And Ireland seems a different country. It would need to be. I never realised then how close I was to the Treaty—born only ten years after it. And brought up in the shadow (and occasionally on the lap) of Dev, where everything seemed so black-and-white and tidy

* Leader of the Cork No. 2 Brigade of the Old IRA.

around the edges. Fed on fake history: all the Irish were heroes/
saints/martyrs, all the English were robbers/murderers/tyrants.
But happily that was counteracted by Eng. Lit. One can't grow
up on a country's literature and hate that country. Maybe
that's part of the long-term answer to the Northern Problem:
expose the Catholics to Eng. Lit. and the Protestants to Gaelic
Lit. But no one would listen to me if I said so.

Cavan. 8 June

There was a strong tail wind and much cloud when I left
Ballymackey at 6.30 a.m. Then heavy cold rain drenched me
to the skin. At Egan's Hotel in Birr a large pot of tea, a piled
plate of home-made brown bread and lavish butter and mar-
malade were served beside a bright fire for thirty pence. A
tubby, elderly priest reading *The Irish Independent* across the
hearth thought me mad to be going North—"Keep away from
Paisley's lot, with your accent." It was impossible to get him
to express any opinion about The Troubles, apart from his feeling that their location is best avoided. He was not being evasive,
I think, just feeling bewildered and bored by it all.

I pedalled on towards Athlone through slashing rain across
brown miles of harvested bog—looking like a child's dream of
a world made of chocolate. Beyond Athlone the sun came out
and I was in Goldsmith country where one is more aware of
the *sky* than of the green undulating, tree-fringed landscape.
An immense melancholy sky—grey and black and silver today,
shifting ever before the wind and often lowering to drench me
again. Despite this being a main road there was little traffic.
The visible locals were few and not very friendly. Many of the
men looked moronic or sinister—sometimes both. A curious
and unexpected impression. Doubtless they would prove to be
neither if one got to know them. All afternoon I seemed to feel
an extraordinary brooding watchfulness over the landscape, a
stillness and silence that was pensive rather than peaceful. And
the little towns had a dispirited air about them. Stopping in
Ballymahon, to picnic in an empty pub during heavy rain, my
pint was pulled by a fourteen-year-old girl proud of her new
dentures. "*Ten* of me own had to come out! The dentist thought
mebbe I'd been eatin' too many sweets, like." Her small brother

came to sit beside me, sucking something puce and repulsive on the end of a stick.

As one goes farther north the farmhouses look more neglected, the cars more battered, the land poorer. Several small hand-painted signs were lurking in thick hedges where no motorist could possibly see them: 'Danger! Cows Wandering On Road!' So unlike the brisk 'Cows Crossing' of more with-it areas. Do these cows need the long acre? Or had it simply not occurred to anybody to eliminate the danger by mending a fence instead of painting a sign? Near here cows were being milked into buckets in the fields. My own part of Ireland was like this forty years ago.

In Granard the Mart was just closing. The pub—one of many—was full of foul-mouthed farmers, some very drunk. Pulling my pint, the young woman behind the bar called, 'Mind yer langwidge, now! There's a lady present!' Whereupon a weatherbeaten old man beside the door—holding a wad of bank-notes in one hand and a double whiskey in the other—replied swiftly, "I don't see no lady here, on'y a tough woman in throusers!"

At 7.0 pm all Cavan's B. and B.s were full. I felt disinclined to go farther, after cycling 104 miles, so I am now in the allegedly posh Farnham Arms Hotel. And I am moved to wonder—would our tourist figures be declining even without The Troubles? Peeling paint everywhere, filthy smears on my bedroom wall, no bedside lamp, no hot water. Personally I don't want hot water in June but many people paying £4.75 for a tiny room might expect it. The receptionist tells me that The Troubles have hit the tourist trade so hard nobody could be expected to keep up such a place. But at least they could keep it clean.

In the huge lounge-bar a sofa cushion has been ripped across, apparently with a knife. Its foam-rubber guts look like cold porridge. The only other drinkers this evening were two silent German anglers, gloomily considering their beer, and a talkative young mining engineer just home after two years in Canada. He pointed to an anti-contraceptive letter in his *Irish Times*. "Why are they *still* going on about it? If you ask me it's all to take our attention off inflation." I know exactly how he feels.

It's hard to believe—especially after a period abroad—that in Ireland we are still arguing about legalising the sale of contraceptives. I remember arriving home from Baltistan last year and feeling that I'd come from the Third World to some dotty Fourth World consisting only of Ireland.

It seems strange to be keeping a diary about travels in Ireland. A vague little sadness follows like a cloud-shadow after the realisation that I have grown remote enough from my own country to look at it with something of the detachment I might feel in Asia or Africa. Is this what it is fashionable to call 'loss of identity'? Can't be helped, even if it is. And there are compensations. It's a form of somewhat belated growing-up—being weaned from that Mother Ireland on whose not entirely infection-free milk so many of my generation were reared. A lot of Irish people are now going through this process. The Northern Troubles have forced us to reconsider our personal versions of nationalism. Ten years ago I wrote in a newspaper article that if a war were to break out for the purpose of uniting Ireland I would wish to take part. Now that attitude seems to me immoral. Or was I only pretending to myself, because such a conflict then seemed impossible? And are those in the Republic who now give verbal support to the Provos also pretending to themselves? It's hard to gauge the extent to which the Provos can depend on voluntary Southern help. Involuntary help they can always obtain in a crisis, since we are not a race with a death-wish. Beyond a doubt an enormous majority in the Republic is anti-Provo and becoming more so every month. But how potentially violent is the small minority? How fanatical? Is the Fighting Irishman stage or real in 1977? And does Ireland's weird national sex-life come into the picture anywhere? Even if one doesn't accept a direct link between sexual frustration and aggression, Irish Christianity's anti-sex complex must have very peculiar effects on some unfortunates.

When people in the Republic show sympathy for the Provos does it mean they condone their crimes? Or have they succeeded in mentally separating the crimes from the aims? Certainly some feel the aims justify the crimes. After one ghastly bombing in Belfast, a County Cork farmer remarked cheerfully to me, "You can't make an omelette without breaking eggs. We wouldn't be free down here if your father or mine was all that squeamish"—an argument which is hard to demolish without embarking on a detailed analysis of Irish history which few County Cork farmers would relish. Yet such people can be weaned off Mother Ireland only through education. They must be persuaded to look calmly at the Northern Protestants' point of view, however much they may abhor what they see. Now they won't admit it even exists, for which the Irish Government's stance from 1932 until very recently is largely to blame. Given that stance, it's surprising that so many of us have already outgrown the anti-Partition cult. But some have outgrown it merely because the North has become too hot to hold; not because they see that the Unionists have a point of view which is valid, however badly some loyalists may have behaved in its defence.

In these northern counties of the Republic it seems that more people are willing to look at the Unionist viewpoint—though of course this is also the area where one finds the most active support for the Provos. But I am thinking now of those who are not extremists. At least they have some contact with the Northern Protestants, as individuals, in a way we don't. South of the Dublin–Galway line there is little sense of personal involvement with Northern Ireland; it seems much further away than Britain, where so many people have lived and worked, or even than the USA. But beyond Athlone I noticed the North beginning to impinge, if only through complaints about the tourist trade; most of the Northerners who used to holiday in the Midlands or the West do so no longer. And as one moves nearer the border changes in attitude are marked. Instead of Northern Protestants being seen as an amorphous, objectionable mass, people tend to comment on the good qualities of the 'nice' ones and to see them as co-victims, with the Northern Catholics, of the 'nasty' extremists on both sides. Some Northern Catholics might consider that a too-charitable interpretation of history. But one doesn't complain, nowadays, about an excess of charity. Though perhaps one should. Perhaps the only thing of real value—the only thing that can help to sort it all out—is a dogged concentration on the truth, however hard it may be to establish or uncomfortable to live with.

A Few Small Clarifications

We are repeatedly told, usually by churchmen, that the Northern conflict is not about religion. Maybe not. But it so often seems to be that any account of personal impressions of its nature must be prefaced, if it is to have the slightest value, by an exact statement of the writer's own religious standpoint.

Once an English journalist asked me, in all seriousness, if my wanderings could be traced back to my frustrating experiences as a pupil at an Irish convent boarding-school. The question fascinated me, as an indication of how durable certain stereotypes are. That young woman was astonished to hear that my schooldays really were among the happiest of my life. On other subjects she was quite well-informed yet she genuinely believed that most Irish schoolgirls suffer hell under the domination of puritanical, sadistic nuns, many of whom are probably themselves repressed nymphomaniacs. This notion would not be surprising in East Belfast but it disturbed me to find it embedded in the mind of a London journalist. It was not of course a malignant prejudice. The young woman was perfectly prepared—even glad—to discard it on being assured that most Irish convent schools, while slow to encourage intellectual freedom, are no more psychologically unhealthy than the average English public school. But the persistence in Britain of such cartoon notions about Irish Catholicism adds another pinch of misunderstanding to the Northern witches' brew.

My parents were enthusiastic amateur theologians and I grew up listening to them quarrelling savagely about things like Transubstantiation, Predestination and Original Sin. As an only child I often had no choice but to endure these doctrinal gymnastics—on long car journeys, for instance—but the boredom was worth it because I thus became aware of religion as something that really mattered to individuals, and could be felt and thought about. It wasn't just something to be accepted prepackaged from priests. I also learned to appreciate, at a very young age, the difference between Irish Catholicism and The Rest. My father often remarked that it was unreasonable to judge Roman Catholicism by its aberrant quasi-Jansenistic Irish version. (Just as it is unreasonable to judge Protestantism by the uses to which it has been put in Northern Ireland.) Yet I was not allowed to overlook the benefits Ireland has derived from Catholicism, despite its local defects. Not the least of these were on the practical level, in the provision of educational and medical facilities and trained personnel of a standard which for a long time the State could not afford to provide.

Although my parents were essentially orthodox Catholics they had a light-hearted approach to the peripheral taboos. Long before Vatican II they never fussed much about eating meat on Fridays or darning socks on Sundays. They were heart-broken when I drifted away from the Church during my early twenties yet they never tried to argue me back. Nor did I ever have any feeling, during childhood or adolescence, of being pressurised by priests or nuns. This may be one reason why I escaped that urge to uproot from Ireland which afflicts so many Irish writers. (The urge to travel is quite another matter.) There was nothing in Ireland that I felt I had to get away from, either as a person or a writer. On the contrary, it was the place I had to get back to, wherever I went.

There is a popular theory that lapsed Irish Catholics are psychologically incapable of cutting the umbilical cord and so remain permanently uneasy about the eschatological consequences of their rebellion against Mother Church. The motives for one's defection clearly have a lot to do with this. In times past a common motive was conflict between personal ambitions and Catholic moral teaching. Then guilt was almost inevitable, the defection being based not on a genuine experience of the Church's inadequacy for the person concerned but on a defiance, for practical reasons, of the inconvenient laws of an institution still reluctantly revered. Nowadays, however, things are different. The majority of lapsed Catholics of my age, or younger, seem to bear no such burden of fear-full guilt.

At a stage in human development when so many people elsewhere are making alternative ethical and/or spiritual

arrangements, it is hard to see orthodox Christianity becoming
a civilising factor in Irish society. To me, as to many others,
the inability of the Churches to exercise the slightest restraint
on Northern excesses is their death-knell. The mess is too nasty
to be cleaned off the ecclesiastical carpets. They will have to
be thrown away. And their replacements will have to be woven
by Irish men and women of every sort working together on the
loom of forgiveness. All this will take time but one has to look
far ahead when considering Northern Ireland. To think only
about the present and the immediate future is to invite despair.

The clergy, from curates to cardinals, are the inevitable
scapegoats when people set out to criticise Irish Catholicism.
But do they deserve all the blame? Some time ago Louis
McRedmond wrote an article in *The Tablet* in which he recalled
his Catholic childhood in a small town not far from my own
home. He maintained that in Ireland the Church *is* the people,
and if the people seem priest-ridden to outsiders it is because
they want to be so. My own experience certainly confirms this.
As a family we did not want to be priest-ridden: and we weren't.
When I 'lapsed' a quarter of a century ago—long before such
an event could be spoken about above a whisper in rural Ireland—no priest ever attempted to 'get me back'; the local
clergy knew perfectly well that I was not, and never had been,
within their disciplinary reach. I am still living in that same
little town, on good terms with the clergy of all denominations
and with the nuns in the convent next door to my house. No
doubt prayers are wistfully said for my salvation but nobody,
clergy or lay, has ever tried to make me feel ill-at-ease because
of my defection.

Several Northern clergymen eagerly asked me, 'Why did you
decide to leave the Roman church?' Two were obviously hoping for an anti-Roman tirade which could be put to good use
in the pulpit on the following Sunday and all looked dis-
appointed when I explained that 'decision' did not come into
it. My lapse was not something I consciously willed; it was
something that had to happen in the course of my maturing.
But I never felt that the world would be a better place if it happened to everybody. Nor did I ever wish that I had been
brought up outside the confines of the Catholic Church—rather

the reverse. Perhaps illogically, a Christian upbringing seems to me a good launching-pad, even for those who do not find Christianity a suitable dynamo to power their adult lives.

I suppose I am now an agnostic humanist, though I don't much like the clinical sound of that. Nor am I sure of its accuracy, unless the humanism may be restricted to just one of its dictionary meanings—'doctrine emphasising importance of common human needs and abstention from profitless theorising' (e.g., breakfast-time discussions about Transubstantiation, Predestination and so forth). And unless the agnosticism leaves me free to believe—or at least to feel that I would like to believe—in some immaterial influence pervading the universe and entitled to reverence. I have an ineradicable respect for all the great religions and even for some of the little cranky ones, trying though these can be.

My drift away from Christianity is nowadays such a normal process for so many Europeans that some readers will wonder why I have gone on and on about it. But Ireland is very much on the edge of Europe, in more than the geographical sense, and religion—or the lack of it—is central to the theme of this book. How the individual thinks and feels about it profoundly affects his reactions to Northern Ireland—and, sometimes, the Northern Irish reactions to him.

Perhaps what the English most resent about the Irish is not our bombs or our bombast but the fact that we *seem* so like them, and in many ways *are* so like them, and yet on certain issues we are unalike enough to appear dishonestly elusive if not downright treacherous. The average Englishman can be securely and legibly labelled, but often our labels don't stick or prove hard to read. One memory from my childhood perfectly illustrates this point.

The year was 1944 and I was aged twelve. On a harsh, dark March afternoon, at the start of the Easter holidays, a squealing gate hinge made me look through the kitchen window. I saw a young man entering the cobbled yard from the garden, which meant that he had climbed an eight-foot wall—hardly a normal approach for afternoon callers. Yet I was not at all alarmed, possibly because we were a slightly eccentric family and so I was not prone to be made uneasy by the unconventional. Or it may simply have been because the young man looked so amiable. He was tall, broad-shouldered and handsome, and as he stood at the back door I noticed that he seemed rather apprehensive and very tired. I marked his Kerry brogue when he gave his name as Pat Carney and asked, diffidently, if he might see my mother.

In the sitting-room my invalid mother's Bath chair was close to the sulky wartime fire of wet turf. She seemed oddly unsurprised by our visitor's original approach route and my curiosity was further sharpened when she asked me to leave the room when I had shown him in. The temptation to eavesdrop then through the guichet was considerable, but successfully resisted. Ten minutes later Pat was back in the kitchen. He said that he had been invited to stay for a few days and that my mother would like to speak to me.

Then, pausing inside the sitting-room door, I did begin to feel alarmed. My mother was the sort of woman who usually managed to remain in control of situations, however tricky, and never before had I seen her so distraught. A friend was coming to tea so there was no time to waste on euphemisms. She told me that Pat was on the run, wanted for the murder of a Dublin detective-sergeant. He had come to us as a protégé of my father's elder sister who, never having recognised the validity of the post-Treaty Irish government, was an active supporter of the illegal IRA. On no account must any caller be allowed to see our guest or any trace of his presence. As I continued to stand by the door, paralysed with astonishment, my mother made a gallant preliminary bid to sort out the ethics of the situation. "This young man is a criminal though he regards himself as a patriot. No doubt his elders are chiefly to blame. They are using his muddled, foolish idealism. But we can talk about it later. Now please show him his room and give him a meal."

I walked down the hall in a joyous daze. This was the stuff of which fantasies are made, yet now it had become part of the reality of my own life. I was to prepare a meal for a man on the run who would be hanged if caught. My mother might have saved her breath. Of course Pat was not a criminal, or muddled or foolish. He was a most glorious patriot, heroically dedicated to the reunification of Ireland. And he looked the part, to my eyes, as he stood by the sink chivalrously scouring a saucepan. My father and grandfather had killed British soldiers but no one had ever suggested that they were criminals. One had to be logical. I was badly jolted when I discovered, that evening, how strongly my father disapproved of Pat. But then I reminded myself that he—my father—was very old (forty-two). And I reflected that, at that age, some people just can't have the right reactions any more.

Listening to my parents, I gathered that for some days they had been half-expecting Pat without knowing exactly why he was on the run. Now they were disagreeing vigorously about how they should deal with him and it gave me a certain sardonic satisfaction to observe them both being inconsistent; at twelve one likes the feet of clay to appear occasionally. My father, who came of an impeccably Republican family, should surely have been the one to welcome Pat, while my mother, whose ancestry was Redmondite at best (Unionist at worst) should have been the one to reject him. Instead, my father coldly argued that it was sinful (he was very sin-conscious) to shelter someone who had deliberately killed an innocent man in the course of a seditious campaign against a lawfully-established government. And my mother warmly argued that it was unthinkable, sinful or no, to betray someone whose coming to our home was an act of faith in our humanity. She insisted that allowances must be made for Pat's sick idealism. To which my father, sprung from generations of rebels, replied austerely that it would prove impossible to govern the state if hectic emotionalism were to be accepted as an excuse for murder.

"Very well," said my mother at that stage, "go now to the gardai barracks."

But my father didn't.

It interests me now to remember that my parents never debated the ethics of capital punishment. Presumably they accepted it, in theory, as the appropriate penalty for murder. Yet had it not been commonly employed in Ireland during the forties, as part of the government's anti-IRA campaign, they might well have refused to succour Pat. When such a decision can lead directly to a death sentence it requires more moral courage, or moral arrogance, than either of my parents possessed.

From their point of view an awkward situation was being compounded by the need to impress on me that giving refuge to Pat did not mean condoning his crime. In the end they gave up pretending to unravel this tangled skein for my benefit, which was sensible of them since I well know that they were incapable of unravelling it for their own. Anyway I had already come to my own conclusions and was only listening to their dutiful waffling out of politeness. Yet I vaguely sympathised with their discomfiture and appreciated their compassion— spontaneous on my mother's part, reluctant on my father's. Although they repudiated Pat as a violent man their consciences compelled them to allow for the fact that he saw himself as a soldier fighting a just war: a dilemma that in present-day Ireland has again become familiar to many, even if the disuse of the death penalty has somewhat blunted its horns.

A parallel situation is inconceivable in an English middle-class household. Our drama was a direct product of Irish history—the history of a people who for centuries were unwilling subordinates, accustomed to devious defiance of the law and to making subjective moral judgements in a variety of turbulent situations. Given normal circumstances it would have been hard to find a more scrupulously law-abiding, high-minded and civic-spirited couple than my parents. But when it comes to the test few, if any, Irish people show that bred-in-the-bone respect for law and order which is so fundamental to the English way of life. The average Englishman adverts to this potent force only when it is missing and its absence in Ireland apparently charms/ repels/bewilders/scares/amuses many of our English visitors. Some sense it merely as a pervasive 'difference' which makes of Ireland a foreign country, despite all the superficial similarities to Britain. Others perceive it as a threat to our development as a responsible nation—or, in times of stress, to their own safety.

For the past half-century the uncomplicated English attitude to law and order has been officially encouraged in Ireland. But such traditions do not take root within decades, especially if there is a political grievance to provide restless spirits with an excuse—however implausible—for continuing lawlessness disguised as heroism. Personally I cannot see us ever becoming dependable citizens on the English model. As has often been remarked, we are on the whole more imaginative, individualistic (in the moral rather than the social sense) and argumentative than the English. It is not in our nature to obey any Authority simply because it is there. We have been accused of using up all our docility in our relationship with the Roman Catholic church but this is not strictly true. During the past 150 years many Irish men and women have found it quite easy to remain fervent Catholics while rejecting clerical interference in the military and political spheres—a theological juggling feat at which some Provos are particularly expert.

Pat stayed with us for a fortnight but he and I never referred directly to his peculiar status and he made no attempt to influence me politically. We played round after round of rummy and he gave me lessons in map-reading and taught me how to whistle through my fingers so piercingly that I can be heard two miles away. Also, he often talked anxiously about the world's endangered wild life; he was a keen conservationist thirty years ahead of the fashion. To me this marvellous companion seemed a magic sort of person, an intelligent grown-up who had retained all the wondering enthusiasms of childhood. And my intuition was right. It was Pat's tragedy that he had never outgrown either the innocence or the ruthlessness of youth. Life, for him, had an unreal simplicity and of death he felt no fear. He was a devout Catholic yet his religion had been tailored to fit The Cause. Having seen his vision—an Irish Republic of thirty-two counties—he believed that nothing should be allowed to stand in the way of its attainment. Not even the shooting in the back of an unarmed fellow-Irishman troubled his Christian conscience when the victim had betrayed Ireland by serving a twenty-six county Irish state.

That strange contradiction at the core of fanaticism was very obvious in Pat though I was then too young to see it. Within him existed both a paranoid egocentricity—the sort that dismisses other people's opinions as necessarily false—and a totally selfless dedication to The Cause. One of my mother's favourite theories was that every human being is born a potential fanatic and the test of a civilisation is its ability to 'defanaticise' us. But I was not prepared to acknowledge, during early adolescence, the fanaticism of Pat and his like. Their heroism—so obviously genuine, however misdirected—utterly blinded me to the viciousness (in its consequences if not in its aspirations) of their patriotism.

Perhaps because of my friendship with Pat, it still seems wrong to me, when discussing guerrilla fighters of any nationality, to use the words 'gunmen' or 'terrorists'. In moments of shock, feeling revolted by their deeds, one chooses these terms almost as a form of revenge; I have done so myself, frequently. Yet it is probably true that most guerrillas start out as quite ordinary (though perhaps abnormally immature) people, and then begin to act in extraordinarily uncivilised ways under the pressure of uncivilised situations that are usually not of their own making. To reject and despise them as individuals, without any attempt at understanding, is merely another sort of sterile violence.

When the modern guerrilla fighter seems to disqualify himself for consideration as a human being we tend to forget that every form of war has a brutalising effect. In 1855, from the trenches before Sevastopol, a young soldier wrote to his aunt: 'Man-shooting is the finest sport of all; there is a certain amount of infatuation about, that the more you kill the more you wish to kill.' A nasty confession, all the nastier for being made with such élan. Yet one never thinks of that soldier as a gunman or terrorist. He survived Sevastopol, and a lot more besides, to become one of the most eminent Victorians. All his long life he frankly enjoyed killing men (preferably coloured) to enrich his Queen's Empire, and his reward was to be made a Field Marshal and a Viscount.

No doubt Lord Wolseley was in many ways a good chap: and so was Pat. My parents became very fond of him and deeply concerned about him; night after night they argued patiently in futile attempts to make him see the error of his ways. Very soon he seemed a member of the family—quite an achievement, in view of the strains imposed on all the adults concerned by his presence in the house. Had he been detected under our roof, my father would not have perjured himself by denying any knowledge of his identity, and so would certainly have been imprisoned; as his sister was soon to be, on Pat's account.

Our guest was careful never to go too near a window and any knock at the door sent him rushing upstairs. Remembering how I relished all this melodrama I wonder now if I fully understood that we were truly dicing with death. But my light-hearted approach may well have helped by easing the tension generated between the three adults. Pat knew that I took the game seriously enough to keep all the rules, and I was made deliriously proud by his entrusting to me the addressing and posting of his letters. One morning I went into his room to leave fresh linen on the bed and saw an automatic by the pillow. For years this was to rank as the most thrilling moment in my life. I tingled all over at the romance of that weapon—symbol of Adventure!—gleaming black and lethal on the white sheet. It never occurred to me that in certain circumstances it could be used to kill the local gardai, the fathers of my playmates. But then it was impossible to associate the gentle, considerate Pat with any form of violence or cruelty.

One evening Pat said good-bye instead of good-night and when we got up next morning he was gone. We heard nothing of him for several months but his luck did not hold. Eventually he was captured while asleep in my aunt's house and tried in Dublin before the Military Tribunal. Then he was hanged by the neck until he died, at eight o'clock in the morning on 1 December 1944. His real name was Charles Kerins.

I continue to think of him as Pat. And even now I prefer to remember only that he was brave. Brave enough to refuse all sedatives in the condemned cell and to walk to the scaffold unaided, in full possession of his faculties, at the age of twenty-five, proud to die, as he believed, for his country.

In Waterford city, where I was then at boarding-school, 1 December 1944 was a morning of violent wind and slashing rain. Just before eight o'clock I was queuing for my breakfast. I knew of Pat's attitude towards his sentence and at the moment of his hanging, when the gong in the hall was signalling us to enter the refectory, I experienced an almost hysterical elation. Then, curiously enough, I ate my usual hearty meal. It was against the nationalist tradition in my blood to mourn such deaths for that would have been to imply that the sacrifice was not worth while.

Our mail was distributed during the mid-morning break and two worlds met when I stood amongst my classmates and—while they drank their milk and chattered of hockey—read a letter from a friend who had been hanged three hours earlier. Pat had written the day before, to thank me for my 'high-spirited devotion'. With his letter he enclosed a silver ring which I wore constantly from that moment until my fingers and my ideals outgrew it—developments which conveniently occurred at about the same time. But I have it still and I would not part with it.

Charles Kerins' mortuary card described him as 'Chief-of-Staff, Irish Republican Army' which to the unknowing sounds impressive. But in fact the IRA was virtually a one-man show by the end of 1944. In *The Secret Army* J. Bower Bell considers Pat's last months and the significance of his death. 'Kerins eventually left his safe house at Dr Kathleen Farrell's* and returned to Kerry to let the heat cool.' (Staying with us en route.) 'He felt the police were very close and knew of the house; nevertheless, he left some papers and guns behind to be picked up. The year 1944 was so bad that he could not find a single man left to go by the Farrell's and collect his dump. In June he came back to Dublin and hired a pony cart to move the things from the Farrell house. He called in a disguised message over the tapped phone that he would be over that evening, June 15. There was no sign of the police when he arrived at 50 Rathmines Road and he slipped in quietly. Late that night the trap finally closed. The police arrived with squad cars, ambulances, tin hats, coats of mail, and machine guns. They prised off the side-door lock and went straight up six flights to the room where Kerins and Dr Farrell's seventeen-year-old son were sleeping. The detectives burst through the door. Kerins had a Thompson under the bed but he never had a chance to use it for he was seized before he was fully awake.... On October 9, as expected, he was found guilty and sentenced to hang ... and with him died the last fragile symbol of IRA continuity. For the first time in generations the line had been broken. There no longer was

* My father's sister.

a Chief of Staff or a GHQ or an Army Council or even an IRA.
The prisons and the camps held those who would not quit but
few of these men looked forward to more than their own freedom and the chance to lead quiet private lives.... The IRA
had become an anachronism for most Irishmen. The time for
physical force had passed: partition would be ended by political
agitation, not gunfire in the streets. The Irish Minister of Justice, Gerald Boland, announced in pride that the IRA was dead
and that he had killed it. He had been helped by the RUC,
the British police, the Irish Army, and of course by the IRA
itself, but to all intents and purposes he spoke the truth.'

A new offensive against the British in Northern Ireland was
begun in December 1956 but by the following July the IRA
were again on the defensive. They fought on, however, for
another four years, causing £700,000 worth of damage in
Northern Ireland and making it necessary for the Stormont
government to spend half a million pounds a year on their
security forces. But on the whole this was not a 'killing' campaign and by the standards of the seventies very few lives were
lost. Then in February 1961 a public statement, drafted by
Rory Brady, was issued 'To the Irish People'. It said, 'The
leadership of the Resistance Movement has ordered the termi-
nation of the Campaign of Resistance to British Occupation
launched on December 12, 1956.... All arms and other material
have been dumped and all full-time active service Volunteers
have been withdrawn. The decision to end the Resistance Campaign has been taken in view of the general situation. Foremost
among the factors motivating this course of action has been the
attitude of the general public whose minds have been deliberately distracted from the supreme issue facing the Irish
people—the unity and freedom of Ireland.'

To put it in more realistic terms, the Irish general public,
North and South, had matured enough, politically, to see the
folly of IRA methods. In the South they had said so at the polls
in October 1960 when only 3 per cent of the electorate cast
a first-preference vote for Sinn Fein. And not even the IRA's
genius for auto-brain-washing could overcome the lack of
money to buy arms.

During the sixties some IRA leaders came to accept what

a few of their predecessors had unsuccessfully preached during the thirties: that they could do more for Ireland by 'going political' and opposing social injustices than by sticking to their guns. Many traditionalists disapproved, especially when the new thinking led to a recognition of existing political and legal institutions and when Marxist influences became apparent. They were able to say 'I told you so!' in August 1969 when Paisley-inspired Orange mobs attacked Belfast's Catholic ghettos and on one night burned 500 homes. The RUC had proved unwilling or unable to defend the Catholic population and an armed IRA was needed again.

How had it come about that in two cities of the UK—Belfast and Derry—the discredited IRA was able to regain support because it was genuinely needed to protect certain areas? There is no short answer to that question; here an historical digression becomes essential. But I will be as brief as possible. Anybody who wishes to study Northern Ireland's history in detail is advised to consult the bibliography.

In 1603 the Gaelic Ulster chieftains were defeated after a nine-year war and the province was planted with Protestant colonists from England and Scotland. In other parts of Ireland a Plantation usually meant confiscating the land and replacing the Gaelic aristocracy with English landowners but in Ulster the colonists were of all social classes. By 1703 only 5 per cent of the land of Ulster was owned by the Catholic Irish. The planters' towns were fortified against the Catholics and it was illegal to employ Catholics within their walls. Often, however, this law had to be ignored for lack of colonists, so the descendants of the Gaelic landowners were permitted to slip into the towns, from their hovels on bogs or mountains, to scrape a living as servants. As John Darby has written in *Conflict in Northern Ireland*, 'The sum of the Plantation then was the introduction of a foreign community, which spoke differently, worshipped apart, and represented an alien culture and way of life. It had close commercial, cultural and political ties with Britain. The more efficient methods of the new farmers, and the greater availability of capital, which allowed the start of cottage industries, served to create further economic differences between Ulster and the rest of Ireland, and between Catholic and

Protestant within Ulster. The deep resentment of the native Irish towards the planters, and the distrustful siege mentality of the planters towards the Irish, is the root of the Ulster problem.'

In 1641 Catholics massacred Protestants; in the 1650s, during the Cromwellian campaigns, Protestants massacred Catholics and in retaliation Catholics massacred Protestants whenever they could which wasn't very often. In 1690 the victory of William of Orange over James II at the Battle of the Boyne provided the raw material for a peculiarly potent Protestant myth. It also led to the formation, two years later, of a Protestant parliament in Dublin which acted firmly against Catholics, excluding them not only from parliament but from the army, judiciary and legal profession. Further sordid details of the Penal Laws may be found in the history books. I personally would prefer to forget them but they do help to explain the Irish Problem. They must be partly responsible for our uncertain attitude towards law and order and also for the extent to which Irish nationalism came to be identified with Catholicism, despite our many Protestant Nationalist leaders.

During the eighteenth century the Presbyterians also suffered under a milder yet not easily tolerated version of the Penal Laws. Towards the end of the century the Society of United Irishmen was founded to establish an independent Irish Republic. Its membership was both Catholic and Presbyterian and after the uprising of 1798 three Presbyterian clergymen were hanged. Several exclusively Catholic or Protestant secret societies flourished at about the same time: the Defenders, the Peep O' Day Boys, the Hearts of Oak, the Steel Boys and— most important of all—the Orange Boys, who grew up to become the Orange Order. The original Orange aim was to wreck Presbyterian–Catholic co-operation, oppose independence for Ireland and unite all Protestants in the struggle to protect the country against seditious Catholics.

On 12 July 1834 a woman was killed in Belfast's first large-scale sectarian riot. Other riots, causing many deaths and serious injuries, took place in 1857, 1864, 1872, 1876, 1878, 1886 and 1898; on some of these occasions more than 2,000 police and troops had to be called out to restore order.

Even in the old Gaelic days Ulster had never been very closely involved with the other provinces (except when fighting them), and during the nineteenth century it became more and more 'a place apart'. While the rest of the country remained virtually untouched by the Industrial Revolution, Ulster's prosperity increased and it suffered less than other regions during the potato famine, described by John Darby as 'undoubtedly the most far-reaching event in nineteenth-century Ireland'.

A separate legislature for Ulster was first mentioned in 1834 when there was talk of the Act of Union being repealed and a Dublin parliament being restored. Fifty years later the vigorous Home Rule campaign of the 1880s provoked the Ulster Protestants to organise themselves (with generous help from the English Tory party) into a powerful political bloc which disintegrated only in 1972. The Orange Order supplied the foundations and in February 1886 Lord Randolph Churchill, Independent Tory member for Woodstock and spiritual ancestor of Enoch Powell, wrote as follows to the Irish Lord Chief Justice Fitzgibbon: 'I decided some time ago that if the GOM* went for Home Rule, the Orange card would be the one to play. Please God it may turn out the ace of trumps and not the two.' It did indeed prove to be an ace and ninety years later the British government must be wishing they could play the Irish game without that particular card.

In 1912 the renewed threat of Home Rule spawned an Ulster Protestant army, the Ulster Volunteer Force, which set about training and arming 100,000 men. It was officered by the Ulster gentry but commanded by an Englishman, Lieutenant-General Sir George Richardson, KCB, veteran of the Afghan, Waziri, Tirah, Zhob and Kunnan campaigns, who had led Indian troops to the storming of Peking in August 1900.

Towards the end of that year Patrick Pearse—headmaster of the school where my father was then a twelve-year-old pupil—wrote: 'It is symptomatic of the attitude of the Irish Nationalist that when he ridicules the Orangeman he ridicules him not for his numerous foolish beliefs, but for his readiness to fight in defence of those beliefs. But this is exactly wrong. The Orange-

* Gladstone.

man is ridiculous in so far as he believes incredible things; he is estimable in so far as he is willing and able to fight in defence of what he believes. ... Personally I think the Orangeman with a rifle a much less ridiculous figure than the Nationalist without a rifle; and the Orangeman who can fire a gun will certainly count for more in the end than the Nationalist who can do nothing cleverer than make a pun.'

Patrick Pearse was not as tough as he liked to sound but he did manage to direct the Irish Volunteers, in response to the UVF, and the Liberal government soon had reason to fear a three-sided civil war. The Home Rule bill was to become law in 1914 and the harassed Liberals began to negotiate furtively with Redmond, the leader of the Irish Party, in an attempt to reach a compromise which would placate the Ulster Unionists without driving the Nationalists to armed rebellion. But Redmond showed no enthusiasm for further tampering with the bill. His constitutional party, after decades of disappointment and frustration on the Home Rule issue, was already losing support to those who favoured military action. In the end, however, he agreed to a modification which would allow those Northern counties with a Unionist majority to opt out of Home Rule for six years, during which time they would continue to be governed by Westminster. This silly arrangement satisfied nobody. The Ulster Unionists showed their contempt for it by proceeding with their plans for armed rebellion while many who had been 'moderate' Nationalists became converts to the same idea.

In March 1914 the British Army began to move against the UVF. Then fifty-eight cavalry officers stationed at the Curragh, in County Kildare, refused to serve against Ulster Unionists. Asquith, who had not been involved in the original decision to take action in Ulster, quickly decided that it would be wiser to pretend to ignore the UVF. The officers retained their commissions and five weeks later the UVF welcomed, at Larne, a boat from Germany loaded with 25,000 rifles and 3,000,000 rounds of ammunition. In July Erskine Childers—an Englishman, father of our late President—used his yacht *Asgard* to land 900 rifles and 25,000 rounds of ammunition (also from Germany) at Howth. But on 4 August 1914 a stop was put to everybody's gallop. When the Home Rule bill became law on 18 September a companion bill suspended its operation until the end of the war and, as J. C. Beckett has noted, 'Redmond's support of the government was well received by nationalists in general, and recruits for the British army came forward by the thousand. . . . War quickly stimulated the Irish economy: there was soon plenty of money in circulation, and the farmers had never been so prosperous. Nationalist Ireland as a whole seemed quite happy to wait for peace to bring home rule, and in the meantime to enjoy the profits of war.'

On 1–2 July 1916 thousands of those UVF men who had originally been armed to fight against their King (so that they might ever remain his loyal subjects) died fighting for him in the Battle of the Somme. However tiresome and inconsistent Unionist loyalty might look to outsiders in peace-time, it shone like pure gold on the battlefield. The discipline and courage of the 36th (Ulster) Division were such that on 2 July Sir William Spencer wrote: 'I am not an Ulsterman but yesterday as I followed their amazing attack on the Somme I felt I would rather be an Ulsterman than anything else in the world.'

Meanwhile, back in Ireland, the Irish Volunteers had staged an ill-organised uprising in Dublin on 23 April 1916. I use the word 'staged' deliberately, for to me it seems that the Easter Week Rebellion was an exercise in planned myth-making; and such a successful exercise that sixty years later even the most 'de-nationalised' Irish man or woman has to make a tremendous effort to examine it objectively. Its long-term effects will probably be debated for centuries to come. Only this much is certain: in January 1916 Pearse could not have recruited for his cause one-tenth of the numbers who were proud and eager to help Britain defend poor little Catholic Belgium. But by mid-May, when fifteen of the insurgent leaders had been shot in Kilmainham gaol after trial by court-martial, the public attitude had changed dramatically.

Easter Week may have been, in military terms, an inept bit of nonsense. But because of Britain's reaction it made of Catholic Ireland a nation—not once again, but for the first time. And Britain very quickly got the message, spurred on by the need to soothe public opinion in the United States where the powerful Irish minority had been infuriated by the executions. On 11 May Asquith told the House of Commons: "The government has come to the conclusion that the system under which Ireland has been governed has completely broken down. The only satisfactory alternative, in their judgment, is the creation, at the earliest possible moment, of an Irish Government responsible to the Irish people."

Given the Ulster Unionists' inflexibility, what Asquith's statement had to mean was two Irish governments responsible to two sections of the Irish people. In 1920 three counties (Donegal, Cavan and Monaghan) were chopped off the ancient province of Ulster to leave the new statelet of Northern Ireland manageable under 'a Protestant parliament for a Protestant people'. The Catholic one-third of the population thus became a group who had to be kept in that safe two-to-one minority; and for over fifty years this balance was maintained, despite the higher Catholic birth-rate, through policies which ensured the required rate of emigration among Catholics.

The Government of Ireland Act (1920) also established a parliament for Southern Ireland. But so many Southerners were opposed to partition that, in Professor Beckett's words, 'Southern Ireland as a political entity was still-born'. In the North 232 people were killed in sectarian riots in 1922, including two Unionist MPs, and almost 1,000 were wounded—figures with a contemporary ring. As Liam de Paor has put it in *Divided Ulster*, 'A settlement desired and welcomed by no party in Ireland had been imposed.'

My paternal grandparents and their elder daughter were 'out' in 1916; my father and his younger brother tried to run away from Castleknock College to join the Volunteers but were retrieved in time. I grew up to think of the GPO in Dublin, from the steps of which Pearse read the Proclamation of the Irish Republic, as a sacred spot. The 1916 myth, like malaria, is in my bloodstream. But fortunately the fever it caused in youth is not recurrent. Ireland's modern miseries help one to build up powerful anti-bodies against it. If one believes, as I do, that Ireland's future well-being depends on an increasing closeness to Europe—and particularly on an uninhibited recognition of our special ties with Britain—then clearly Easter Week was a mistake. But it was a noble mistake, the sort one would expect of a mystical poet-leader like Patrick Pearse. It is impossible for me to condemn it though increasingly I regret that it ever happened. Obviously I would not feel thus had Ireland been able to develop a distinctive way of life based on ancient Gaelic traditions—the dream of the 1916 leaders. But, for that, Irish independence came centuries too late and our attempts to revive an extinct culture led only to humbuggery. We forced the Irish language on generations of reluctant children whose parents could speak only English. Our Gaelic sports clubs would not allow their members to go to a rugger or cricket or soccer match. We hypocritically pretended to sit on the fence during the Second World War while with one foot we kicked the ball for Britain when nobody was looking. We cultivated a dishonest smugness about the extent of our independence, when in fact we were and remain economically bonded to Britain by sterling and dependent on her for the employment of our emigrants. In 1937 we produced a disastrous constitution which might have been specially designed to alienate forever the Northern Protestants. We showed an exaggerated deference (now slightly waning) to the Catholic church as the one feature of our national life which really does set us apart from Britain. And every year we ritually polished myths that would have been better left to get so rusty they fell apart.

Would we have been deprived of anything worthwhile had Easter Week never happened? Certainly we would have gained a lot had the fifteen leaders of the Rising lived their normal life-span as co-architects of the New Ireland. Patrick Pearse, for instance, had founded his own schools because he believed that the Irish educational system was 'a murder machine', that teachers should 'keep in touch with educational thought in other lands' and that education should be all about the development of the individual personality. He urged 'Freedom to the individual school, freedom to the individual teacher, freedom as far as may be to the individual pupil'. And at St Enda's he proved it possible to run a school efficiently while putting those theories into practice.

In 1912 Pearse had accepted the emasculated third Home

Rule bill, largely because it gave Ireland control of her own educational system. But for the attitude of the Ulster Unionists, he and many others would almost certainly have remained resigned to Home Rule and never become myth-makers. Not everyone remembers now that the violence which ravaged Ireland between 1916 and 1923 began as a reaction to the establishment in Ulster of a private army of 100,000 men. The Ulster Unionists—themselves led by two non-Ulstermen, Carson and Bonar Law—had shown the way.

During the thirties Northern Ireland's unemployment rate rarely fell below 25% and sectarian rioting was frequent. But the Second World War brought relative prosperity and the post-war Stormont government successfully expanded industry. Of Northern Ireland's 150 new factories many belonged to international combines whose representatives had never heard—and would not have heeded—Lord Brookeborough's advice to employers, given on 13 July 1933: 'There are a great number of Protestants and Orangemen who employ Roman Catholics. I feel I can speak freely on this subject as I have not had a Roman Catholic about my own place. ... I would appeal to Loyalists, therefore, wherever possible, to employ good Protestant lads and lassies. ... I want you to remember one point in regard to the employment of people who are disloyal. ... You are disfranchising yourselves in that way. You people who are employers have the ball at your feet. If you don't act properly now, before we know where we are we shall find ourselves in the minority instead of the majority.'

As living standards began to improve for the minority, they also benefited from the introduction into Northern Ireland by Westminster—against Unionist advice—of the Welfare State. Free secondary education, made available by the 1948 Education Act, led to a spectacular rise in the number of Catholic university graduates and when the IRA formally 'retired' in 1961, and the moderate Terence O'Neill became Prime Minister in 1963, it seemed that civilisation was at last overtaking Northern Ireland. But that was not to be. Both the extreme Protestant religious leaders and the traditionalist Unionist political leaders (two groups which often overlapped) condemned this 'weakening process' and resolved to halt it.

It soon became clear that Terence O'Neill, though well-intentioned, was not a man who could achieve much for the Catholics while being relentlessly opposed by Ian Paisley and his Loyalist associates. Some reforms were carried out, but the pace was too slow and the O'Neill approach too uncertain. In 1967 the Northern Ireland Civil Rights Association was formed and the violent Paisleyite reaction to its non-violent campaign for social justice started the present troubles.

We are all so impressionable, and the media are on the whole so unanalytical, that even I—with all the foregoing facts stored away in my memory—had most of my disapproval focussed on the IRA when I crossed the border. Yet the Provisional IRA campaign is an effect, not an original cause, of the latest act in Northern Ireland's 350-year-old tragedy. It would never have started if the extreme Loyalists—frantic at the sight of the thin edge of the liberal wedge—had not gone into action during the sixties, and if the security forces had not failed to control them when they ran amok. (On occasions the police actually *joined* them in their attacks on Catholics and Catholic property.)

At this stage in Northern Ireland's history it is of vital importance to get the facts straight. The errors of the past have to be remembered and acknowledged before they can finally be forgiven and forgotten. What is the point of patching things up somehow, through sheer war-weariness, and stuffing skeletons back into their respective sectarian cupboards for another ten or twenty years? Those skeletons need to be identified, and given a decent burial, and then the cupboards can be left open to air.

As Liam de Paor has observed, 'One of the minor effects of partition was to create tiresome difficulties of nomenclature'. To many these difficulties may seem childish—verily the least of Northern Ireland's problems—yet within the region itself they are often of considerable consequence. And an alertness to nomenclature can be useful to the outsider as a method of assessing a stranger's thoughts and feelings about Ireland's past, present and future. One example is Derry versus Londonderry. Several people told me that when Northerners meet casually the conversation is often manipulated to bring in the city on the Foyle; thus everybody's political stance is quickly revealed. However, Derry is in fact a bad choice as Professor Moody makes plain in *The Ulster Question*: 'Though the official name of the city, as of the county around it, has been Londonderry since 1613, the ancient Irish name of the place, Derry, has continued to be used by most people locally and throughout Ireland; and though some Unionists use Londonderry on principle, it is, on balance, I believe, less emotive to use Derry. In Orange tradition it is Derry's walls (not Londonderry's) that are the symbol of "no surrender". On the other hand there is much to be said for using Londonderry to describe the county, an area that had never been known as Derry or by any one Irish name before the city of London's connection with it.'

I grew up with the deep emotions aroused by rival nomenclatures. As an adolescent the term 'British Isles' made me positively aggressive and until quite recently it made me wince. Now the pendulum has swung the other way and I rather favour it as a recognition of certain psychological and cultural facts, themselves the outcome of completed historical processes which it is much too late to reverse. It therefore pleased me to hear many youngish Northern Catholics casually using 'British Isles' as a natural description of these two islands.

In Northern Ireland one has a wide choice of names for the rest of the island: the Twenty-six Counties, the Free State, Southern Ireland, the South, Eire and the Republic of Ireland. The first of these is favoured by anti-partitionists; it implies that the division of the country is essentially artificial, arbitrary and temporary, and pending reunification the Dublin Government's territory deserves no more dignified description. The Free State is the most generally used, within both communities, and as it became obsolete elsewhere with the introduction of our 1937 constitution, when I was aged five, it took me some time to get used to it. Southern Ireland and Eire seem to be used by Unionists who don't much like the region in question (or at least its present administration). Some of them were

rather peeved when I pointed out that 'Eire' simply means
'Ireland' in Gaelic and for English speakers to employ it is either
inane or—if it is used to describe the Republic—inaccurate.
I believe it came into fashion in Britain, after 1937, as a result
of its being tendentiously used on our postage stamps. 'Down
South' or 'the South', used by either side, seem to convey
amused tolerance of Southern whims, or even affection, but 'the
Republic' is used by only a tiny, liberal, forward-looking
minority, most of whom have spent some time living outside
Northern Ireland among people who think it proper to refer
to a country by the name it has elected to use. A snag here
is that one must avoid the adjective that would normally be
derived from the 'Republic of Ireland' usage. To speak of Republican attitudes, policies, feelings—not to mention soldiers
or guns—would be very ambiguous. Personally I prefer to use
the South and Southerners, which seem the least offensive terms
from everybody's point of view—except perhaps that of ped-
antic geographers.

The choice of names for Northern Ireland is also wide:
British-occupied Ireland, the Six Counties, Ulster, the North
and Northern Ireland. The first is used only by maniacs, the
second by moderate anti-partitionists. 'Ulster' is the favourite
term of most of the region's residents but is grossly misleading
since three of Ulster's nine counties are within the Republic,
and Northern Ireland is equally misleading since Donegal is
further north than most of Northern Ireland. But at least
'Northern Ireland' has the merit of being the region's legal
name, according to the Government of Ireland Act (1920), and
throughout Ireland an acceptable abbreviation is 'the North'.
(No wonder the English have given up trying to fathom either
end of a country that keeps its most northerly county in the
south. . . . Though now I come to think of it, New College,
Oxford was founded in 1379. Which just goes to show how
much the English and the Irish have in common.)

Next—what noun is appropriate to Northern Ireland? 'Province' won't do since one-third of the province is on the wrong
side of the border. 'State' implies more self-determination than
Northern Ireland has ever had and 'country' or 'nation' are
blatantly absurd. 'Colony' has overtones that would be resented

by both communities and 'statelet' sounds too patronising, though outsiders might consider it more precise than anything else; so one is left with the unsatisfactory word 'region'.

What to call our neighbouring island is less tricky, though even here there are hidden pitfalls. To refer to the UK in the Bogside Inn, or unthinkingly to say 'England' instead of 'Britain' in Presbyterian areas planted from Scotland, would not be diplomatic. On the whole, however, Britain is acceptable; and my own favourite term—'across the water'—is commonly used by both communities.

On religious labels, most writers seem content with 'Protestant' and 'Catholic' though obviously in Northern Ireland as elsewhere some Protestants would prefer 'Roman Catholic'. Usually, however, the Northern Protestant himself refers simply to 'Catholics' unless he belongs to that school of non-thought which favours 'Papish bastards', 'Fuckin' Fenians' and other such vivid epithets. Yet the Protestant label seems to me unsatisfactory; Catholics are Catholics but what are Protestants? Are they Church of Ireland, Presbyterian Church in Ireland, Non-Subscribing Presbyterians, Free Presbyterians, Evangelical Presbyterians, Reformed Presbyterians, Pentecostals, Baptists, Congregationalists, Quakers, Christian Scientists, Methodists—or what? Of course I exaggerate, though all these sects do flourish in Belfast. According to the 1961 census the proportions are: Roman Catholics 34·9 per cent, Presbyterians 29·0 per cent, Church of Ireland 24·2 per cent, Methodists 5 per cent, Others 6·9 per cent. But there can be considerable animosity between the Church of Ireland and the Presbyterian Church in Ireland, not to mention the abhorrence felt by Free Presbyterians for any church that has made even the most timid ecumenical gesture and the loathing felt by every other church for the Free Presbyterians. It can only make for further confusion if one refers sweepingly to 'Protestants' as though the saintly Archbishop Simms and the diabolical Mr Paisley were kindred spirits. So where necessary I have named particular sects.

The main political and paramilitary groupings are fairly straightforward if one ignores the recent proliferation of Unionist splinter parties and uneasy coalitions, which we may happily

do as this is not a book about politics. The almost entirely
Catholic Social Democratic Labour Party is heir to the old
Nationalist party, which was a direct descendent of the pre-
partition Home Rule party. The Northern Ireland Labour
Party is not, unfortunately, very important; it has never had
a normal backing from the working-classes because the Orange
Order saw to it that they voted Unionist. The Alliance Party
is the voice of tolerance crying in the wilderness; it is the only
party in Northern Ireland that outsiders could imagine themselves voting for—but most Northerners regard it as wishy-
washy and distrust it as a middle-class intellectual's creation. It
wishes to abolish sectarian politics yet its support is mainly Protestant; because it favours the link with Britain many Catholics
see it as merely a non-sectarian splinter off the Unionist Party.
That party, despite its having held together for fifty years as
the Stormont junta, consisted of disparate elements which were
united only by their determination to keep Northern Ireland
in the UK and free of Romish influences. In a genuine democracy, which did not have to devote so much energy to repress-
ing a dissident minority, the various Unionist groups would certainly not have stood shoulder to unlikely shoulder for half a
century. I use the past tense because under the pressure of
recent events the Unionist Party has at last fallen to bits and
is now (one hopes) in Humpty-dumpty's situation.

Some of these bits have links with some Loyalist paramilitary
groups. But it is impossible to find out what actually goes on
in the shadowy corners where nobody at present has any real
power—except that derived from the use of arms—and where
everybody is trying to manœuvre into a position from which
power may one day be seized. What of the illegal UVF, for
instance? Or the Orange Volunteers? Or Tara? Or the UFF?
How close is their relationship with the UDA? With Paisley's
Free Presbyterian church and his Democratic Unionist Party?
With the more extreme Orangemen? With each other? And
what of the Catholic paramilitaries and *their* splinter groups?
How strong are all these organisations, in manpower and
weapon-power? How well or ill disciplined? Many people are
prepared to air their theories in reply to such questions, or even
to whisper 'facts' that must not be passed on. But obviously

nobody who really knows talks. And on these points my own enthusiasm for fact-finding was tempered by the knowledge that nowadays in Northern Ireland excessive curiosity can leave you dead down a side-street.

The Catholic paramilitary groups are less numerous though it is becoming increasingly difficult to judge how many gangs are operating rackets in defiance of their leaders. During the 1969 IRA renaissance the movement split into two mutually antagonistic armies and the bitterness between them eventually led to such merciless feuding that it was unsafe to gaol Official and Provisional prisoners in the same compound. By 1969 the Marxist Officials had already set up a left-wing 'national libera-tion front' dedicated to destroying the Dublin and Stormont governments; which governments would of course have to be recognised, *de facto*, if they were to be opposed through political channels. But the Provos despised this newfangled waffling about making a revolutionary philosophy work. They rigidly refused to recognise the three governments concerned and reaffirmed their allegiance to 'the 32-County Republic pro-claimed at Easter 1916, established by the Dail Eireann in 1919, overthrown by force of arms in 1922 and suppressed to this day by the existing British-imposed Six-County and Twenty-Six County partition states'. A few years ago a breakaway group of Officials set themselves up as the Irish Republican Socialist Party, known as 'the Irps'. The Officials are also known as the Stickies (or Sticks) because during Easter Week they affix Easter lilies to their lapels with gum instead of with pins. (Those lilies are the Republican equivalent of the Remembrance Day poppies.)

Now only one nomenclature puzzle remains—to outsiders the most baffling of all. What is a Loyalist? As far as my own observation goes a Loyalist is someone obsessionally afraid of Gaelic Romish domination who clings to the link with Britain as his one sure safeguard against this fate. He frequently asserts that he is loyal not to the British parliament, which he pro-foundly distrusts, but to the Crown. He is not overfond of his British fellow-subjects across the water and sulkily suspects the English and the Southern Irish of being closer to each other in spirit than either is to him. He is ever on the alert for a 'betrayal' to be hatched between London and Dublin and is not insensitive to the financial benefits accruing from his position within the UK. But he wishes these did not have to be shared with disloyal papists who have done nothing to deserve them and sometimes use their dole money to buy bullets. (As he does himself, but that is quite a different matter.) In certain circumstances he is prepared to kill, maim, rob, burn and go to prison for the sake of maintaining the link between himself and Queen Elizabeth II. On paper he sounds just about the least likable sort of extant human being yet when one is sitting in his home having a cup of tea with himself and the wife, or drinking a pint with him and his friends in the pub, he can be very good company. In theory he hates Catholics (and in practice, if he becomes a unit in a mob) but almost without exception I found him polite, kind, generous, helpful and welcoming—though I was an unexplained stranger with a very Catholic name and an unmistakable Southern brogue. Moreover, as the barriers went down he often appeared bewildered, unsure, frightened and generally pathetic—not at all the dour, hard-headed, thick-skinned, unimaginative character one had been conditioned to expect. He suspects that Queen Elizabeth—inexplicably—doesn't want him any more and he is beginning to realise that the rest of the world sees him as a peculiarly unsavoury relic of the Dark Ages. This of course means that the rest of the world is wrong. But it is nevertheless uncomfortable to have been made aware of such universal if misguided disapproval. Life is hard, in these days of rapid change imposed from outside, for people who have been bred to cherish and boast of their inflexibility (No Surrender!) and who have been reared in a far corner of Europe so insulated against modern thinking that it makes even Southern Ireland seem cosmopolitan and progressive.

The Loyalist hard-liner is often someone victimised by his own prejudices no less than he victimises others because of them. If he could discard them, as he might a worn garment, Northern Ireland would be more than half-way to peace. But such prejudices are like the very marrow in the bone and to expect individuals to get rid of them suddenly—or even gradually—is absurd. The most one can hope for in the foreseeable

future is a changed climate that would render the more dangerous prejudices passive rather than active.

Meanwhile the non-Loyalist—though not at all disloyal—
Northern Protestant will have work to do, removing the anti-
Catholic devices built into the structure of Northern society
over the centuries.

3

Journal of Borderline Cases

9 June

Today I left Cavan town soon after eight o'clock—a sunny morning with a strong cool wind and swift white clouds. In Belturbet post office advice about cross-border routes was offered by a friendly clerk and a tall old farmer with a leathery face. They thought a cyclist might be able to get across, if the water was low, where the bridge used to be. "It was blown up twice," explained the clerk, "so now they'll leave it that way." When I asked who had blown it up, and why, they obviously thought I was 'leading them on' and changed the subject. But I genuinely wanted to know. I have a very limited understanding of these matters.

Beyond Belturbet the hilly third-class road passed a few poor little farms and presented two crossroads without signposts. Uncertain of the way, I approached a depressed-looking farm dwelling. As I crossed the untidy yard I called out "Anybody at home?"—not realising (stupidly) the effect an unknown voice would have quarter of a mile from the border. As I stood at the open door the whole family faced me silently like figures in a tableau, eyes full of fear, everybody motionless. A thin bent granddad stood in the centre of the kitchen floor leaning on an ash-plant, his hat pushed back off his forehead. A woman of about my own age, with unkempt foxy hair and a torn pink jersey, had been making bread and stood with floury hands held over a basin. A young woman with impetigo, a ragged skirt and sandals not matching was just inside the door holding an empty pail. A skinny, freckled little boy had been pulling a cardboard carton full of turf sods across the floor and he it was who broke the silence by beginning to cry. It is many years since I last saw that degree of slovenly poverty in my own part of rural Ireland. (Yet the inevitable television set stood in one corner.) But it was the fear, not the poverty, that shook me;

that instant of pure terror before my harmlessness was recognised. Then everybody relaxed—except the child—and the women came out to the road to give me precise instructions. They didn't think the stepping-stones would be above water today—and they were right.

Round the next corner a concrete roadblock supported a NO ROAD sign. Then I saw a river lined with willows and alders. Its fast brown water was swirling and glinting in the sun below the trees' fresh green, and it seemed incongruous—yet obscurely reassuring—to find such a troublesome border taking such a lovely form. Standing on the remains of the old narrow bridge (it must have been very attractive) I looked at a newish county council cottage twenty yards away—deserted, all its windows blown in, yet a framed photograph of a County Cavan football team still hanging on an inside wall. Across the border was a thatched cottage half-hidden by trees: probably it was empty, too. I could see not a sign of life anywhere and suddenly I remembered the Turkish–Soviet border at Ani. Though there are no watch-towers here one gets the same feeling of animation artificially suspended by politics. I looked down at the rusty carcass of a bus filled with boulders; the locals' attempt—plus these submerged stepping-stones—to replace the bridge. How much more efficiently the Baltis or Nepalese would have coped, with so many boulders and trees available!

Back on the road I was nearly run down by two Irish Army Land-Rovers going towards the non-bridge at top speed. As I turned off onto another byroad they raced back towards Belturbet. Pedalling slowly along a deserted hilly road parallel with the border, I looked north when the high hedges permitted. Fermanagh was a long ridge of wooded or cultivated land with little houses that even from a distance were perceptibly neater than most Co Cavan homesteads. Within only a few miles I passed several abandoned farmhouses, cottages and hovels; it must be easy to go to ground hereabouts. Most gates had been improvised from old bedsteads, tar-barrels and/or bundles of thorn. I surmounted one bedstead to attend to my morning duty, leaving Roz in the ditch and paying no attention to an approaching vehicle. But it stopped beside Roz with a squeal of brakes and three young soldiers clutching rifles came over the 'gate' so quickly that it collapsed. As my activities were at a crucial stage I could do nothing but squat on, causing the Irish Army to retreat in such confusion that one youth tripped over his rifle.

The next cross-border road was about half a mile beyond a little town where a tactful publican said it was tough work this weather on a bike—no doubt by way of easing any embarrassment I might feel about my early thirst. His business had suffered greatly because of The Troubles and he did not lower his voice when condemning the IRA. "I'm not a cruel man but I'd hang the lot of them. Shooting's too good." He recalled how along the border things had been improving—significantly, if slowly—since 1952, when Dublin and Stormont agreed to run the Foyle Fisheries between them. After that they worked together to drain the Erne and develop a hydro-electric scheme. And for over twenty years the Great Northern Railway has been operated jointly by the two governments. "What with all that," he said, "and people everywhere getting less religious, the border would've faded off the map by the end of this century—in spite of the politicians. But now it won't. Thanks to these Provo bastards—if you'll excuse me. Ten years ago we were all relaxed around these parts, after the O'Neill–Lemass meetings. It's hard to explain it, but people on both sides just didn't feel the border *mattered* any more. And now look at us—afraid to lie down in our beds at night!" I found it interesting that he, who was Old IRA as he proudly told me, directed all his animosity towards the Provos. This over-simplifying always happens when a situation is both very complex and very emotional; it's a retreat from laborious thinking into easy feeling.* What a disservice the Provos have done the Northern Catholics! All over the world people felt such sympathy for them when their plight was first publicised in 1969 and now most of that sympathy has been quenched by the excesses of their 'defenders'. If we in the South, who grew up knowing the background, are beginning to say, "To hell with them all!"

---

*During later wanderings in the counties of Leitrim, Cavan, Monaghan and Donegal I often came across this 'fading border' theory—or perhaps I should say 'memory'.

how can the uninformed English be blamed for feeling the same only more so?

Not far from the pub a glum young soldier was on duty behind a shoulder-high pile of sandbags with his rifle pointing across the quiet street. Even such an embryonic army-post seemed bizarre in the middle of this dopey Irish townlet. On one level it was hard to take it seriously, a reaction the Provos apparently share. Yet deep down it stirred a flicker of disquiet. Am I becoming morbidly super-sensitive to intimations of violence? In other words, too soft? To acclaim brave warriors has for so long been a part of our tradition that one feels half-guilty about no longer liking the thought of young men being trained to kill other young men.

The gardai checkpoint on the edge of the town was manned by an extremely handsome and chatty young guard. He held me in conversation for ten minutes and assured me that I would be perfectly safe across the border where the people are "not so bad as they're made out to be". As we talked three huge trucks laden with gravel from a County Fermanagh pit came through the barrier *en route* to a Co Cavan building-site. "Dozens come across every day," the guard explained. "At this rate we'll soon have one of the Six Counties back."

Soon I had passed two signposts, the first saying, 'Unapproved Road', the second 'Co Fermanagh Boundary ½ mile'. This last both amused and irritated me. It is a not-so-subtle reminder that the Republic refuses to recognise the state of Northern Ireland and still claims jurisdiction over the whole island of Ireland, which naturally keeps Unionist ire on the boil.

There is nothing to mark the border; if there were it would long since have been blown up unless heavily guarded day and night. Yet a more peaceful countryside could not be imagined. Rolling farmland—contented cows—quietness—hay-smells—churns by the roadside. Hard to believe that occasionally those churns—solid monuments to the regular rhythm of rural life—do *not* contain milk ... Soon one notices neater gardens, more fresh paint, real gates, trim wooden fencing and newer cars—with British registration numbers—in the farmyards. And the road surface begins to improve.

Upper Lough Erne was all sparkling wavelets between green islands. It is about eleven miles long with fifty-seven islands, some heavily wooded; a few are still inhabited by humans and a few by herds of wild goats. Lisnaskea seemed all grim grey stone houses and empty streets. There was a lot of nasty fast traffic on the main road to Maguiresbridge where I suddenly realised what was missing—parked cars. In most Northern towns parking on the streets is now forbidden. But the publican said with a twinkle, "It's OK to park bikes—if you lock them." (Why? A sizeable bomb would fit in Roz's saddle-bag.)

I detected myself immediately glancing around that pub in search of symbols to give me my bearings. These were not hard to find; a Redemptorist mission collecting box on the bar, an advertisement for a local Gaelic Athletic Association club dance, another for a Feis Ceoil that had taken place three weeks earlier. Any one of these would have been enough. I was displeased to find myself adapting so quickly to the divide—call it religious, ethnic, economic or what you will. But it's so central to all of life in the North that the outsider at once feels compelled to allow for it. Not to do so would simply show insensitivity to the local atmosphere. And could conceivably, in certain areas, be dangerous.

Despite the hot noon sun a turf fire burned brightly in the bar grate. The only other customer was an ageless sort of man who looked like an unemployed farm-labourer. Both he and the publican were polite but not relaxedly friendly. They refused to comment on even the most trivial aspect of The Troubles and plainly my being from the Free State by no means endeared me to them. They asked why I was cycling around the Six Counties and seemed to think that 'wanting to get to know the North' insufficiently explained such eccentric behaviour. Perhaps in future I had best explain that I am hoping to write a book about the area.

The bridge of Maguiresbridge is an attractive seventeenth-century effort which I crossed to leave the main road. Narrow, hilly boreens (perfectly kept) took me to Marble Arch Glen through superb countryside with the Benaughlin and Cuileagh mountains on my left above stretches of dense woodland. Towards Enniskillen lay miles of placid farmland and ahead I

occasionally glimpsed Lough Macnean, said by anglers to provide the best coarse fishing in Europe. Leaving Roz locked to
a gate I approached Marble Arch on foot, wishing it had been
given some name less redolent of diesel fumes and traffic caco-
phony. For more than a mile my path followed the leaping,
clear-brown Claddagh river through a National Trust wood
between the tallest ash trees I have ever seen; apparently limestone encourages their growth. The path ended at Marble
Arch. This extraordinary complex of dark cliffs, deep pools,
piles of giant boulders and shadowy grottoes is the lower en-
trance to the subterranean labyrinth of Cuileagh, first explored
in 1895. Now it is popular with pot-holers but a stern notice
warns visitors against solitary underground adventures.

I climbed out of the dim, cool, still wood onto the windy
brightness of high green uplands. In every direction I could
see distant mountains and often the glint of lakes. Late prim-
roses grew around silvery chunks of limestone on the close-
cropped turf and small clouds sailed fast in a very blue sky. On
the next, higher hill dazzling white lambs bounded away from
me but their mothers now have such heavy fleeces that they
could only waddle. I found one dead ewe, trapped on her back
by the weight of her wool with a sad, puzzled lamb lying beside
her. Strange piles of stones, amidst groves of ash and hawthorn,
looked pagan and mysterious; their arrangement seemed not
fortuitous. I walked on and on through this innocent brightness
and beauty thinking how unlikely that, two miles away,
three men were blown to bits a few weeks previously. And a
few days previously a farmer, whose house I passed on the way
back to Roz, was made to drive a bomb to the nearest village
and park it outside the police-station. Odd that the atmosphere
of the place has not been tainted—no bad 'vibes'. But there
are other vibes. Ernest Sandford's splendid new guidebook tells
me that in parts of Fermanagh some people still use a combination of herbs and magic to cure both human and animal ail-
ments. I can believe it.

My first Enniskillen pub, though new and luxurious, was not
unpleasant. The affable young man behind the bar explained,
"We used to be on the corner over there. Then after the bomb
we built this place." According to him, inflation is 'making a

nonsense' of the compensation system. If your property was blown up in 1974 compensation is paid according to its 1974 value—and where does that leave you, when you are rebuilding in 1976? The government, he felt, should do something about this injustice. I cravenly said nothing. But I wondered how many governments would treat an anarchic region as generously as Westminster is now treating Northern Ireland.

In the street I asked a young woman wearing a Pioneer pin the way to the post office. "First to your right," she said—and then called after me, "Careful not to miss it! It's in a caravan since it was blown up, inside a wire barrier." (I notice Catholics tend to say 'since it was blown up' and Protestants 'since they blew it up'.) Everybody seems unselfconsciously matter-of-fact about the extraordinary way they live now. Yet the process of adapting to this sort of permanently watchful existence *must* be damaging. The annual statistics say that Northern Ireland's citizens are no more at risk from bombs and bullets than from road accidents. But it's the nature of the threat that creates tension, not the numbers of victims.

The grey-faced post office clerk was the first (and so far the only) person to react unfavourably to my accent. He was chatting cosily to another customer when I entered the caravan, then his face and voice hardened for dealing with me. But can he be blamed if an instinctive hostility is triggered off by a 'Catholic' accent? Who knows what he and his colleagues suffered mentally and/or physically when the post office was blown up?

This evening I realise that I've been suffering from 'anticipation neurosis', a condition automatically cured by being *in*, instead of approaching, the feared situation. Once over the border my nervousness evaporated completely. I just feel a bit guilty now towards all my jittery friends. At home I soothed them with assurances—perfectly sincere at the time—that I would avoid Northern pubs. Yet already I've been in three. And not, as cynics may think, because my love of beer is stronger than my fear of death. Some obstinacy mechanism— a form of pride, really—begins to operate when there is a question of changing normal habits because of pressures being put on society by factions one cannot respect. (Also there is the uni-

versal delusion 'It can't happen to me', which no doubt is necessary to prevent people going to bits under stress.) Anyway, how
else, in Europe, can one meet the locals? Outside of Europe
it's easy, so many are so eager to befriend the traveller. But
in Northern Ireland, especially, where it's prudent now to
suspect strangers, even a teetotaller would have to frequent
pubs or forever hold his tongue.

13 June

I have fallen in love with Fermanagh—especially the rough
border stretches, all mountains and moors and wide silent lakes.
In places one can still imagine how it must have seemed to the
English in 1606, when the touring King's Deputy and his
retinue had to sleep in their tents because throughout the whole
county there was not even an attempt at a town. The assizes
had to be held in a ruined monastery, the only building
big enough. Fertile ground here for Orange myth-making!
The good land going to waste, populated only by savage Gaels
living mainly on curdled milk in cramped wattle huts without
chimneys—a people ignorant of and indifferent to the fast-
changing world of Renaissance Europe. So what a good thing
that along came the industrious planters to develop this wilderness, just as their relations were in due course to develop the US,
Canada, Australia, New Zealand, large areas of Africa—all
places populated by other savages who were mostly easier to cope
with than the Gaels, possibly because they weren't the same
colour.

It helps to remember that the Protestants have been in
Northern Ireland longer than the Whites have been in the US.
It *is* now their country as much as the Catholics'; they have
no other. Had the Gaels been 'subdued' as effectively as the
Red Indians and the Aboriginals there would be no disputing
that point in the 1970s. But apart from anything else Gaelic
labour was needed, just as convict labour was needed to develop
Australia. Then religion (can't get away from it) frustrated
widespread miscegenation; and was reinforced by the settlers'
feelings of racial superiority—something linked to yet other
than the religious difference. Not to mention the blood-pride
of the Gael—a strong and silent pride, far removed from

sentimental word-spinning in Celtic twilights. Something old as the bogs and tough as the oak in them. I can see it still on the lean dark faces of the hill-farmers here. And feel it still, too, occasionally, stirring in my own mongrel blood of the Pale. So there could be no merger of races; and recurring rebellion throughout the rest of Ireland kept the pot of sedition and suspicion simmering in Ulster—and sometimes boiling. And here we are ...

If the Unionists were not now entitled to call Northern Ireland their own country it would logically follow that half the population of the world should be shifted or conquered to right ancient wrongs. Perhaps the snag is that there are too few Unionists; were there several million their claim to Northern Ireland would be more obvious. Because there are only one million, too many people vaguely feel they could and should be made to toe the Republican line—especially as their treatment of Catholics has made them seem a people who deserve punishment. But if it were formally accepted by the Northern Catholics, and by Dublin and London, that Northern Ireland is the Unionists' homeland by right—not merely because nobody can think of any way of wresting it from them—might they not then treat the Catholics more justly, seeing them at last as fellow-citizens rather than as subversives? Looked at this way round, the ball is now in the Catholics' court. If they could bring themselves to accept that 350-year-old wrongs cannot be righted and are best forgotten, then the way would be clear for the Unionists to relax, clean out their reeking stable and start again—for the first time free of fear lest someone might somehow suddenly dispossess them. Perhaps enough allowance has never been made for the constant insecurity they have suffered since their makeshift state was set up in 1920. Nobody behaves well when feeling threatened.

This line of thought is cheering. It offers some hope since the non-IRA Catholics are far more mentally and emotionally flexible than the Protestants and so are more likely to compromise. I have left the British out of my long-term reckoning. Less than a week here has convinced me that they have no important role to play in the future of this region. The Unionists can't have it every way and in fact must cease to be Uni-

onists and become Northern Irishmen if they want their claim
to own and rule Northern Ireland generally recognised.

14 June

This Fermanagh farmhouse is large, substantial, spotless—
the cleanest home I've been in since visiting Switzerland. No
need to add that it's Protestant. Sam and Betty are staunch
moderate Unionists who spent ten years in Canada but came
back when Sam's unmarried elder brother died. Their two sons
are at school in Enniskillen and soon—they hope—will be off
to study 'across the water'. Certainly not in Belfast; they
haven't gone near the place for a decade and think I'm mad
even to cross the Bann. Had life been normal they would have
preferred their boys to stay in Northern Ireland and of course
George would have got the farm; now they are considering selling it when Sam wants to retire. "I'd rather see them away
out of it," says Betty. "What is there for them here but risk
and uncertainty? It said on the radio 16,000 left Northern Ireland last year and would you blame them? It's peaceful enough
in South Fermanagh for people our age. But with boys you
never know ... What is there for them but work—or mischief?
Young lads need a bit of fun. Surely they could go over the
border to dances and so on—we've cousins in Leitrim—but
you'd be uneasy with them toing and froing in the dark. We
had our honeymoon in Killarney but we wouldn't have any
mind to travel the Free State now."

Yet Betty and Sam go to Donegal for a week-end three or
four times a year 'to get away from it all'. Most Fermanagh
people can't think of Donegal, Leitrim and Cavan as belonging
to another political entity. These are close and familiar
counties, part of their traditional 'home territory' though
largely Catholic—and far safer, they feel, than Protestant
Antrim or Down. In this area partition often seems merely ludicrous. Many of the 'settler' farmers in the mountains have
absorbed an amount of 'native' culture and there have even
been some mixed marriages. One is told in a whisper that So-
and-So's maternal grandfather was a Catholic—'But there was
no ill-feeling about it. We've always been easy-going round

here. 'Live and Let Live'—did you see that motto up on the old corn-market in Lisnaskea? That's the way we'd like to keep it in Fermanagh.'

In both communities many of those who grew up pre-partition still see the border as contrived and undesirable, something imposed on innocent country-folk by a bunch of squabbling politicians. It saddened me to talk to such old men up on their windy, lonely, lovely bogs overlooking both North and South. They are a link with something lost that can never be found again. Their children and grandchildren, whether Catholic or Protestant, seem much more British; some of the former might be shocked to realise how hybrid they have become under the influence of the British media, educational system, social welfare system and all the rest.

One old man, met below Cuileagh, reminded me that in Ulster the Gaelic civilisation lasted longer, in a pure form, than anywhere else. He was Church of Ireland but scorned myths, Orange or Green. For an hour he stood talking to me in the sun, leaning on his spade, while his son and grandson loaded turf into a trailer. He had left school at the age of twelve and all his life laboured happily on these hills. He loved books, he said, and when he was a lad an old rector had died and left him a whole boxful. He quoted Gibbon, Chesterton, Wolfe Tone, Macaulay, Yeats, Thackeray, Milton, Mangan, T. S. Eliot—and of course the Bible. His wife died last year and his married daughter wants him to move into Enniskillen. ''But I'm better off on my own. Her place is full of children watching television. It's not a place you could be at peace in, with the books.'' A man after my own heart.

Making my way down that mountain, on a rough sheep-track, I asked myself—who would have developed Ulster had the province not been planted? The Gaelic chiefs? But they had a vested interest in keeping it the way it was. Yet *somebody* had to interfere if it were ever to catch up with the rest of Ireland, never mind the rest of Europe. Perhaps the plantations were inevitable, however deplorable; history taking its course, wearing down an anomalous people as rivers wear down rocks on their way to the sea.

After supper this evening Betty's sister and brother-in-law

called for a ceidhle* with the news that a neighbouring farm has gone up for sale. Much speculation: "They say John's heart isn't the best and he thinks Jane has to do too much"—"But it could be they know Robert won't ever come back. And isn't he better off where he is?"—"All the same, I wouldn't be sure John could ever be happy inside himself off the land. You'll find 'tis Jane behind it." It is accepted that John will settle for less than the real value of the place because he is a responsible citizen who wouldn't sell to a Catholic. Catholics will bid and bid high ("Where do they get the money?" asks Betty grimly), but it was carefully explained to me that it wouldn't be fair to the security forces to give the Provos another foothold so near the border. Everybody had been warned about this at the Hall; "Wasn't that so?"—and Betty looked to Sam for confirmation. But Sam's usually open and friendly face had closed and hardened. The Orange Order is a semi-secret society and Betty should not have forgotten where I come from. I hastily changed the subject.

Betty, however, was not at all abashed. She is naturally communicative and guileless and soon returned to the mystery of Catholic wealth. Her brother-in-law then reported what he had been told in Omagh by a decent man who wouldn't spread rumours. It was proved now, and there was no more doubt about it—the Provos were being supported in their efforts to buy land by the Allied Irish Banks, backed by the Bank of Manhattan, which had been given orders by the CIA. Sam nodded knowingly, while the two women exclaimed in horror and alarm—yet relishing the drama of the revelation. In silent astonishment I considered this new myth, gleaming from the mint. Is it needed to reinforce some of the old Orange myths, now being slightly devalued by Northern Ireland's unwonted exposure to the outside world? If Rome seems a little less menacing than it did, why not coin a CIA threat? Anything to keep Orangemen united and on the defensive against Catholics, who are always supported by evil outsiders. Or is all that supposing a more calculated origin for myths than they actually

* Many Gaelic words are still heard in Northern Ireland. Down South 'ceidhle' means a session of traditional Irish dancing; in Fermanagh it means dropping in on a neighbour for a cup of tea and a chat, either casually or by invitation.

have? How *do* they start? By a sort of spontaneous combustion of the public imagination? Or through one tiny seed of truth having an Orange or Green spell put on it by professional myth-ographers so that it grows into a monstrous tree of falsehood? The Provos do get funds from Irish-Americans with more money than sense who see them as the pure-bred descendants of Tone, Pearse *et al.* And the AIB in Northern Ireland (and maybe in the South, too) does pay them protection money. Given those two seeds you can grow any number of myths, especially at a time when so many outlandish things are happening on the international scene.

Northern Ireland induces contradictory moods. For a while I'm elated and hopeful because of the sheer likeableness and good sense of the people I meet; then it seems possible that they will be able to sort out their problems sooner rather than later. Yet within an hour I can be cast into deep gloom by conversa-tions that reveal the hard unchanging core of those problems. I have now been four days with this family and it is impossible to think of them as stereotyped bigots. The evening I arrived we sat by an unnecessary fire (lit to underline how welcome I was) and Betty assured me, "There's no ill-feeling around here and never has been. We'd all go to the end of the earth for each other. I respect anyone who lives up to their beliefs and our Catholic friends feel the same." Did the lady protest too much? I don't think so. I have seen for myself how good relations are in all sorts of little ways—ways which seem to reflect a genuine wish on both sides to live in civilised harmony.

Yet the very fact that I automatically used that word 'sides' is ominous. Nowadays Sam and his friends can be told at their Loyal Orange Lodge meeting not to sell to papists for security reasons. But even if there were no such convenient 'instant rationalisation' available, they would still have been reminded not to sell to papists, period. He and Betty and their friends aspire to tolerance yet no ordinary individual can escape from the wheel of intolerance to which their community has been bound for centuries. And if someone did escape—what then? If Sam insisted on selling land to a papist, what would happen to him? The Orange Lodges do not encourage violence—we are told. They don't really have to; thousands of Orangemen are well-armed and worship the sort of Old Testament God who is always gratified by the elimination of his enemies. And of course The Troubles have made it much easier to disguise bigotry as patriotism.

By now I have cycled many miles around Fermanagh but have seen only two members of the security forces—a pair of good-looking, cheerful, helpful RUC women police constables in Enniskillen. No other police, no UDR, no British army patrols, nothing to flaw the impression of a traditional rural community going about its daily tasks in a contented neighbourly way. A Protestant lends medicine for a sick Catholic cow, a Catholic fetches a spare part for a broken Protestant tractor, everybody goes to the funeral of an Orangeman who always spoke out against the fiddling of the voting register. All seems as it should be and what's the fuss?

The fuss is when any member of either community breaks an unwritten sectarian law. Or when paramilitaries need to 'borrow' your car or telephone—or simply want all the money you have in the house, or a cheque will do if you've no cash handy. The effect of what goes on behind the scenes is noticed only when the stranger arrives unexpectedly in someone's farmyard, or at someone's door, and sees the momentary fear on faces that an instant later will have become smiling and welcoming.

It is strange to sit in a comfortable farm kitchen—with cattle lowing nearby, bright copper pans on the walls, a sheep-dog and two tabbies on the hearthrug, Queen Elizabeth II in coronation robes over the mantelpiece—and suddenly to realise that this is, and for fifty-five years has been, a society governed under the surface by guns. In past years the guns of the B Specials, the RUC and at intervals the IRA; more recently the guns of the UDR, British army, Provos, Stickies, UDA, UVF, UFF, and countless individual gangsters who have not found it hard to acquire weapons under prevailing conditions.

Most Protestants in this area believe that the present troubles would never have become so acute but for the disbanding of the B Specials and the disarming of the RUC—two measures insisted upon by the Hunt Report. To the 'B.s', especially, they say, should go most of the credit for keeping the IRA down during 'the peaceful years'. The B.s were unofficially yet openly the military arm of the Orange Order, a semi-private force of 10,000 men who kept their guns in their homes and were subject to none of the normal British controls under which their successors in the UDR now chafe. Their duty was to protect the state from Taigs—which they did, and nobody questioned their methods. They were rough, tough bigots, obviously not as depraved as Green propaganda would have it yet the authentic descendants of the dreaded eighteenth-century Peep o' Day Boys. Catholics feel an hysterical hatred for them and cannot see that it was possible to excuse the creation of the force, if not its subsequent behaviour, by reference to the papists' opposition in 1920 to the founding of the state of Northern Ireland. Unfortunately the fact that so many ex-B men joined the UDR, when it was established to reinforce the disarmed RUC, deterred those moderate Catholics who might otherwise have enlisted in the new regiment.

The vicious circle of gun-law has not really been broken by the 1970 reforms. Since then gun-clubs have proliferated throughout the North where there are more firearm licences held than in any other part of the UK. Also, dangerous attitudes have been bred by half a century of government-condoned illegal violence. Protestants often think it necessary and normal to have firearms in the house for self-defence against the IRA; Catholics often think it allowable to attack the security forces of a state that has never shown much regard for impartial law-enforcement.

15 June

This morning I asked Betty where in Lisnaskea I could find a certain sort of shop and she gave me two addresses. This evening when I told her I had got what I needed at So-and-So's she smiled and said, "That's my brother! He just opened up the business a few months ago but I didn't want to influence you so I said nothing!" A tiny detail, yet telling a lot about the ethos of the upright Northern Irish Protestant farming family.

In Lisnaskea I visited a young couple who have left their

myths behind them and face into a lonely future—if they stay in Northern Ireland. James comes from a Co Down Protestant family, Una from a Co Armagh Catholic family. I first met them a few years ago when they were living in Dublin, giving both sets of parents a chance to recover from the shock of their marriage. Now two children have arrived and reconciliation—with reservations—has taken place; yet they would not care to live in either of their home-towns. They returned to the North for mixed reasons. James's job is unusual and there was little scope for him down South; also—this was obvious, though not explicitly stated—they feel that not to have returned would have been a personal surrender to sectarianism. They are pioneers who instinctively respond to challenges in a positive way. It helps their personal relationship—Una explained—that both had abandoned Christianity before they met; therefore there can be no recriminations about undue influence having been used by either side. But now they have no niche in Northern society and they find discrimination cutting both ways. For over a year Una could not get a suitable job because she had been to a Catholic school and on their return from Dublin James, who works for a Protestant firm, was made to realise that as a non-Orangeman he cannot expect quick promotion.

I was amused this evening by the verbal fencing that took place when Una and James called at the farmhouse to collect me for a pub-crawl. They were of course invited in—to have let them turn away from the door without refreshment would have been unthinkable—and plainly it was at first deduced from their surname that they were Protestants. (Though surnames have become a rather unreliable guide over the centuries; and first names can be ambiguous, too, despite many being unmistakably 'sectarian'.) Then a chance remark seemed to imply Catholic links and once doubt had been raised Betty and Sam could not rest easy until the matter had been clarified. They would have treated them—and I believe felt towards them—no less kindly if they knew them to be Catholics; but they just had to be *sure*. Schools are of course an almost infallible guide to religion, followed by sports clubs, home addresses and employers' identities—though the higher one rises on the social scale the less reliable are these last two indicators. Una and James must often encounter this situation and at first they good-humouredly evaded the various trip-questions. Then Una went slightly on the defensive and this seemed to be the signal for James to end the game by giving the facts.

20 June

I have spent the past five days cycling from village to small town to farm through the counties of Londonderry and Tyrone.

My first glimpse of the Brits came near Omagh, where an open Land-Rover slowly overtook me with two boy soldiers and a happy-looking tracker-dog gazing out from the back. When I waved and smiled the youths saluted and the dog stood up and wagged his tail. Then came an incongruous-looking war-machine. No doubt it would have seemed commonplace to those who have been following the fortunes of Northern Ireland on television over the past several years, but to me it was a most extraordinary unidentifiable object, at once comical and sinister as it trundled through the quiet countryside.

In the next village I asked the Catholic youth behind the bar if he thought it would be a good idea for Britain to withdraw her troops. He sighed. "Of course we'd thank God to be shot of them—but not now. Not the way things are." The only other customer agreed. He, too, was a Catholic, a middle-aged commercial traveller from Derry. "If the Brits went I'd be on the boat with them," he said.

"They're not *all* bad," continued the youth, "just a mixed bunch, like anyone else. My father hates the lot—he'd see 'em all dead, never mind gone home. But I say most of 'em don't know what it's all about—*they've* nothing against us."

I clutched happily at this straw of tolerance. How splendid—I thought—if the young are beginning to question parental prejudices! But then the youth went on, "Things are much worse round here since The Troubles. In the old days everybody mixed and got along—and mostly the older people still do. But me and my friends, we keep well away from the other lot. Mixing isn't safe. Tartan gangs come out from Derry and the RUC pretend not to see them."

I asked how my companions felt about a united Ireland and

the youth shrugged. "D'you want us down there? I wouldn't say you do—not since we got so troublesome!"

The commercial traveller smiled. "And wouldn't we lose an awful lot? Just to be sensible about it ... I'm not fussy. If it came and worked I suppose I'd be glad enough. I was brought up to think that's what I should want .... But I'm damn sure I wouldn't kill anyone to get it."

On my way into the next village (mainly Protestant) I came upon a gaily decorated stretch of main road. Right across it was freshly painted, in three lines of huge red, white and blue letters, NO POPE HERE, UP ULSTER, WE WANT DEMOCRACY, REMEMBER 1690. In the local hotel lounge hung a large photograph of a smiling, eager-looking, handsome young man; the black marble plaque underneath was inscribed in gold letters: 'Murdered by the IRA in 1972. At the rising up and the going down of the sun we will remember him!' Unfortunately they will. And, in a way, who can blame them?

The barman—small, slight and sandy—seemed quite determined to remain aloof from the Southerner. But when I persistently chatted on he thawed and asked, "Do you still talk down there about the Black North?" I had to admit that now it's even worse, that most of us don't talk at all about the North because we'd rather forget it. Then he and I and the three obvious Orangemen who were having their lunch-time beers discussed The Troubles for an hour. They were virulently anti-Westminster yet they favoured an indefinite continuation of Direct Rule because a Southern take-over seemed the only possible alternative.

In several Protestant pubs or hotel bars I have had to spend over an hour getting across the simple message that I am well-disposed towards the entire population of Northern Ireland. This seems a strange struggle to be taking place in Europe though I am used to versions of it further afield. When for half an hour grunts and nods, with heads averted, are the only responses from my fellow-drinkers, I am sometimes tempted to give up. Yet if I burble inanely on about the weather and inflation and the scenery, and then mention that I hope to write a book about Northern Ireland, the barriers almost always suddenly go down. And when they do it is astonishing how freely people talk, as though they had been waiting years to meet an outsider who wanted to hear their point of view.

Most Northern pubs are owned by Catholics because Protestants have an uneasy feeling that it is sinful to sell alcohol. Yet they drink it with enthusiasm so thousands of good Orangemen who would never otherwise allow a penny of theirs to stray into Green pockets are obliged regularly to patronise 'the others'. This curious example of double-think makes it quite difficult for me to find Protestant pubs for my heart-to-heart talks with Unionists, who naturally won't open out within earshot of papist bar-attendants. However, I have been greatly cheered by my sessions with mixed groups in Catholic pubs. Many everyday issues still unite the country folk and in some villages I rejoiced to hear the two sides teasing each other about religion—with no hidden barbs.

To meet the women folk, and the sort of men who don't drink in pubs—a considerable minority, even in Ireland—I have been stoically frequenting cafés and tea-shops and dutifully partaking of unwanted beverages and fattening foods while engaging my neighbours in conversation. And isolated farms are easy prey. The arrival of a talkative female on a bicycle usually causes some alarm at first but then I am seen as a wonderful break in the monotony and often it is hard to get away.

I now find myself in the vaguely embarrassing position of being able to distinguish between Catholics and Protestants by appearance—or is it by 'aura'? One would prefer not to react to other human beings in sectarian terms but this is what Northern Ireland does to travellers. In London I often play an ethnic game, spotting people I guess to be Irish and then asking the way to find out if my guess is correct. It usually is and this subject fascinates me. Emerson pointed out that in England every religious sect has a distinctive physiognomy. And some twenty years ago Michel Leiris, the French anthropologist, argued that facial expression should come under the heading of 'behaviour' rather than 'physique'. Were I asked to describe the difference in the North I could only say that to me the Catholic face seems in the whole more humorous, more happy and less 'controlled'.

These past few days have been still, warm and overcast, with the flanks of the Sperrins muted brown and olive-green, or grey-blue in the distance. I stopped one morning in the mountains to watch sheep being sheared by three men with 'Protestant' faces. When they had slowly decided that I was harmless, and invited me to the farmhouse for elevenses, they revealed 'Protestant' feelings, too—of animosity towards London for conspiring with Dublin to betray them, and towards Dublin for having undermined London's loyalty to the Loyalists. They considered the Unionists misunderstood, misinterpreted, misused and about to be misled into some cunningly disguised trap which would have them all in the 'Free State' before a rabbit could hop. They blamed 'that Paisley' for a lot of it because his raving and ranting had got decent Unionists a bad name. They agreed with his anti-ecumenism—they were old-fashioned Presbyterians and wouldn't want to pretend otherwise—but they didn't like the way he put it over. And they wouldn't ever be for stirring up hate—'There's enough of it around'. I liked them enormously. There is something very disarming about these rugged 'no surrender' types with their high principles, straightforward talk, tough attitudes and soft hearts.

Beyond the sheep farm a little lonely road climbed high between small emerald rock-flecked fields. Low rounded mountains overlooked green valleys dotted with neat white dwellings. The turf-cutters on the dark-brown bogs straightened up to wave and sometimes marshy land glistened black and silver. Along high steep banks grew vivid clusters of pink and purple bog-flowers and the may and gorse were still blooming—great clouds of white and gold resting on the fields. There was no traffic until I had free-wheeled down and down to level, rich farmland, sheltered by many stands of beeches, elms and chestnuts.

The North's towns and villages seem unnaturally subdued. There are so few cars, so many lines of concrete-filled barrels down the main streets to prevent parking near shops, so few people about and such grim police barracks—fortified, inside giant wire cages, against bombs and machine-guns. These jolt one, in prim-looking little towns, after cycling for hours through tranquil countryside. We are used to thinking of the village police-station or gardai-barracks as a place into which anyone can wander at any hour, without even knocking, for advice and sympathy about a lost cat or a stolen bicycle. It is very much part of our way of life that the police should be acceptable and accessible, not driven to defend themselves from the public like an army of occupation. Until the policing problem has been solved, how can normality be restored anywhere in Northern Ireland?

Of course not all Northern towns are prim. And when you come to a dejected, neglected main street, with litter in the gutter, cracked (or missing) windows, green brasses on the hall-doors, untidy displays in the shops and an indecent number of pubs (boarded up against bombs and bullets) you can be sure that most of the inhabitants are Catholic. In one such town, in a decrepit pub, the only other customer pulled my pint because the barman was 'out the back'. Strangers are never left alone for an instant in Northern pubs. When I asked "Have you had much trouble around here?" the reply was cheerful. "No, thanks be to God, we've been terrible lucky. There was on'y the supermarket burned down, and a garage and tailor's shop blown up, and the RUC post mortar bombed. And there was two police shot dead just round the corner there. But mostly we're very quiet." I looked hard at him, suspecting irony, but he had meant exactly what he said. Everything is relative. Then the middle-aged barman returned and made his comment. "It's a shame we couldn't have the police back same as before and be rid of the army. Those two RUC lads shot here was fine fellas—everyone loved 'em, Catholic and Protestant. 'Twas some outsider done it for sure. But look at Belfast these times with the army—they've destroyed the place entirely. I wouldn't go there now to save my life".

I suggested that even more of Belfast might have been 'destroyed entirely' without the Brits as a buffer state; but the barman, who was very well-disposed towards the RUC, would not accept this. Yet I have met other Catholics who view the army as a comparatively benign force while concentrating all their hatred on the RUC and the UDR—seeing the latter as B Specials in disguise, which too often they are.

4

Derry is Different

Heavy traffic makes for joyless cycling on the wide, dull main road from Limavady through industrial suburbs to Derry. This morning a head wind kept my speed down to four m.p.h. and lavish broken glass along the verges gave Roz her first puncture of the trip. I passed closely guarded housing estates where the soldiers' families live. Later I was told that they are 'bussed' to shop in towns where they are not identifiable. It seems unlikely there could be any such town in Northern Ireland; probably this is a delicate way of saying 'To Unionist shopping areas in mainly Unionist towns'. What a life for those wives and young children! All the boredom and tension of being posted in a rebellious colony without the compensation of getting to know some exotic corner of the globe. In and around Derry one suddenly becomes very aware of soldiers speeding to and fro, always with rifles pointing at a population which feigns to ignore them completely.

Four miles upstream from the broad Atlantic inlet of Lough Foyle, Derry overlooks the river. On both high, steep banks its buildings rise in tiers from the water's edge; warehouses, dwellings, shops, churches, new housing estates—and new ruins. The river is spanned by an unlovely double-decker steel bridge, opened in 1933 and named after Northern Ireland's first Prime Minister, Lord Craigavon. I paused half-way across the bridge and looked back at the mainly Protestant Waterside. Wide shopping streets lead up to thousands of little working-class houses, quite recently built on the highest ridges; and to the south of these, on lower slopes, detached Victorian/Edwardian villas are now scarcely visible amidst the mid-summer leafiness of tall trees. Turning west again, towards the old walled city, I gazed beyond it into Donegal. Derry is almost on the border and the Republic's most northerly county forms an important part of its natural hinterland. No wonder so many apolitical foreign visitors, who know nothing of Northern Ireland's problems, regard the partitioning of this tiny island as utterly nonsensical.

Despite Derry's splendid setting, one's first impression is of physical squalor. Uninspired new buildings contrast with scenes of destruction, demolition, reconstruction—and bare ugly sites awaiting further uninspired buildings. But this morning, as I explored many hilly streets, unexpected laneways and attractive unbombed corners, I found some ancient spell being laid upon me. Not that this city, as a city, can claim to be ancient. It was only in 1614 that a group of London guilds provided labour and cash for the creation of the last walled city to be built in Europe. In 1649 and 1688–9 this investment was justified when Derry withstood two famous sieges—hence 'the Maiden City'—and thus established itself in Northern Protestant folklore as a main source of communal pride.

Sieges apart, Derry's history goes back to the dawn of Irish Christianity. In 546 St Columba founded his first abbey here on a tree-crowned hill; the Irish word 'Doire' means 'a place of oaks'. And one quickly becomes aware of Derry as a city where—despite centuries of discrimination and discontent—the Catholic and Protestant strands within Irish Christianity have in some subtle way become interwoven. At present the city's population of 51,000 is about 60 per cent Catholic and 40 per cent Protestant and within hours of my crossing Craigavon bridge at 8.30 am I had been told by seven citizens that 'Derry is Different'. By which they meant that Derry people, whatever their religion or politics, are not temperamentally inclined towards Belfast's brand of implacable sectarianism.

Approaching the battered Guildhall at noon, I found the open area in front cordoned off. There was some leisurely police and military activity and an elderly woman explained, "They had a wee bomb went off up Shipquay St last evenin' and they think now maybe there's another in that shop"—she nodded towards a shoe-shop beside a military check-point and we watched a magnificent cream-coloured army Alsatian sniffing up and down the pavement in front while his handler

exchanged quips with two young woman traffic wardens across
the road. "The soldiers always look more cheerful when there's
somethin' goin' on," observed my companion. "It's the standin'
about all day doin' nothin' makes 'em mad. Bored, they gets.
That's what it is—plain bored. Then they'll beat up anyone
they can lay hands on. People say they're vicious but I say
they're bored. I've six sons m'self—I knows all about young
lads!" She was the sort who would have made tea for the Brits
when they first arrived in Derry and the Catholics ran to welcome them, waving tricolours and cheering in a delirium of
relief at having someone to defend them from the RUC and
the 'B men'. Perhaps she would still like to make them tea, if
she dared. But no Catholic dare, now. August 1969 seems a
long way away; the Provos hadn't been invented, then. Near
us a few people were standing around waiting, perhaps also
bored and hoping for a big bang to relieve the monotony. But
most got on as best they could with their shopping and talked
about something else. In the bookshop up Shipquay St—the
steepest main street of any city in Ireland—I remarked to a
friendly assistant that I found the public indifference to bombs
extraordinary. She sighed. "It's bad we don't notice any
more—we've got too tough."

Slowly cycling into the Bogside I saw a huge proud notice:
YOU ARE NOW IN FREE DERRY. To prove it, lamp standards
and pillar-boxes are painted green, white and orange in hori-
zontal stripes; and there are several crude life-size murals of
heavily-armed Brits with monkey heads and faces—unwitting
shades of Hanuman! Many new rows of houses or blocks of flats
already look irreparably neglected or vandalised and much
black paint has been thrown at their walls—sometimes to
deface large, carefully-painted tricolours or Easter lilies, or
legends saying BRITS OUT! REMEMBER 1916! UP THE
REPUBLIC! Are these paint splashes the work of the
Stickies? Or the Irps? Or do Tartan gangs from the Waterside
across the Foyle recklessly steal into the Bogside at dead of
night? In the midst of so much sordid vandalism the memorial
to those shot on Bloody Sunday stands immaculate and inviol-
able—the visible sign of yet another powerful myth. And
nearby, painted in large letters across the front wall of the

Bogside Inn—the main Provo pub—are the words INFORMERS WILL BE KILLED. For a moment I took this casually, as just another bit of swaggering adolescent graffiti. Then, with a chilly feeling inside, I realised that the slogan is nobody's sick joke. It is a statement of fact. How free is Free Derry?

Having already been so warmly welcomed in this city by so many total strangers, it surprised me to be at once made to feel uneasy within the Bogside Inn. The barman was disinclined to chat and I was pointedly ignored by the twenty-five or thirty men—mostly youngish, and no doubt mostly Provos—who were drinking at the long bar. Presumably they were unemployed (always one of Derry's major problems) and I wondered where they got the money to drink so much on a Monday afternoon. It's hard to describe the atmosphere. To say that it felt sinister is true but sounds ridiculous—though why should it? Given enough people with hostile attitudes, it would be odd if a place didn't feel sinister. But I hadn't been expecting any such atmosphere; everyone had assured me that Provos like a chance to put their case across to visitors.

When I was halfway through my pint an old man—the only person there of his generation—moved to stand beside me. Having found out why I was in Derry, he began to talk nostalgically about the good old days before The Troubles. He was twenty at the time of partition—"And the mistake then was the way our lot wouldn't go up to Stormont and grab fair shares for us. Too many ideals we had then, with no sense to them." He was obviously a man of some stature in the Bogside, who could loudly say such things in a Provo pub. He went on to deplore every form of bigotry but warned me against going into pubs 'across the bridge' where the population is mixed. Reminiscing, he recalled that a few years ago in the Inn every man kept his gun before him on the bar-counter while he drank. "You should have come up then. We had journalists and book-writers and professors and Communists and anarchists and all sorts. From everywhere they were coming, to 'study' us." He laughed aloud at the memory. "'Twas terrible easy to fool 'em—they'd believe any nonsense. Now they've all gone home—no more excitement. The commies got a terrible let down. They thought Derry was the start of their revolution in Britain. But Irish Catholics aren't Eyetalians. We've got our own ways of running revolutions."

I have been trying to analyse my extreme unease in that pub. Why did I not feel free to try to break down those Green barriers, as I have been quite successfully tackling Orange barriers elsewhere? The answer must be 'fear'. I was afraid of being suspected of gathering intelligence. 'Informers will be killed ... ' Informers *have* been killed. Melodramatic? Neurotic? Probably. I certainly feel rather down in my own estimation this evening. Especially as a Derry friend with Provo 'connections' has just assured me that even if I were suspected of spying I would not be killed, only beaten up or knee-capped. It seems the death-penalty is reserved for traitors from within the ranks.

23 June

I feel like a bloated sponge this evening, having spent the past two days 'absorbing' in the Bogside, the Creggan and Brandywell. These are Derry's Catholic areas where, true to Northern Irish form, everyone has slightly different opinions and theories about The Troubles. It interests me that no one ever mentions the moribund (or is it dead?) People's Democracy movement, which played such an important part at the start of The Troubles. In times of stress the present and the immediate future—or a past no more remote than last week—are all that matter to most people. And rumours multiply fast. Most seem not worth recording but I'll jot down one to give the flavour; it was repeated to me today, with relish, on four separate occasions. Among the Brits in Derry there are said to be an average of two deaths a week from self-inflicted wounds—some straight suicides, some following on attempts to get an honourable discharge. Possibly this is fact, but I find it very hard to believe. Another popular story sounds like rumour but I've good reason to believe it's true. A few days ago the Brits raided a Bogside house to lift a junior Provo and found a very senior Provo with him. They didn't want to arrest the leader, having presumably been ordered not to do so, but he insisted that if the junior were lifted, so must he be. Neither was, and the Bogside is still laughing.

Nowadays it could—and very likely would—be fatal for a Catholic to fraternise with the army. Yet enlisting in the army can be more practical for a Catholic than joining the RUC. Quite a few Derry mothers would like to see their sons safely in a British uniform and away out of Northern Ireland, despite their being unable to return home freely on leave. Some parents only learn that their children are in the Provos when their home is raided or they hear that the youngsters have been 'lifted' elsewhere. (In other families everybody is involved, from great-grandad to the five-year-old learning to make petrol bombs.) When adolescents are picked up for trivial offences some parents are relieved because this may save them from serious crime.

One English community worker told me that there are many fine young men among the Provo internees—well-intentioned, genuine, intelligent. He also knows three top Provo leaders who took to guerrilla warfare not because of passionate patriotism but because their family life had fallen to bits. All three seemed good, kind, decent, normal men when he first knew them. He described the case of a devoted husband and father whose third child was born an idiot. The mother was so devastated that she refused to have any more children and being a rigid Catholic she also refused to use contraceptives. When her husband appealed for help to his local clergy, doctors and social workers he got little sympathy and no practical advice. Within two years he had left his wife, become deeply embittered and joined the Provos for whom he brilliantly organised some truly horrible crimes. Yet he remains devoted to his children and often sends them gifts through the 'special messenger' who told me his story.

Opinions vary widely about the behaviour of the Brits during house searches. Obviously this is partly because the behaviour itself varies widely—so much depends on the regiments involved and the officers' attitudes—and partly because people's feelings towards the Brits do likewise. Several Catholics assured me that many stories of military misbehaviour are pure Provo propaganda, though unfortunately of the sort that can bring into being what it alleges. A search-party may be provoked to misbehave by a hostile reception, itself provoked by Provo 'in-

citements to hatred'. Another responsible informant described
how the homes of innocent people were seriously damaged
because the troops wrongly suspected they had been fired on
from a particular house. One Catholic woman argued, "It's
all a matter of how you take them." Her home has been
searched four times by different regiments but no harm was
ever done. The first time the family was away so a glass panel
of the hall-door had to be broken. Otherwise, "You wouldn't
know they'd been in the place—except they left it tidier than
they found it." On later occasions they were received politely
and behaved politely. This repeated searching Mrs A— blamed
on the Provos, of whom she is a well-known, outspoken and
sharp-tongued critic. In retaliation for her sort of opposition
they often give the army an anonymous tip-off to raid so-and-
so's house.

A few years ago, at the height of the Provos' anti-Brit propaganda campaign, the UNA provided a community worker
whose task it is to act as a neutral witness during house searches;
his word is usually accepted by both sides when disputes arise.
Soldiers are searched before and after a raid to eliminate friction about the planting of evidence and petty thieving. Yet even
now a regiment has to be more strictly disciplined towards the
end of its tour. When thinking, 'This time next week we'll
be in Germany' the troops tend to become indifferent to local
reactions and, sometimes, to work off long-suppressed grudges.
The Brits versus Paddies feud frequently makes grown-ups
behave like not very bright five-year-olds. Two nights ago,
when the weather had just broken and it was raining heavily,
an absurd incident took place at a nearby army border check-
point. Soon after 1.0 am a young Catholic couple were asked
to get out of their car while it was being searched. The husband
explained that his wife was ill and could not stand around in
a downpour. While arguing the point he tossed an empty
cigarette packet onto the road and was accused of breaking
the law by littering the public highway. This wrangle continued for over four hours until the two soldiers concerned
went off duty—by which time the unwell wife must have been
feeling a lot worse than if she had stood for ten minutes in the
rain.

Irrationality flourishes in this climate. Recently the Provos organised a riot at MacGilligan Camp, for which purpose they and their UDA and UVF fellow-internees declared a truce. Mattresses were thrown onto the wire barricades and set alight with the aid of boot polish; the central heating was disrupted; the new kitchen was burned. The catering staff, however, promptly improvised in the old kitchen and continued to serve hot meals on time. Yet the Provos were outraged because their mattresses had not been immediately replaced and threatened to go on hunger-strike.

I had a long talk this evening with a distinguished citizen who knows every physical and psychological corner of Derry. He said that a powerful underworld is developing fast here because the drinking and betting industries are being taken over by the Provos, just as they were by the Mafia at the end of the US liquor war when he himself was living in America. Also, as the normal discipline of society weakens more marriages are breaking up, the illegitimate birth-rate is rising fast and alcoholism has become an acute problem.

Traditionally this is a city of masterful women. For generations the main local industry was shirtmaking and while wives went out to earn, husbands stayed at home with the children. One can still clearly see the results of this in many families where women vigorously insist on their menfolk either supporting or not supporting the Provos. As The Troubles have progressed, from the first fine careless rapture of necessary self-defence to the founding of an efficiently-run underworld, more and more women, even in strongly Republican families, have tried to restrain their sons from 'joining the lads'.

It seems there has never been much foreign influence in Derry though at first the People's Democracy Movement attracted (having itself been inspired by) left-wing students from many countries. The media tended to exaggerate this student solidarity until it became—to some newspaper readers—of Sinister International Significance. I was told a glorious true story which is well-known but still seems worth writing down. To Derry during the thick of The Troubles came a keen young English press photographer, intent on a scoop. A Provisional told him that for a substantial consideration this could be arranged and next day the two met at a place from which the photographer was driven (blindfolded) to a field above the Creggan. There he spent an ecstatic hour photographing *very* sinister 'Foreign Influences' training local boys. When he had been reblindfolded and driven away his Provo friend took the rifles from the Chinese waiters' nervous hands, helped them to remove their unfamiliar paramilitary uniforms, paid them a meagre percentage of the scoop fee and sent them back to their restaurant in the city centre.

In real life, many Provos join either the British or the Irish army for their training. Some also join the Irish army on their release from prison if they wish not to resume a guerrilla career; but many voluntarily continue the fight, having been made more ruthless by their time inside. Others leave Ireland and either work for the cause in Britain or settle down there to a normal life. According to a Protestant informant the pattern is rather different on the Orange side. All but the most extreme of the Protestant paramilitaries 'retire' on being freed, which often means having to emigrate.

This afternoon, in a small Bogside pub, I met two young men who were obviously longing to talk to someone new. (Many young Derry people tend to be wary of strangers though their elders have more than their share of informal Irish friendliness.) They introduced themselves as Sean and Liam; both are philosophy graduates of Queen's and have been on the dole, living with their working-class families, for the past year. I asked could they not get jobs across the water and they said, "Only on building sites, or driving buses." Besides, they don't want to be too far away from their families at present. Sean's mother is a widow and as he has two younger brothers and three younger sisters he reckons she needs him around to help her impose discipline. I would reckon so, too. Liam's father is a semi-invalid (a TB leg was removed) and his mother's nerves have gone since 1969, when a gang of RUC men on the rampage badly beat up her three sons in her presence. Liam said that his family had always been moderate Nationalists, totally opposed to the IRA in all its manifestations, and there was no conceivable excuse for the RUC's invasion of their home. Beside him on the bar-counter he had a paperback copy of my favourite novel and when I remarked that nowadays not many twenty-four-year-olds read *Middlemarch* for fun he pointed out that George Eliot makes a nice change from the Bogside of the seventies.

Neither Sean nor Liam needed much prompting to reminisce about the heady days when this part of Derry became 'Free'. As teenagers they went out to watch the rioting, as their contemporaries elsewhere might go to a football match, and they often became hoarse through cheering the rioters on. "From a safe distance," they added wryly. They had grown up very aware of the importance among their peers of physical skill and courage but obviously they were philosophers before ever they went to Queen's. Liam said his most sickening memory was of three small boys hysterically seeking the autograph of a Provo who had just killed a Brit. That quenched his enthusiasm for cheering. Sean's worst memory was 'The day an eighteen-year-old on the dole showed me ten £10 notes—his fee for shooting a Brit—and said 'Easy money!' He didn't even pretend to give a damn about Irish freedom or Civil Rights. Maybe at the time I was a wee bit inclined to join the lads but that put me off forever."

Until the ages of seventeen and eighteen, respectively, Sean and Liam had never once conversed with a Protestant; and this was normal for boys of their generation. As students at Queen's they at first felt themselves to be in an alien world; segregation was spontaneously kept up despite the liberal academic atmosphere. This was not through overt hostility or bigotry but because it seemed the natural thing to do. "I'll never forget the sense of jittery isolation," said Liam. "There are thousands of Catholics at Queen's, but somehow knowing 75 per cent of the population of Belfast is Protestant got me all unnerved. During my first year I came home as often as I could. Yet I was ashamed of myself for feeling like that in my own country. It seemed so absurd. I saw then how you could trace it straight back to separate schools. Not to bigotry in my home—there wasn't any. And apart from that we're not sectarian-minded here in Derry, the way Belfast is. Derry is different."

"But where do you begin?" said Sean. "Even if integrated schools could somehow be opened in the morning they wouldn't do a damn bit of good while so many parents keep on about Orange thugs and Fenian bastards."

These two young men, like many other Derry folk, admit that by 1968 the constitutional *status quo* had been accepted by the majority of Catholics and reunification had become an idol which was worshipped ritually at certain times, such as Easter Week. "Just the way the English go to church on Christmas Day," explained Liam. Now, among the young, Provo propaganda has to some extent revived anti-partition fervour. Sean believes that many Provos have built their individual identities on the 'Freedom from Britain' ideal and therefore can't give in without losing *themselves*. He sees this as a much more important motive for keeping going than 'material profit'.

Though the Catholic areas here are No-Go for the police—in that lies their Freedom—one sees many army foot patrols with the last youth of four walking backwards to cover his companions. The pale, immature faces are usually tense and angry; it is more manly to look angry than to look what you feel—fear-sick in your stomach because you may be shot in the back any time from any window of any one of those identical dreary little houses. In fact a Brit is unlikely, now, to be shot at in the Bogside. But Provo policy might suddenly change, or an unruly 'volunteer' might have a grudge of his own. And, however unlikely, the possibility is enough to scare an eighteen-year-old with MAM tattooed on his skinny forearm—a boy who may well be in the army only because he couldn't get a job at home.

As I cycled past one patrol, under a deep blue sky with the sun glinting merrily on the glass splinters strewn across the street, I suddenly felt nauseated by the sheer mindlessness of the violence that has erupted here. That young Irishmen and young Englishmen should be trained to be able and willing to kill each other, in 1976, seems intolerably barbarous. I've never been a pacifist but maybe Northern Ireland is making me one. Somehow this afternoon the thought of a responsible government legally training and arming its young men to kill seemed even worse than a gang of paramilitaries doing the same thing. By 2076, will our legalised killings seem as outrageous to Europeans as hanging for the theft of a sheep seems now?

Fortunately these depressed moods never last long and I am on the whole finding Derry the reverse of gloomy. It seems exhilarating, stimulating and curiously exciting—almost intoxicating, even before one has visited the Bogside Inn. It is exciting not in any morbid sense (at least not nowadays) but as a city of lively people trying to restore their communal self-respect through their own efforts. Almost everybody I've met has been involved in some sort of community work. Nor is this because I've been seeking out do-gooders. Any chance contact is liable to interrupt a sentence, look at his or her watch and disappear in a flurry of apologies to edit a community newspaper, or direct an inter-denominational drama group, or attend a meeting on Summer Playgroups or Tenants' Rights or battered wives or homeless old people or deserted children or alcoholics or prostitutes. The Maiden City's recent ordeals have certainly not broken her spirit.

24 June

In Derry, Belfast is referred to with shuddering horror. Today an apparently level-headed man told me that he wouldn't dare walk alone through certain areas of his capital city. It's odd how it goes; some English people think it's dangerous in Co Waterford, some Co Waterford people think it's dangerous in Derry, some Derry people think it's dangerous in Belfast—and I wonder what Belfast people think?

This morning I had a long talk and many cups of tea in a small terraced house with a Catholic mother of eleven. Her oldest son is in the British army; her second son is with the Officials in Belfast and won't speak to the rest of the family; her oldest daughter is engaged to a Provo. "We were always quiet folk—never no trouble, me husband's a Pioneer—and now look at us!"

The last time the soldier son came home on leave (rashly, I would have thought), the prospective son-in-law was on the run and staying for a few days; so the two young men had to share a bed. "I was afraid they'd get irritated and do damage.

Maybe just start some disagreement over a pillow or somethin' and tear away at each other. There's so much hate around now—and all them young fellas is used to killin'.'' It occurred to me that, for next time, there was an alternative solution to the bedding problem which might not prove unacceptable to either the Provo or his betrothed. But such a suggestion would have been ill-received in that decent Catholic household. Personally I rather like the idea of a Brit and a Provo tucked up snugly together. It speaks well for Derry; it surely couldn't happen in Belfast. When the betrothed joined us she told me her mother was just talking silly. The two young men get on very well though her brother is a perfectly genuine 'Brit' who intends to serve Her Majesty faithfully for as long as she'll have him.

I lunched in a pub with two Catholic couples, all secondary school teachers, and towards the end of our session an amount of hostility to the South showed through. General amazement was expressed at the Catholic Hierarchy's continuing to imagine it necessary for the state to buttress Catholic moral law. It was pointed out that in Northern Ireland, where contraceptives are freely available, the birth-rate among both Catholics and Protestants is higher than in the South where our constitution forbids the sale of contraceptives. One teacher declared that Britain's unwritten constitution is a far more satisfactory foundation for a civilised state than our written, dogmatic effort; and this was generally agreed. Again I was told that the Unionist distrust of Catholics was partly the Catholics' own fault for refusing to recognise the state of Northern Ireland when it was founded. The Southern Protestants' co-operation with the Dublin Government was mentioned admiringly as an example of how things should be. Nobody stopped to consider the vast difference between the two situations; the co-operation of the Southern Protestants was encouraged by the Dublin government's tolerance, which was fostered by the unthreatening size of the Southern Protestant minority.

At one stage we were joined by a Dublin man who has lived in Belfast for twenty years and seemed a lot keener on Irish unity than my four Northern companions. When I asked what he would do with one million resentful Protestants, after Irish unity had been forced on them, he replied crisply, "What they did with the Taigs over the past fifty-five years." But he was at once angrily shouted down; among the North's minority many now seem as much anti-South as anti-British or anti-Unionist. The Protestant hurt at what is interpreted as Britain's indifference to Loyalist loyalty is paralleled by the Catholics' awareness of Southern indifference to Northern woes.

When our Republican hard-liner had moved on we were joined by two of Derry's most active community leaders, Des and Mike. They talked enthusiastically for half an hour but the Derry political scene, whether official or unofficial, is too much for me. It is teeming and seething with plans, ambitions, ideals and schemes produced by dozens of creative, constructive people. However, Des did help by explaining the origins and functions of Northern Ireland's many community groups.

These began to mushroom during 1969-70 and soon there were about 400 of them in Belfast, Derry and Dungannon—and scores elsewhere. They were inspired by popular distrust of the police in Catholic areas, by dissatisfaction with political parties—Orange or Green—and by impatience with an increasingly inefficient administration at both local and central government levels. Based on the belief that 'God helps those who help themselves', they at first concentrated mainly on protection, then began to work on employment and social amenities. The Provos could be said to have started as a badly-needed defensive community group which grafted itself onto the IRA tradition; the UDA and other Protestant paramilitary organisations grew out of the failure of the security forces to protect Protestant areas from Provo bombs in 1970-71. But now there is (or should be) a sharp distinction between community groups, which are helped by the government's Community Development Officers, and paramilitary organisations. In certain areas community vigilante patrols still operate and the paramilitaries sometimes attempt to take over these ready-made reinforcements. Des said it is hard to judge how effectively Belfast's big community groups have been infiltrated by extremists.

Over the years, as the politicians have become more powerless, discredited and divided, community groups everywhere have gained strength. Originally they were strictly sectarian but now they are beginning to co-operate and to form Community Associations, of which Derry's is perhaps the strongest. Within these Associations each group retains its local character and there has been talk recently of forming a Northern Ireland Federation of Community Groups. Des finds this idea very exciting. At least a certain number of working-class people— Orange and Green—are sharing their common problems and trying to get on with their own thing. But this development is so much against the interests of Unionism/Orangeism that it may well be sabotaged.

Des—a Catholic—incidentally made one very interesting point; if he is in a London pub and hears Northern accents he goes to join the group feeling sure of a welcome and not inwardly asking the involuntary Northern Ireland question— 'Which foot do they dig with?' But he never equally spontaneously approaches a group of Southern Irish.

Every day in Derry I hear several sad little stories. One of the teachers told me about going to visit her sister in a notoriously 'Orange' town for a niece's First Communion day. Near her in the Catholic church knelt a little girl of seven whose veil was all askew; she was with her Protestant father because her Catholic mother—a constable in the RUC—had been blown to bits a few weeks previously by a Provo bomb. The congregation greatly admired her father for having had the courage to go to Mass—a form of worship abominated by Orangemen— on this very special day in his daughter's life. But they were apprehensive, with good reason, about his future safety.

Most Northern Catholics are intensely (sometimes I'm tempted to think obsessively) conscious of job discrimination. I asked this group if Direct Rule has helped here and all agreed that slowly things are improving. They believe the Ombudsman is trying hard but quite often, in certain areas, Catholics refuse to work for Protestants when given the chance because of their well-founded fear of intimidation. Also, action can be taken only when people complain and many won't for fear of the consequences. Des gave a good example of how ruthlessly discrimination was applied under Stormont. A classmate at his Derry school tried to get a post office job but was failed in a simple examination. Subsequently he won a scholarship to Queen's and he is now a very young professor of some abstruse branch of science at the Royal Institute in London.

Des invited me to go with him to the Waterside on one of his community projects so Roz was put in the boot and off we went across Craigavon Bridge to a sprawl of new housing estates high above the east bank of the Foyle. Although the Waterside is often thought of as 'Protestant Derry' one-third of the residents are Catholics—or were, until very recently. There is now a two-way cross-Foyle movement because so many feel safer in exclusively Orange or Green areas. This is the sort of thing that could soon undermine everybody's proud boast that 'Derry is different'.

Certainly much of the Waterside looks Protestant. It is far tidier than the Green districts, many of its electricity poles and kerbs are painted red, white and blue and its walls say UDA RULE, UVF HERE, FUCK THE IRA. Yet its pale small children seem no less numerous than the Catholic young and have just as many sweet-rotten first teeth and lollipop-stained chins. These new housing estates were atrociously planned; they have no shops or post office within reasonable reach and no playing spaces. We listened to many complaints about the local Tenants' Association and the women seemed just as dominant and vigorous as their sisters across the Foyle. Several parlour mantelpieces were adorned by what appeared to be life-sized phallic symbols; eventually I identified them as rubber bullets mounted in brass at the relevant angle—an indication that the Waterside people either have exceptionally clean or exceptionally dirty minds. The former, Des insisted, because if the latter they would have doctored the pointed tip. It is horribly easy to see how these objects could kill a person if they hit a vulnerable spot.

All Derry's social workers are deeply worried about a problem to be found now in cities all over Europe—the psychological effects of uprooting slum communities and re-housing them in comparative luxury. People who have been 'dropping in' on each other all their lives no longer visit, or depend on each other in emergencies, though they are still neighbours. Keeping up with the McCanns has suddenly replaced the old values and countless respectable families, who before always managed to pay their way, are in debt. During times of tension neighbourly support becomes more important than ever and its weakening here has contributed to a spectacular increase in mental illness and alcoholism among women.

Des and I talked at length to an elderly widow in a hideously carpeted little room strewn with expensive broken toys and crammed with shoddy new furniture; the large television, on spindly legs, supported a variety of seaside souvenirs. Annie lives with her married daughter who works in a factory and the five children are at school all day and the son-in-law "had to go across the water because when he was out of a job for a long while he got tangled with the UVF. They pay regular, like the Provos. Then the RUC was after him and he'll hardly come back—'twouldn't ever be safe". Annie is very fond of her son-in-law and was most upset when she accidentally discovered his connection with 'that lot'. She began to take a drop more than she should and when he went off and she was alone every day she only had the drop to cheer her up. "Everything got worse for us all when there was no string on the doors." She meant that in their new housing estate you could no longer put your hand through a letter-box, pull the key out on a string and enter a friend's house without knocking. "No one ever needed to be worried or lonesome or in want in my old street. Now it's gone—all pulled down." And what to some town-planner is a triumph—one slum less—to her is a disaster.

When Des had driven off to a meeting about Spastic children I cycled slowly across the Waterside to a mainly Catholic housing estate where I was to meet one of the Community Centre leaders. From this height Derry looked very lovely in the light of a cloudless summer evening. Across the smooth, wide Foyle lay the Bogside and Creggan and the big Republican graveyard on a steep green slope scattered with white tombstones. The clear strong Atlantic air must contribute quite a lot to the Derry people's aliveness. Around me were miles of unhuman new council estates and yet—somehow—no part of Derry is depressing. It embarrasses me now to remember what I expected to find here: a city of sullen, suspicious underdogs, slouching and lounging through ruined streets.

Bernie was sitting in the sun outside her little house, waiting for me. A cigarette hung from her mouth as she rapidly knitted a winter woolly for her two-year-old son—the youngest of sixteen children, four of whom died as babies. She is aged thirty-nine, looks much younger and is expecting the next in December—"A free Christmas present for the lot of us". She dresses neatly and smartly and keeps her raven hair glossy—"Jimmy wouldn't like a streel". (Clearly Jimmy appreciates her deference to his viewpoint.) The two eldest girls, aged nineteen and seventeen, have been working in a factory since they were sixteen, but the best-loved (I suspect) eldest boy, aged eighteen, has never been able to get a job. For the past year his mother has been torn between sensibly urging him to go across the water and selfishly keeping him at home on the dole. (Jimmy, I gathered, doesn't have much say in these matters.) Every day Bernie worries more about the lad—"With nothin' to occupy the mind and no pride from earnin', you wouldn't know but he might end up in the Kesh." Hoping I wasn't being tactless, I asked what in fact the lad did do with his time. Bernie chuckled. "Don't you fear he's idle! With Jimmy and meself out workin' all day, and the two youngest not at school yet, he have plenty to occupy him in the house! And right good he is, too, with the wains. Like another father to them."

We were joined then by Jimmy's sister, Bridge, whose husband was one of five men killed a few years ago in an indiscriminate machine-gun attack on a local Catholic pub. Bridge was left with nine children—the eldest aged twelve, the baby a Mongol—and she did *not* look younger than her years. Together the three of us walked to the Community Centre, a shoddy but adequate building paid for and constructed by the locals. In the hallway a wall-plaque commemorated the 'Five Innocent Victims' of that pub attack. At all times the strong outer door is kept securely locked and only opened when the 'porter' is quite sure of the identity of those seeking admission. Last year the Provos tried to take over this centre by 'getting at' the younger members. They manœuvred a man onto the committee but when he failed to gain control he was ordered to resign. Power-sharing is not part of the Provo way of thinking, either. The only Protestant involved in this centre—he is almost the only Protestant on the estate—has been elected to the committee four years running by popular vote. I separately asked six people would this be likely to happen in a reverse situation—if a Protestant Community Centre had one Catholic member—and they all reluctantly said 'no'. They seemed almost ashamed to admit to an outsider this defect of Northern Irish society. My question might have been used to launch an attack on Protestant bigotry in general but instead everyone briskly changed the subject. Many little details are accumulating to reinforce my unexpected first impression of the greater virulence of Orange bigotry. This morning I was told by a Protestant minister that Derry's inter-church meetings can take place only in Protestant or neutral buildings. Many Northern Protestants have such a superstitious fear of Catholicism that a minister seen visiting Catholic territory could get very rough treatment from his parishioners.

After the meeting we returned to Bernie's house for tea and Swiss roll. Jimmy was standing on the doorstep—two foot over a jampot and stoutish, with thick fair curls and an air of being constitutionally content. He had the two-year-old in his arms and, as we came round the corner, was gazing devotedly at him as though this were the first instead of the sixteenth product of his loins. On the step below him sat his eldest daughter—slim, dark, good-looking—leaning affectionately against her father's legs. This happy family picture would have made a most moving anti-contraceptive poster. Bernie had just been telling me that a few years ago, after a tricky confinement, her doctor advised sterilisation—and at the memory of this attempt to deprive her of her rights she flushed with rage. In the loving atmosphere generated by this enormous family the slick idea 'only two and do well by them' seems meretricious. It all depends on what you mean by 'doing well', I suppose.

25 June

Today I visited 'The House', a touching example of the sort of practical Christianity that flourishes in Derry. It is in fact two old two-storeyed terraced houses, just under the Walls of Derry overlooking the Bogside, and it shelters twelve homeless, hopeless men who would otherwise be sleeping out. No government department or charitable foundation supports it; it was thought up by and is entirely the responsibility of the not rich local people. They provide food, furniture and fuel, do the laundry, mend clothes, clean rooms—and, most important of all, give affection, sympathy and understanding. Most of the men are winos but a few are 'mended'. Any resident can wander in and out at any time he chooses, up to 11.0 pm, and cook his own food and make his own tea. When I arrived unexpectedly everything was neat and tidy and five men were sitting around the Rayburn watching the antics of a tabby kitten.

I was given a pint mug of very sweet stewed tea by a fifty-year-old with a sad, vague, kind face. He told me he has been 'dry' for the past two years, because the Legion of Mary had made him feel he's 'wanted', and now he is the unofficial but generally accepted warden of The House. Beside him sat an old man with a tidy, pointed beard, thick spectacles and very beautiful hands. He was not quite sober and had a difficult accent but I gathered he had recently been in hospital and had only decided he wanted to get better because nuns from the local Mercy Convent visited him every day. "Angels, they are," he declared indistinctly. "Angels without wings." There is more to Northern Ireland than meets the headlines.

Mrs C— came in then; she is one of the founders of The House and visits it daily to do various domestic chores. She remarked of the Brits, "These lads will go home the cleanest men that ever left a war." A few young women from strongly Loyalist areas are given passes to visit the military barracks for dances; otherwise there is no mixing between troops and locals.

I spent most of the afternoon with Brian, a Catholic in his early thirties who is a skilled mechanic, a part-time voluntary community worker, a Trade Unionist and a shrewd commentator on local affairs. He has straight, shoulder-length shiny fair hair, a long strong face and plenty of self-confidence tempered by modesty. If the North's community groups are throwing up many such leaders the future is not without hope.

An ardent Republican in his youth, Brian 'got off that scene when the guns came in'. But he still has many Provo friends and believes the ordinary people should maintain their personal links with the paramilitaries. "Nothing can really change unless we communicate, discuss, argue, explain viewpoints. No matter how much we disagree with the other chap we *must* talk to him—and not just about the weather or the racing." He thinks it 'bloody silly' of the British government ever to be toffee-nosed about meeting the paramilitaries of either side. "These guys have already proved they can bring the state to its knees. You must talk to them, you must admit nothing can be sorted out without their co-operation. It's bullshit to talk about 'beating the terrorists' as though they were a sort of foreign element in the community. They're part of it, they grew out of community needs and discontents in the first place and no matter how much people may hate and fear them now they're still part of it. It won't ever be possible to 'isolate them' effectively. That's typical, half-baked political pie-in-the-sky—maybe fit for consumption in Westminster but just a joke here."

Brian bases all his hopes on the paradox that now the Northern Irish, Green and Orange, are slowly drawing closer to one another. He feels that already most Catholics would prefer an independent Northern Ireland in which some neutral agent (the UN?) kept a watch-dog force, rather than an independent thirty-two county Republic. Some qualified sort of independence has to come, he is convinced, eventually. But what the Catholics have to resist is any manœuvre that could lead to UDI without firm safeguards for them; some extreme Loyalists now yearn for this as the only constitutional rearrangement that could restore the Orange top dogs to their previous position.

Many Northern Catholics argue that violence had to be used to overthrow a thoroughly corrupt and unjust régime, that no number of non-violent marches, protests or demonstrations could have demolished Stormont. One jibs at this but, as Brian said, the sequence of events from 1963 to 1972 makes it hard to deny. "And so," he went on, "we're all being a bit hypocritical when we condemn the Provos. They did a lot of the dirty work and the whole Catholic community is enjoying the benefits. It's just a pity they've caused so much grief to innocent people. If they'd been clever enough only to destroy property and kill civilians and avoid racketeering they'd have a lot more support today. As it is, people have forgotten their real achievement. Since they forced Britain to take over, things have improved a lot. London just won't tolerate discrimination. And this is having a good effect on Catholic morale. Can you imagine what it feels like to be a second-class citizen in your own country? We're always being told we've no sense of civic responsibility but we've never before had the chance to get on, or to feel free and equal members of society. Being ambitious and industrious wouldn't have done us any good—and then the people who kept us in that position blame us for being shiftless and lazy. I'm happy enough with Direct Rule. For the moment it's the only solution. There has to be an awful lot of reconciling all round before anything else will work. And it gives us time to sort ourselves out. At Britain's expense, of course. But that's fair enough. She did a lot to get us into this mess."*

Brian reckons that the dividing line between crime and patriotism is becoming increasingly blurred in Derry. A spell 'inside' confers status on an unemployed youngster; the gaol-bird is a folk-hero and no one enquires too closely into the reason why he was gaoled. Among the Provo volunteers one now finds both witless riff-raff and seasoned criminals willing to do anything for money. Such types are never admitted to the Inner Circle and so have no worthwhile information to give if caught. Brian reserves his deepest contempt for the 'fireside Provos' who never risk anything themselves but egg on local youngsters. These include certain priests—one of whom I met yesterday, though Brian was not aware of this and expected me to be shocked by his information.

Repeatedly Brian revealed the contradictory feelings aroused among Northern Catholics by the Provos. A person of great integrity, he has a natural respect for law and order—but not when the forces of law and order are used to uphold injustice. As a humane man he abhors brutality but as a realist he appreciates the improvements the Provo campaign has indirectly

* In *Violence in Ireland: A Report to the Churches* (published September 1976) the anonymous authors—a working party appointed by the Catholic Hierarchy and the Irish Council of Churches—make strenuous efforts to prove that Republican violence was not responsible for the fall of Stormont. But in the end they have to admit that it was, 'indirectly', though they rightly emphasise that 'the main objectives of Republican policy have not been achieved by violence or the threat of it. ... It would probably be widely agreed that the events of 1968–76 have removed any possibility that might earlier have existed of the re-unification of Ireland in the foreseeable future.'

secured for the Catholic underdogs—and therefore, as an honest man, he cannot unreservedly condemn them. Many people with less strength of character tend to resolve this inner conflict by shutting their eyes to one aspect of the Provo phenomenon and becoming implacably 'pro' or 'anti'. Only a few weeks ago I was full of self-righteous scorn for the ambivalent attitudes of so many Catholics to the IRA; now I find myself sympathising with them.

25 June

Since crossing the border I have several times been asked if I feel no patriotic involvement in the Northern conflict, despite my ancestry; and I am able honestly to answer 'None whatever'. Yet occasionally an atavistic sort of patriotism shows through, flashing out like the fire in a diamond when it is caught in a certain light. The day I crossed the border and saw the Union Jack flying in the grounds of a factory near Lisnaskea I felt a spurt of irrational resentment. This reaction had its source far below that thinking level on which I accept that Northern Ireland's Unionists have every right to fly the British flag in their own corner of Ireland. Then again, a few days ago, I felt a surge of exultation when a prominent Unionist declared that he sees a thirty-two county Irish Republic as ultimately inevitable, however undesirable.

The Northern Protestants' insecurity is perhaps in part a result of their lacking any primitive patriotism—an emotion that can be wonderfully strengthening if kept under control. But to take root firmly patriotism possibly needs a more temperate climate than was ever known in post-Plantation Ulster. Three hundred years has been long enough for the Unionists to feel that Northern Ireland is their homeland, yet the emotion it inspires looks less like patriotism than like an aggressive sort of modern nationalism. My definition of patriotism is an awareness of loving and *belonging to* a place, whether or not the vagaries of politics decree that *it* belongs to *you* at any given date. Thus I can feel patriotic about Northern Ireland—as I never could about England—*without feeling possessive*. People feel and think and react in such various and often contradictory ways on different levels—and maybe politicians made such messes because they try to get everybody neatly operating on only one level.

Just a few days in Derry make one appreciate how stunted its social evolution has been. There is a striking difference between a working-class population that is so by nature, because of the general level of intelligence of its members, and one that has simply not been given the opportunity to develop its talents—or to use them in an appropriate manner if they have been developed. It has become a cliché to say that the North's present troubles began with Britain's Education Act of 1948 and since arriving in Derry I have seen for myself, several times a day, how true this is. Before 1948 the vast majority of Catholic children had to remain part of an uneducated, inarticulate mass. Whatever their abilities, they could not hope to get to secondary school—much less university.

Tomorrow I leave for Belfast. So often I've fallen in love with a place and been heartbroken when the time came to go, but here I can look forward to coming back quite soon. Derry feels such a friendly little city, despite all the soldiers, policemen, civilian searchers, security officers, street-barriers and checkpoints. One very quickly gets used to the abnormal. Today I found myself cycling up a steep hill in the Creggan right behind an army Land-Rover with two guns pointing directly at me—and I was half-way up the hill before I registered them. Derry motorists prefer not to drive near army vehicles lest they might be involved in a stoning; but for a cyclist it's a relief to be in a city where motor traffic is so restricted. I'm astonished, and slightly alarmed, by the casual security approach to bicycles. Although Roz could carry a ten pound bomb in her large saddle-bag she is never thoroughly checked. Yet today, crossing the bridge, I saw a most respectable-looking gentleman standing beside his car while two soldiers removed all the hub-caps. Had he been unable to satisfy them about his identity and 'purpose of visit'? Or were they just miserably bored and giving themselves a job?

Repeatedly here one asks oneself, "Who is afraid of whom—and why?" At first I was bewildered by the apparent non-existence of shops in parts of the Bogside. Then I realised that they are all tightly shuttered and reinforced against—whom? In the dimness of one big grocery store, which from outside looked like an abandoned building, a friendly proprietor asked jokingly (or half-jokingly?) how it is I'm not afraid to go wandering alone through Provoland. (He had sent his youngest assistant out to guard Roz while I shopped.) I could give no coherent reply and the question made me realise that I don't fully understand my own reactions to Free Derry. Illogically, I feel safer there than in those areas where I'm protected by the RUC. Is this because the average Bogsider would identify me as a Southern Catholic and therefore not an enemy? Whereas in other areas there are Tartan gangs, UVF gunmen and lone Orange wolves who might see a Southern Catholic as their natural prey? Yet that doesn't make sense, for to counteract the 'average Bogsider' one has the Provo, who sees himself as the rightful ruler of Free Derry and might choose to see me as a spy of some sort. Perhaps the answer is that I'm unduly suggestible and that Free Derry exhales an atmosphere of light-heartedness. Whatever the Provo intimidation, the people have at least got out from under the oppressive Orange cloud. And however uncertain the present and future may be, there is in the air a tremendous sense of having been released.

5
Men of God

The Irish abroad are often asked, "Is it *really* a religious war?" (Sometimes they ask each other, too.) The best short answer is in Garrett Fitzgerald's book *Towards a New Ireland*: 'The most fundamental obstacle to reunification is the sense of distinctness that is felt by a large proportion of Protestants in Northern Ireland—a feeling of not belonging to the rest of the Irish community, with whom they share the island of Ireland.... The sense of a separate identity is almost completely confined to Protestants, and today to Protestants in Northern Ireland for the most part. The core of the problem lies amongst this group.... It is true to say that the inter-community conflict in Northern Ireland is not a religious war, in the sense of a war about religious dogmas, but it would be a mistake to underestimate the underlying importance of the divergence in attitudes of Protestants and Catholics on a number of issues of fundamental importance to the running of a State. ... In particular the Catholic church's claims in the educational sphere, in medicine, and in matters of public morality are seen as impinging on what many Protestants regard as their liberties. ... The Irish problem is quite simply the fruit of Northern Protestant reluctance to become part of what they regard as an authoritarian Southern Catholic State.'

If this is accepted, it means that clergymen are the officers in Northern Ireland's mental and emotional war, little as they may fancy the role, and for this reason I tried to meet as many of them as possible of all denominations and ranks. Without exception they received me kindly and were immensely helpful though to some a Southern writer named Murphy must have seemed a very suspicious object. My discussions with clergymen took place all over the six counties, in villages, towns and cities, at various times between June 1976 and July 1977. But for reasons of coherency and anonymity I have gathered into one chapter most of the reflections inspired by these Scenes from Clerical Life.

Ever since the creation of Northern Ireland, Protestant clergymen have openly and vigorously meddled in politics to an extent that would have been unthinkable, at any period, for Catholic clergy in the South. Some of them even became professional politicians and few branches of the Unionist Party lack enthusiastic clerical members. Moreover, for almost fifty years membership of the Orange Order—a Protestant religious semi-secret society—was one of the qualifications for joining the Unionist Parliamentary Party; and many Orangemen habitually voted as instructed by the Master of their Lodge. On both sides, in the North, religion and politics have merged into a single tribal emblem or driving force. As my publisher remarked, when I was discussing this point with him, "Religion has become a symbol of many motives—man lives more easily by symbols."

Nowadays the Orangemen's primitive myths and frenetic aversion to ecumenism look like a tatty remnant of something that even when new was not very attractive. Their virtues endure, but are far too killjoy and rigid to win much sympathy—or even to be acknowledged as virtues—in the 1970s. Indeed, Protestantism generally is at a certain disadvantage when neutral non-Christians compare it to Catholicism. It lacks the panache, the assurance, the dignity and the subtlety of the older form of Christianity. At their most ceremonial and solemn, the Protestant churches can only imitate but never quite achieve those effects which the Catholic church produces without even trying. To me Protestantism seems like an industrious, sober, earnest, upright, plain-looking and rather dreary yeoman farmer. Whereas Catholicism is an arrogant, ruthless, perceptive, sophisticated and very handsome aristocrat, accustomed to getting away with things because he never doubts that he is entitled to do so. Naturally one has more respect for the wholesome farmer but the dissolute aristocrat is a good deal more attractive and interesting.

Orangeism is Protestantism at its least refined, the farmer with his boots off and his feet on the tea-table. I am not implying that all Orangemen are boors. By the time I left Northern

Ireland some of my best friends were Orangemen—and I write that sincerely, with my tongue nowhere near my cheek. But the Orange tradition is an uncouth mixture of ignorance, xenophobia, self-deception, suspicion, rabble-rousing, fear and aggression. Inevitably it produces a great deal of loutish behaviour, which its leaders seem unwilling or unable to correct. One example is the custom of calling a football 'The Pope' and ritually kicking it around a field. Some outsiders find this funny but I am not amused. It is impossible to imagine, in the wildest corner of Ireland, groups of Catholic peasants having similar 'games' with footballs named 'Queen Elizabeth'. They might feel towards the Queen no less animosity than the Orangemen feel towards the Pope—though I doubt that—but there is sufficient restraint in their tradition to ensure that animosity does not employ such uncivilised outlets. It may be argued that it would be better if the Catholics did have symbolic footballs instead of bomb factories. But this argument is false. In sectarian—as distinct from political—feuds the Orange assassins have been both more active and more sadistic than the Green.

Given the peculiar nature of Orangeism, the outsider—especially the outsider from the South—has to make a sustained effort to get at the real person beneath the Orange topsoil of neuroses. (A similar effort has of course to be made with extreme Republicans whose neuroses are almost equally numerous.) But this effort often proves well worth while. There are many Orange clergymen whom it is a privilege to meet because of their sincerity, their unexpected and touching innocence, their real spirituality—in a word, their sheer goodness. Of course this goodness co-exists, most confusingly, with a virulent form of unchristian bigotry; otherwise the individual concerned would not be an Orangeman. But it is of prime importance for us in the South to recognise that all Orangemen are not *merely* bigots, that at least as much genuinely religious—as distinct from political—fervour exists within the Orange Order as within any other Christian organisation.

Almost every feature of Northern Ireland's situation contains a paradox. The Orange paradox is that Orangemen have acquired a deserved reputation for narrow fanaticism while all the time they are fighting to preserve a liberal and tolerant

society such as they erroneously imagine exists in Northern Ireland. We have now got to the intricate kernel of the whole problem. A liberal and tolerant society, comparable to modern Britain's, has never existed in Northern Ireland because Northern
Protestants (not only the 100,000 or so Orangemen, but virtually the entire Protestant community) have felt compelled since
the 1830s—and even more since 1920—to discriminate against
Catholics lest Romish authoritarianism might demolish Protestant freedom.

That of course is an over-simplification, like almost any statement ever made about Northern Ireland. There have been
other complicated reinforcing motives for discrimination—economic, racial and political. But without the religious cement,
these would most probably have crumbled by now. Many
Northern Protestants are spiritually—and some are physically—descended from the Scottish Covenanters; a study of
those brave zealots of the seventeenth century throws considerable light on what is happening in Northern Ireland 300 years
later. One spiritual descendant was the Rt Hon. J. M. Andrews.
Speaking as Grand Master of the Orange Order, he stated in
June 1950, "I observe from reports in the Press that there are
a few Orange brethren who feel that we are exclusively a religious Order. While I agree that we are mainly a religious body,
the Order has been in the front rank for generations in preserv-
ing our constitutional position. The Orange ritual lays it down
that it is the duty of Orangemen to support and maintain the
laws and constitution. It is fundamentally important that we
should continue to do so, for it we lost our constitutional position within the United Kingdom 'civil and religious liberty for
all', which we are also pledged as Orangemen to support, would
be endangered." At first sight, when one looks back over
generations of total disregard for the civil rights of Catholics,
this seems just another example of the celebrated Orange
double-think. But—as they say in the playground—"Who
started it?"

We Irish are always being accused of looking backwards too
much. Sometimes, however, we don't look back far enough—
or carefully enough, or honestly enough. If we are going to
search for the roots of the Orange/Green conflict we must go

all the way back to Luther and Calvin. And then we must accept what we find, the fact that all over Western Europe, and much of the rest of the world, people now take for granted a degree of spiritual, intellectual and political freedom which has Lutheran doctrine as one of its main sources. This 'liberty for all' is what the Northern Protestants believe they are trying to defend, in their muddle-headed, stiff-necked, ham-fisted way. When they look South they see a government with so little respect for individual freedom of conscience that divorce and the sale of contraceptives are illegal in the Republic. And they know the statistics: in 1861 in the twenty-six counties there were 466,000 Protestants, a hundred years later there were 144,868. The Orangeman sees 'persecution' behind these figures and in a way he is right. Yet it was never the straightforward persecution of a minority of alien ex-rulers by a vengeful native majority which had at last come to power. Other statistics, showing what a remarkable proportion of the Republic's national wealth remains to this day in Protestant pockets, amply prove that. Rather was it an insidious and relentless form of spiritual blackmail operated by the Catholic church. On the surface everything looked fine and the Irish could (and often did) boast loudly—and to an extent justifiably—about how their government bent over backwards to accommodate the Protestant minority. But under the surface that minority was being steadily weakened by the Vatican's *Ne Temere* decree of 1909 which ruled that no Catholic could marry a Protestant unless both parties solemnly promised to bring up all the children of the marriage as Catholics. Many Protestants who would otherwise have made a career in Ireland emigrated in search of a partner and many of those who remained either stayed single or were forced to raise Catholic families. Normal social relationships between the two communities had to be restricted since Protestant parents were understandably reluctant to expose their young to nubile Catholics. The Irish are not natural segregationists; whether Protestant or Catholic they are far too easygoing and gregarious to put up ideological barriers between neighbours. But the *Ne Temere* decree made a certain aloofness mandatory for Southern Protestants if they wished their community to survive and thus they came to be regarded as unreasonably stand-offish or bigoted. Few Catholics ever tried to see their point of view; there was no recognition of the gross insult to Protestant integrity implied in the decree—which was rarely defied. Like the Orangeman, the average Catholic is immovably convinced of his church's rightness.

A few years ago Rome relaxed the laws governing mixed marriages and most national hierarchies promptly adjusted their local regulations. But the Irish bishops, showing a crass insensitivity to the Northern tragedy, ignored this opportunity to improve interchurch relations all over Ireland. They well deserve their reputation for being more Catholic than the Pope.

During the past decade relations between Church and State in the Republic have been closely analysed by several writers and I particularly recommend *Church and State in Modern Ireland* by Dr John Whyte and *Minority Report* by Jack White, both published by Gill Macmillan. This is a subject about which it is alarmingly easy to give wrong impressions. Only an Orangeman would suggest that the Catholic hierarchy rules the Republic from some secret subterranean office beneath Leinster House, equipped with a hot line to the Vatican. Since the state was established the church has rarely interfered directly with its running; yet the Irish Republic is undeniably governed according to a moral code approved by the Catholic church. The clergy do not need to interfere directly because they have almost complete control over the education of 95 per cent of the population. Therefore the vast majority of elected representatives would never even consider legislation that might conflict with Catholic teaching. They have been brought up to regard as a deadly sin the taking of personal decisions about moral issues. To sin by breaking church laws is one thing—and presumably is as easy for Irish Catholics as for anyone else—but to say that breaking church laws *is not necessarily sinful* remains for most Irish Catholics a psychological impossibility.

In such an atmosphere, there has never been any need for the bishops to move into that subterranean office. Recently a zephyr of change has been felt; a few politicians are actually talking in public about one day legalising divorce and the sale of contraceptives. But opinion polls indicate that most citizens would at present oppose such a revolution so the politicians may do no more than talk for some time to come. In one sense it is all very democratic. A Catholic parliament for a Catholic people—no problems, no friction, everybody backing up the Ten Commandments as interpreted at Maynooth and disregarding the tiny Protestant minority. But another minority is gradually expanding, a minority of liberal Catholics and forthright agnostics who will not be so easily disregarded and in due course will make a Catholic parliament seem very undemocratic indeed.

To get the perspective right, we have to view the much-despised Orange bigotry, fear and intransigence against this background. Two wrongs don't make a right but one wrong can make another wrong seem less wrong and that, I feel, is the case here. To Northern Protestants, whether Orangemen or not, a united Ireland means their having to accept minority status under a government that is voluntarily and happily subservient to Catholic bishops.

A common Southern Catholic comeback—which gets nobody anywhere—goes as follows: "But look at the laws in the North! On Sundays Catholics can't get a drink! They can't take their children to the public playgrounds they're paying for through the rates! They can't get onto golf-courses or into swimming-baths if Unionists are in control! What sort of civil liberty is that? Isn't it worse than anything we have against the Protestant way of thinking in the South? And 34 per cent of the population have to go along with rules made by another religion—down here it's hardly 5 per cent!" To which one can only reply that the percentages involved are irrelevant since it is the principle that counts. And that on balance, though neither set of church-inspired laws is desirable, the North's interfere less than the Republic's with fundamental human rights. (To me, nothing is more fundamental than the right to a pint on a Sunday; but I must not allow myself to be swayed by personal prejudice.)

Those interested in studying the details of Orangeism are recommended to read Tony Gray's *The Orange Order* (Bodley Head). Published only a few years ago, it is an objective, well-written, witty and not unkind study of a very odd phenomenon. An institution like the Orange Order is utterly foreign to the

British way of life in the twentieth century—another Northern
paradox, since the Orangeman is so deliriously proud of his
Britishness. Therefore outsiders tend to underestimate its importance, seeing it as a typically Irish bit of dottiness which
cannot be of any real significance today in any part of the UK.
Yet, as Tony Gray points out, 'It infiltrates every aspect of
life in Ulster and is largely responsible for the very existence
of Northern Ireland as a separate state and for the way in
which the Unionist Party has run that state for the past half
century.'

The Orange Order began in the 1790s as a Church of Ireland
(Anglican) lower-class movement which united groups of
armed men pledged to defend Protestant farms in Co Armagh
from the attacks of the Catholic Defenders. (These were
members of an anti-landlord agrarian secret society; they were
fiercely anti-Protestant yet their secret oath affirmed loyalty to
the Crown.) Nowadays, however, Orangeism is associated
equally with the more fanatical elements in all the Protestant
churches. It prides itself on being ecumenical in its own sense
of that term. In *Orangeism: A New Historical Appreciation* by the
Revs. Dewar, Brown and Long, Mr Long points out that 'The
argument that the Orange Order is a divisive influence on Irish
Protestantism is utterly wrong.... The charge is ill-founded
for the Order has embraced every shade of Protestant opinion
and is as comprehensive in its theology as its members are in
their ways of living.' Despite this claim, there is increasing disquiet among Southern Protestants, and among the more liberal
Northern Protestants, because of the extent to which their
churches still officially and publicly identify themselves with
Orangeism; for instance, by flying the Union Jack from church
towers on Orange festivals. To the uninitiated this might seem
a harmless gesture; to Northern Catholics it is a reminder that
the Church of Ireland and the Presbyterian Church in Ireland
aid and abet anti-Catholic campaigns such as that which
brought the power-sharing Assembly to an end in May 1974.
A few years ago there was a certain amount of controversy
(though not enough, some thought) when the press photo-
graphed a Church of Ireland clergyman in the act of blessing
a battalion of armed UDA paramilitaries.

Throughout Northern Ireland one meets clergymen of all denominations who are openly sympathetic to paramilitaries of the same colour. When I called on one Provo leader the door was opened to me by the local parish priest; to give him his due, he blushed. He had expected to find his host's young daughter on the doorstep. That Provo, however, was a rabid atheist; so one could charitably argue that the parish priest was visiting him to reclaim his soul.

At first I found this aspect of Northern life very shocking. But as one studies the background, and talks to the clergymen concerned, one realises that it is unreasonable to expect them to be immune to the infections in the atmosphere. Men of God are only human. And it is inevitable that some Catholic clergy will feel justified in giving tacit encouragement to organisations which claim to be fighting to free a down-trodden minority, while some Protestant clergy will feel compelled to support those who are fighting to protect Northern Ireland from Rome. The education of many Northern clergymen is geared to the propagation of myths; and the ecumenical movement, which could be described as a major de-mythologising campaign, is anathema to most Northern Protestants. One Catholic bishop said to me plaintively that he was tired of going to ecumenical services attended only by himself and his parish clergy. So strongly do many Northern Protestants feel about ecumenism that a Church of Ireland rector admitted he dare not take part in an interchurch service organised by Catholics in the next parish—which his own bishop was coming some distance to attend. "It's all right for the bish.," he said. "His Lordship can say 'Amen' and get home fast but I have to live with the people around here." Another rector told me that within a few days of his return from an interchurch conference on Peace in Northern Ireland, a local gang of Orange youths badly beat up his seventeen-year-old son. The boy could have identified them in court but his father sensibly chose not to go to the police lest his son might not survive the next attack. He summed the situation up very succinctly: "Under our system, you can govern people only to the extent that they wish to be governed. And by now big numbers in the North, on both sides, do not wish to be governed."

Elsewhere, a Presbyterian clergyman described to me his sense of outrage and betrayal when he attended a Presbyterian conference in Dublin some years ago and found many Southern ministers opposed to the Orange stand on ecumenism. He attributed their deterioration largely to the corrupting influence of the Republic's Romish atmosphere. But he also blamed his Southern colleagues for associating too freely with 'high-church' Anglican types. By most people's standards, you would have to travel far and search hard in the Republic to find just one 'high-church' clergyman. But then the Northern Presbyterian is not 'most people'.

We are so accustomed to thinking in terms of Orange versus Green that we tend to forget the Presbyterian versus Church of Ireland game. The land-owning gentry and their offshoots in the professional and commercial worlds are Church of Ireland but most members of that community belong to the poorer classes; they are to be found in their thousands in the Belfast slums. The Presbyterians are strongest among the middle-classes, farming, business and professional, and can boast of many rich self-made men in their congregations. Neither side has forgotten that they fought each other during the Civil and Cromwellian Wars, that the Church of Ireland devised a code of penal laws to subdue Dissenters and that Anglicans have always been reluctant to recognise the validity of Presbyterian and Methodist orders. Moreover, Presbyterians despise Anglicans for not showing a proper understanding of Old Testament laws, such as that regulating the observance of the Sabbath. None of this is easy for the newcomer to take seriously. But quite soon you find yourself accepting as normal—or at least unsurprising—the white-hot passions generated among ordinary people by the minutiae of doctrinal differences.

Near one small town, I stayed in a house with an unusual and very attractive garden. A few weeks previously my hostess had agreed to open the garden to the public on a Sunday afternoon in aid of some irreproachable cause sponsored by the Church of Ireland. When the opening was advertised the local Presbyterian community lapsed into a state of shock. Then it pulled itself together and tried to organise a protest. When this failed it sent a representative to distribute suitable biblical texts among these godless neo-papists who were wallowing in sin by admiring a garden on the Lord's Day.

If it were not for a shared antipathy to Catholicism, these divisions within Protestantism would no doubt be more obvious. I was sometimes amused by the cross-currents as I moved—in the same village or town—from manse to rectory to parochial house. Quite often when the minister or rector heard that I was going on to see his opposite number, a degree of veiled (and occasionally unveiled) antagonism appeared. This differed from the open hostility that might have been expressed towards the local Catholic clergy; it was tinged with guilt, whereas criticisms of the Catholics were tinged with self-righteousness. Obviously it was felt that really one shouldn't criticise one's fellow-Protestants to a Southerner, but the differences that separate these two branches of the Reformed Church were too deeply felt for decorum always to prevail. In contrast, the Catholic clergy never criticised their Protestant colleagues as people though they had a lot to say about the vileness of the political system that for so long was supported by the Protestant churches.

In Northern Ireland, the Church of Ireland is probably the least powerful and influential of the three main churches yet it bears the heaviest responsibility for trying to bring about religious reconciliation. As an episcopal church it is closer to Catholicism than to Presbyterianism; as a Reformed church it is closer to Presbyterianism than to Catholicism; as part of the Anglican community it has a greater potential for flexibility and sweet reason than either of the other two (or would have, if it could somehow disengage from the Orange Order). Ergo, it is the natural bridge. In certain areas its rectors may risk being lynched by their flock if they become too exuberantly ecumenical. But at least they won't be decollared, unfrocked, unmansed or whatever the term is for describing the disposal of a recalcitrant Presbyterian minister by the Elders of his congregation. Reliable clerical rumour has it that after the Bishop of Conor's sermon at the funeral of Lord Brookeborough—in which the living Lordship hinted that possibly the dead Lordship had been marginally less than perfect—a deputation of apoplectic Orangemen requested the Archbishop of Armagh to sack the Bishop of Conor. But the Archbishop expressed a personal disinclination to accede to this request, even had it been technically possible for him to do so.

Moderate Presbyterian ministers have to be a great deal more circumspect than was Bishop Butler. One told me that he had recently attended a supper party given by a Catholic bishop for a few of his non-Catholic clerical friends. A good time was had by all but subsequently most of the guests had to write embarrassed little notes apologising for their inability to return the episcopal hospitality. Despite this precaution some of them suffered for their indiscretion; I learned a few months later that my Presbyterian friend had been demoted to a small rural manse. Nor are abrupt transfers unknown in the Church of Ireland. One rector found himself on the move because he had prayed publicly that the area's newly-elected Catholic MP, of whom his congregation naturally disapproved, might be given 'wisdom and strength'.

An English Anglican army chaplain remarked to me that until the chaps with their collars turned the wrong way can get together themselves, and develop genuinely good relationships—as distinct from formal appearances together in public— little reconciliation is likely between their respective flocks. He didn't realise that here we have yet another vicious circle. I met several clergy, including a few Orangemen, who were so shattered by events since 1969 that they have already formed real friendships with their opposite numbers. But the Protestants among them are forced to be so discreet, lest their flocks might get restive and stampede, that the benefit of their personal goodwill is being confined to their own lives.

Only the Catholic clergy have no worries about lay opposition to ecumenism. This is not because the laity are too cowed to criticise priestly decisions but because the idea of ecumenism arouses no fear of a 'takeover'. The average Catholic feels sure—without really stopping to think about it—that if there is any taking-over to be done his church will do it. I have never met any Irish Catholic layman or woman, North or South of the border, of any background or age-group, who was even mildly suspicious of ecumenism. Some such people must exist somewhere but it is evident that—quite apart from their lack of fear—the ecumenical idea genuinely appeals to the Irish Catholic temperament. Their natural leaning towards it is discouraged, even today, in some Southern parishes where the clergy still think of Protestants as heretics. But I hope it is significant, and not just chance, that I met not one Northern Catholic parish clergyman who was against the ecumenical movement.

This brings us back to the profound differences that exist between Catholic and Protestant bigotry. Before crossing the border I had imagined the two communities to be well matched in this respect; but they are not. During five months in Northern Ireland I never heard a member of the Catholic laity expressing hostility to any Protestant church as a religious institution or to any individual Protestant *as such*. Hostility and hate were invariably focussed on systems or leaders which were seen as economic or racial enemies. This applied whether I was with Catholic farmers in the Sperrins, or with Catholic university students in Coleraine, or with Provos in a Belfast ghetto, or with unemployed Bogsiders in Derry, or with affluent middle-class Catholics on the Upper Antrim Road. Clearly what most Catholic lay people feel towards Protestantism is not true religious bigotry but resentment of injustice and scorn for the methods by which Northern Ireland was maintained under Stormont as a Protestant state for a Protestant people. The difference in quality between the two bigotries has one curious effect; many ghetto Catholics, for all their comparative poverty and lack of education, seem essentially more urbane than even the Protestant gentry, most of whom have as yet been unable to escape from their inherited theological ghetto. But how has it come about that the ordinary Catholic layman is able to distinguish between the political and religious barriers that divide him from Protestants—and, in general, to resent only the former? Even more remarkable, what enables him to distinguish (as undoubtedly he often does) between the misled rank and file of the Orange Order and those 'bosses' whom he sees as the real villains of the piece? (Which I suppose they are, if one must have villain-figures.) Here the Catholic clergy deserve a lot of credit. Though they constantly preach against mixed marriages and integrated schools, their sermons are a defence of their own system rather than an attack on anybody else's. In no Irish Catholic church, North or South, no matter how bone-headed and blinkered the preacher, would one ever hear anti-Protestant sermons on the lines of the anti-Catholic sermons regularly delivered in some Northern churches. The Catholic church, for all her faults, has an ancient dignity which rubs off onto the most unpolished of her priests and makes cheap sectarian sneering from the pulpit unthinkable. But this is not to say that Northern Catholics are without misconceptions about Protestant beliefs or about such organisations as the Free Masons and the Orange Order.

Northern Ireland's two communities are probably equally ignorant of or misinformed about each other's beliefs and traditions, with the difference that the Catholics' misinformation has not been fed to them by their clergy to nourish sectarianism.

It helps to stand back and look at these two communities in an international context. One is not accustomed to thinking of Catholicism as a mind-broadening influence but in the North it does seem to have this effect, when contrasted with the suffocating narrowness of Northern Protestantism. Although at home the Northern Catholics are in a one-third minority they are aware—if only subconsciously—of belonging to a world-wide organisation which provides a link with other languages, customs and creative traditions. It is part of the mainstream of Western civilisation, while Northern Protestantism is a stagnant creek that has formed to one side and in which a tiny group of Christians has been trapped. Many Northern Catholics, despite centuries of oppression, dispossession, impoverishment and contempt, derive from their membership of the Catholic church an inner assurance which makes their bigotry that much less aggressive. It is an interesting point, too, that on the Orange side there are no Catholic folk-heroes, while on the Green side many Protestants are so regarded.

And how about guilt?—as the housewife said to the milkman. One earnest young sociologist assured me that he could detect many traces of guilt in Orange bigotry. But I remain sceptical. The elaborate Protestant mythology does a lot to eliminate guilt by distorting the history of Ulster's plantations—an exercise which also serves to boost the Protestant ego while making the Catholic seem a type deserving only of contempt. The average

Northern Protestant is convinced that his forefathers were God-fearing, diligent, sober, honest, thrifty settlers whose virtues entitled them to take over the neglected lands of the superstitious, lazy, drunken, sly, shiftless natives. I wouldn't know exactly what goes on in the collective Protestant unconscious but I suspect it has been too thoroughly saturated with such myths for any particles of guilt to have survived.

Protestant bigotry seems much more abrasive, strident and off-putting—though essentially Protestant attitudes are more humane and humble—precisely because it lacks the supreme, calm arrogance of the Catholic brand. The fanatical evangelical Protestant may imagine that he knows he is right; but the mere fact that he is a Protestant, and therefore free to think for himself (even if he doesn't) puts his religious 'certainties' in quite a different category from those of the Catholics. He is aware, at some level, that there might be other and equally valid ways of interpreting Christianity, that his church is able to shift its ground to accommodate changing opinions within the fold, that his clergy can disagree sharply about such issues as divorce. And so, lacking the confidence of the Catholic in his own church's eternal, immutable rightness, his bigotry *appears* to be more uncharitable and superficially more unyielding.

Education is the area in which clerical influence in Ireland—North and South—may most clearly be seen. Many put all the blame for segregated schools on the Catholic church and this attitude seems to be justified when—as is the case in Belfast—a Catholic bishop refuses confirmation to children who have been sent to non-Catholic schools. In the past, however, there has been nothing to choose between the churches on this point, though now the Protestants are being much more reasonable. An excellent analysis of the history of education in the North since 1920 is given by John Darby in *Conflict in Northern Ireland*.

I went North convinced that integrated education was something which could and should be tackled at once by London: a good example of how easy it is to settle other people's problems from afar. Now my ideas have been drastically modified and I see the problem—in its Northern Irish manifestation—the other way around. Until prejudice has been tackled by the churches at parish level, and until the ordinary people have been led/directed/persuaded/ordered by their clergy to accept integrated education, I see no possibility of its achieving any good even supposing the government were able and willing to insist upon it. A Church of Ireland rector gave me one particularly vivid example of popular Protestant feeling on the subject. He had in his parish a prosperous, reasonably well-educated family whose heir—a stout young Orangeman of fourteen— one day found himself face-to-face with a *nun* (of all creepy things!) when he went to take his oral French examination. Speechless with horror, the lad fled the room. On the nearest telephone he told his mother from what a ghastly situation he had had to extricate himself, at great risk to his academic future. "Quite right, son!" she said. "No child of mine will ever be examined by a Taig! And don't worry about your exam. I'll be on to the Education Authority now this minute!" She had forgotten that in many little ways things have changed since the fall of Stormont. The Education Authority has a new soul above sectarianism and that fourteen-year-old attained instant fame as the hard-done-by opponent of pernicious ecumenism.

In Belfast I found much disapproval, among both Catholics and Protestants, of piecemeal attempts to make integrated education work. It was said that though it might have been tried, with some slight chance of success, during the sixties, it is futile to attempt it now. To make any impact on sectarianism it would have to be a large-scale, officially-backed movement and to pioneer it unofficially, with small groups of children, is thought to be unfair on the children concerned—and possibly dangerous. Moreover, some Catholics argue that as long as Protestants refuse to accept Catholic teachers in their schools, it would be a form of surrender for Catholic children to attend them.

I discussed this subject with almost everyone I met and few thought that mixed schools would help to solve the immediate problems. At least, that was how they put it. "It wouldn't make any difference"—"It wouldn't do any good"—"It's not important"—"People exaggerate its significance". Obviously most Catholics and Protestants still wish to have their children educated in schools which reinforce the religious bias of their homes and on the Orange side there is often a positive aversion to the idea of children mixing freely. To me this is a peculiarly distressing form of bigotry—a corruption of innocence in the name of God. And the *Ne Temere* decree is partly—perhaps mainly—to blame for its being so widespread and durable in Northern Ireland. At present Protestants have an excellent reason—not merely an excuse—for opposing integrated schools. Nobody imagines that if the Catholic hierarchy changed its attitude to mixed marriages the Protestants would soon change theirs to mixed schools. But at least the next generation of Protestant parents would have grown up without the *Ne Temere* threat in the forefront of their minds.

Education provides the inspiration for a wonderful sentence in *Orangeism* where Mr Long writes: 'The 1947 Act was to put back the clock making it possible for anyone as well as a Protestant, perhaps preferable to a Protestant, to teach Protestant children, parents and Churches notwithstanding.' If anyone wants the Orange philosophy in a nutshell, there it is. But poking fun at Orangemen is too easy; in all their pronouncements they leave themselves wide open to be laughed at by a world that has moved on a bit since 1690. And yet, against the Northern Ireland background they are no joke.

In Catholic folklore, the Orange Order has been invested with all sorts of sinister qualities which it does not possess—just as many Orangemen believe the Romish church to be a cesspool of unmentionable iniquities. However, as the manufacturer, guardian and transmitter of Protestant myths, the Order is undoubtedly a public menace. Official Orange attitudes make it virtually impossible for the Northern Irish to overcome the heart-breaking barrier of mistrust that separates two communities which to a visitor seem equally likeable and kindly. Also, the Order is physically dangerous as a reservoir of fighting men, backed by considerable wealth, who would, given a certain sort of crisis, go forth again—as they have done in the past—to kill Catholics in the firm belief that it was their religious duty to do so. (Like Muslims going forth on a Jihad.) Forecasts of bloodbaths, massacres and full-scale civil war have become common during the past few years largely because of what Orangeism has planted and tended in Northern Ireland's political garden. It would be impossible for the Catholic extremists to run a bloodbath, if only because there are too few of them. This is not properly understood in Britain where IRA activities have been allowed—even encouraged—to deflect public attention from the fact that it is the Loyalists who possess both the means and the motive to bring about a civil war. In *The Protestants of Ulster* by Geoffrey Bell—a Belfast Protestant—the point is made that 'Catholic working-class newspapers simply do not project themselves as wishing to dominate Protestants. There is no mention in them of wishing to kill Prod scum, no caricature of Protestants as dirty, smelly and idle.'

I had always tended to regard the 'Jihad complex' in Orangeism as part of the Green myth. But one day a young Methodist minister showed me his collection of Loyalist ballads and after that I could have no more illusions. Here are excerpts from three of the most popular songs:

On the 14th August we took a little trip,
Up along Bombay Street and burned out all the shit,
We took a little petrol and we took a little gun,
And we fought the bloody fenians, till we had them on the run.

I was born under the Union Jack
I was born under the Union Jack
If guns are made for shooting, then skulls are made to crack.
You've never seen a better Taig than with a bullet in his back.

Sunday morning went for a drive,
Took along my colt 45.
Hey, Hey, Hey, what a beautiful day.
Went to Derry not on a hunch,
Knew I'd get a Taig before lunch,
Hey, Hey, Hey, it's a beautiful day.

Towards the end of my time in Northern Ireland I had a strange little experience. I had been invited to stay with a family of whom I knew nothing, in a town I had not visited before, and the surname was to my ears 'theologically' neutral. When I telephoned to announce my time of arrival an elderly man spoke to me and during our brief conversation I got an impression of unusual gentleness and warmth. At dusk I found the neat little bungalow and immediately realised that this was not a Catholic home—but neither was it Northern Irish Protestant. I felt sure of that because of the family's demeanour ('aura' would be a better word but it makes people laugh). Yet everybody had a marked Northern accent and the whole thing was quite baffling.

As we talked I found myself communicating without any constraint, as I would have done among old friends. 'Atmosphere' is something that has fascinated me in many parts of the world; it is so definite and yet so indefinable. In that atmosphere I was aware of relaxing completely, as I had not done for what seemed like a long time. The familiar Northern tension was not there and I felt no need to be careful lest I give offence. Then, after a few hours, the mystery was solved by a chance remark. I was among Quakers.

That was a revealing little episode; until then I had not realised how much Northern Ireland is a place apart. However sincere an outsider's affection and sympathy for the locals, it is necessary to be constantly on guard. There are so many hidden tensions that one can never speak altogether freely, without fear of being misinterpreted, to either Catholics or Protestants. And there is no such thing as objectivity about Northern problems, except among a tiny minority of intellectuals. (Obviously there are numbers of people who genuinely believe themselves to be objective—and try very hard—but that is not quite the same thing.)

It was an enormous relief to be with a family who had no hang-ups and were both objective and perceptive in their comments on The Troubles. But while in that atmosphere I realised something else about the North which greatly saddened me—the extent to which sectarianism in its various forms has damaged the Northern Irish character by coarsening or toughening it. I do not mean with regard to the normal civilities of life, nor am I thinking only of ghetto types or country bumpkins. What I am referring to is as obvious (sometimes more obvious) among the most cultivated sections of society as up the Falls. Nor is it to be confused with Northern bluntness, a quality I admire. I may have chosen the wrong words; it is hard to find the right ones for what is, in effect, a spiritual disorder afflicting almost everybody in the North. Possibly bitterness would be more accurate—though not necessarily bitterness in the form of bigotry, for many tolerant people suffer from what I am trying to define. Perhaps, after all, it is simply mistrust. An ineradicable mistrust of 'the other side', permeating every crevice of the victim's heart and soul. What could be more damaging than that?

6

Belfast Pedalabouts—Mostly Green

Imagine a London in which the inhabitants of Kensington are afraid to visit old friends in Chelsea; in which nobody from Camden Town dares to drink in Hampstead pubs; in which a youth from Wimbledon would be risking his life by strolling through Green Park; in which a change of taxis is sometimes necessary between Putney and Richmond because few drivers are willing to venture outside their native borough. A London suffering from an acute housing shortage though row after row of solid, spacious dwellings stand empty with bricked-up doors and windows. A London where policemen are likely to be shot dead within moments of entering certain districts—and so never do enter them—and where large buildings are frequently razed by uncontrollable swarms of small boys. A London in which only the West End is comparatively safe for all Londoners to shop in, because it has been securely barricaded off from the rest of the capital and is constantly patrolled by large numbers of heavily armed troops. Such a London could happen only in science fiction—we hope. Yet all the world knows that one city in the United Kingdom has been reduced during the past decade to this almost unimaginable way of life.

I did not choose the most auspicious season for my first visit to Belfast. All over Northern Ireland, but especially in the capital, communal relations deteriorate during the weeks before The Twelfth of July. Even in the country, Protestants who normally are well-disposed towards everybody won't salute Catholics and Catholics know better than to approach Protestant neighbours for the sort of help that would gladly be given in March or October. To me this weird annual cycle is one of the most incomprehensible features of an often incomprehensible scene. Are Protestants afraid that without regular practice they might be unable to maintain the necessary (for tribal preservation) inner level of hostility towards Catholics? During the marching season Orangemen indulge in provocation of the most infantile sort. A good example is the butcher's shop which advertised 'Lourdes-cured ham'. This brand of wit is much relished by Protestants and in the peaceful old days was good-humouredly tolerated by Catholics. But the Taigs' years of accepting jeers and sneers merely lowered them in the Orange estimation.

When I crossed the River Bann—broad and brown between flat banks—it seemed much more real, as a frontier, than the border between North and South. It divides the western, more Catholic and more economically underprivileged region of Northern Ireland from the predominantly Protestant counties of Antrim and Down. Antrim is Paisley country; when I stopped at a crossroads petrol station to ask the way a young attendant abruptly (and absurdly) said, "Don't know". Further down the road two youths curtly gave directions while eyeing me with a mixture of suspicion and derision. On the out-skirts of Ballymena I cycled between rows of preternaturally clean bungalows with shining windows, fresh paint, gleaming brass ornaments on gleaming tiled mantelpieces, washed and ironed curtains and not the tiniest weed visible in any garden. An hour later, on a quiet country road, an overtaking car slowed and began to follow me. My heart lurched, as it would not have done west of the Bann, and the next few minutes seemed long. When the ancient mini overtook me the passenger door was opened by one of the two youths to whom I had spoken earlier and I was treated to an indecent gesture. This was such a relief, when I had been half-expecting a bullet, that I almost said "Thank you".

Six miles short of the city I stopped at a new, opulent 'inn'. It was fortified with a roof-high steelwire enclosure and had a car barrier and a 'sentry-box' in which a security man sat doing the pools. But as usual no attention was paid to Roz's bulging saddle-bag. At the bar I got into conversation with two elderly friendly sisters who run a large café in central Belfast. One of their employees—a young man, recently married—had been blown to bits in a pub a few weeks previously. No one mentioned the three men who had been shot dead the evening before in a pub just down the road. Around Belfast there is a marked tendency not to discuss recent local tragedies.

I spent the next two nights with friends in a residential area which looked the epitome of tranquil respectability but had within the past fortnight suffered three sectarian murders. In one case a thirty-five-year-old Catholic pub owner was shot dead in his bed by a man on a ladder. This victim had allowed his bar staff to serve soldiers on patrol who slipped in through a back door for a quick pint during a heat-wave. The Provos do not approve of pampering the Brits. As I went to bed on my first night it occurred to me that I might wake up dead. A gunman could break in and shoot me in my sleep, mistaking me for my brave host. A few weeks earlier he had risked his life on the Antrim Road to give aid to a soldier wounded by a sniper; meanwhile other members of the foot-patrol were firing in the sniper's direction and eight people stood impassively in a nearby bus queue, pretending not to notice.

I was advised to study the religious geography of the city before cycling around it and a friend lent me his detailed British Army Tribal Map of Belfast, which marks the ghetto areas orange and green. Then my host introduced me to the Catholic ghettos. With a prominent DOCTOR notice displayed on his windscreen he was less likely than other motorists to be delayed at security check points, hijacked by bombers or stoned by gangs of bored boys who for the moment could find no more exciting target.

Perhaps because I never see television, and so was quite unprepared, those ghettos really shattered me. Yet I have known far worse slums in Asia. But Belfast is in affluent Europe and why should large areas of it be swarming with undernourished wild children and knee-deep in stinking litter, and strewn with broken glass glinting in hot sun under a blue sky—all on a summer's day.... So many bricked-up houses, reminding me of dead people with their eyes shut—some of them fine substantial buildings from which Protestants had had to flee in terror taking only their resentment with them. So many high brick, or corrugated iron, barricades between identical streets of little working-class homes, to prevent neighbours seeing and hearing each other, and so being provoked to hurt and kill each other.

Sometimes, over the barricades, I could glimpse Union Jacks flying from upstairs windows. And I remembered a friend of mine in another part of the North—a retired naval officer—saying how much he resented the British flag being abused as a provocative sectarian symbol.

A filthy four- or five-year-old boy was playing all alone on a broken pavement with a length of stick; it was his gun and he was aiming at us. One wouldn't even notice him in London or Dublin but in Belfast I wondered, "How soon will he have the real thing?" Already, in his little mind, possession of a gun is equated with bravery and safety, with having the will and ability to defend his own territory against 'the Oranges'. Around the next corner two slightly older children were carefully placing cardboard cartons in the middle of the narrow street. "Are these pretend bombs?" I asked, appalled. "They might not be pretend," replied Jim, driving onto the pavement to avoid one. Even more appalled, I said nothing. Jim looked at me and laughed. "You'll get used to it!" he said. "Almost certainly they are pretend. But hereabouts sensible people don't take chances."

Everywhere stones and broken bricks were available to be thrown at passing army vehicles. Jagged broken bottles lay in gutters, flashing as they caught the strong sunlight. We passed an elaborately fortified barracks and then a famous 'confrontation spot'. "In the afternoons," explained Jim, "you get the locals out here stoning the troops. And the same evening the same people will run across to the sentry-box and ask could they ever use the 'phone to ring the aunt in Armagh."

When we took a wrong turning Jim became slightly tense. At the end of an artificial cul-de-sac—concrete-filled tar barrels were blocking the road to motor traffic—he turned quickly. A group of gum-chewing youths came sauntering round a corner and jeered at the posh car on principle. "There's a wee bit of trouble on the way," remarked Jim. "It's funny, when you live here you develop a sixth sense—you always can tell when something's brewing." He warned me then never to loiter when entering or leaving ghettos. Sectarian assassins do not always pick out individuals; often they just go to areas where they can be almost certain of their victim's religion. But for them actually to enter a ghetto would be too dangerous. Everyday life in Belfast takes some getting used to, yet contrary to my expectations I found the city quite attractive.

Despite its population of 360,000 one never feels trapped in Belfast. On Roz, I could be away among green fields, or on a mountain, or by the sea, within half an hour of leaving the City Hall. And some of the most wretched areas are within sight of brilliantly fresh countryside—though this fact somehow made them seem even more tragic and squalid.

I parted from Jim a little apprehensively and cycled back to slumland to spend the rest of the day with Catholic families to whom I had been given introductions by a community worker. Outside a huge newish block of flats children swarmed raucously on wasteland while half-starved Alsatians snarled at each other; the lower walls of the building were daubed with exhortations to join the Provos, fuck the UVF and defend the Republic. "Best mind them dogs," said Tom, "they'd ate you."

Tom and Maire are in their forties but look a lot older. Tom is small, slim and bearded—a professional cat-burglar who slipped when crossing a roof one night last year and broke his back. Now he is 'out of work' and has to use a complicated walking-machine provided by the NHS. I found his accent very difficult but Maire was quite comprehensible. With the end of her skirt she wiped bright yellow cake crumbs and a smear of tomato ketchup off the leatherette settee and invited me to be comfortable beside her. Then—sitting bolt upright with bony hands clasped tightly in her lap—she told me about her son. He was twenty-two when he was 'executed' last year as a punishment for deserting from the Stickies. (The Official IRA.) He had been married six months previously and his eighteen-year-old bride was with him when he was shot dead in the street. She was nearly three months pregnant and she lost the baby next day. I was shown the wedding photographs, snapshots already dog-eared, taken with a neighbour's camera. His mother had begged him not to join the Stickies— to join the Provos if he must but never the Stickies. It was no good—he wouldn't listen—he thought the Stickies could do more for the poor. "For the likes of us, who never had nothin' but what we get from the Buroo (i.e., National Assistance) and maybe a bit extra when Tom could do an office—he never went near nobody's house, I swear to God!" But soon enough the young man repented his obstinacy, when he was ordered to shoot someone with whom he had grown up on the same street and gone to school. His mother advised him to say nothing but to get away quietly across the water. The snag was that he didn't want to leave Belfast—he had no mind for travelling—he'd never in his life been out of the city except once to go on a football excursion to Dublin. And he was very fond of his parents— a bit spoiled—an only child. "Somethin' went wrong the time he was born and I couldn't have no more. There are days I'm terrible tempted to be bitter and to wish to see them dead that killed him. I know them, too. I know the very fella that fired the shot. I could tell you where he is this minute. Wouldn't you feel the bitterness, if 'twas yourself? But I prays to God above not to be that way. What good would it do, to have another mother with all this sadness on her?"

It was comforting to be reminded that in Northern Ireland Christianity still occasionally fulfills its original purpose.

Next day I met another bereaved mother in a very different sort of home. Aine lives in an area that has only recently become exclusively Catholic; a few years ago it was a mixed estate of respectable skilled workers with Prods and Taigs living happily side by side in solid little red-brick terraced houses. Now the place is a shambles—burnt-out houses, bricked-up houses, the few remaining shops steel-shuttered, the post office (which has been raided eight times) fortified like an army barracks, every front garden a wilderness, the streets strewn with glass, stones and half-bricks, violent slogans on the 'Peace Line' barriers and vicious dogs threatening every unfamiliar passer-by. Yet the interior of Aine's house was neat and spotless; no Presbyterian home in Ballymena could have outshone it.

Aine apologised for her red eyes; she had not been expecting any caller. "I was just havin' a wee cry in the kitchen. Mostly now I'm all right but sometimes it comes over me round this time—when he'd be comin' in to his supper with his dad. They worked together at the plumbin', see. And you know how a young lad loves his food—he'd say, 'Great, Mum! It's onions tonight and you've been cryin'!' People say I'll forget all them details but sure how could I? It was Corrymeela got me where I am now. I could never have come to myself without it. I never felt at Mass what I felt at those prayers together in Corrymeela. Protestants and Catholics we were, all together, and the Protestants knew 'twas one of their lot killed my son and they prayed *special* for me—and it worked! I'll never again be happy, see. But I'm not angry no more."

There were six large colour photographs of Frank on top of the television set and along the mantlepiece; a tall, handsome young man with blonde hair, merry eyes and a kind, open face. In one picture he had an arm around the shoulder of the girl he was planning to marry. "By now I could have been a grandmother," said Aine. Sadie and he had just bought a second-hand car between them—she was a secretary—and Frank had recently moved to a new semi-detached house in a mixed area. Then one evening after supper he gave his mother a lift to the youth club where she helps as a volunteer—"tryin' to keep the kids off the streets". He said good-night and drove on to his own little house and was shot eight times in the head and chest as he sat in an armchair watching television.

Sadie was a Protestant. And possibly Frank's assassin thought it his duty to prevent a Protestant girl's children being brought up in the Romish faith. Any regular reader of Paisley's *Protestant Telegraph* might come to feel thus if he took what he read seriously.

"They well knew it was dangerous to stay," said Aine. "But they were young and happy and they didn't believe it could happen to them. I told them straight—'Go yous away across the water! Yous'll never have it easy here!' But Frank didn't want to go. He loved the fishin' and the hikin' in the hills—down to the Mournes he'd be with his big boots and his knapsack as often as he could get away."

Dan came in then and Aine insisted that I stay for supper. An excellent meal it was, too, though I had interrupted the preparing of it.

Dan and Aine are the sort of Belfast people one rarely hears of—moderate working-class Catholics who refuse to admit that the IRA have achieved anything worthwhile by bringing about Direct Rule and would be thankful if only life could again be as good as it was in 1968. "'Twasn't perfect for the Catholics then," said Dan, "but by God 'twas a lot better than what it is now!" I mentioned the area where I had spent the previous day, with its chronic unemployment problems and its demoralising awareness of always having been discriminated against. Dan nodded. "Aye, surely they have it tough. But how much of it's their own fault? You get a rare lot o' feckless lads up thataway! There's many up there, and if you put them to work on Monday they'd be out sick on Tuesday. Never had no stomach for work, they didn't. You can't shove all the blame on the Orangemen. I've always wanted to do an honest day's work and Thank God I've never been idle. Most o' my jobs I'm doin' for Protestants but they don't seem to care I'm Taig so long as I does the job good and honest. OK—I could never get a government contract—you had to be Orange for that. But in a city there's plenty work besides. Surely we never got a fair crack from Stormont, but didn't we boycott it in the first place? We'd never have got our rights, I know. But we could have put a wee bit of a brake on the Orangemen if we'd mucked in with the politics from the start. And let me tell you, there's plenty Catholics here think the way we do. Without this new bother things would have got better and better for us—or anyways for our children. Now we're destroyed, with the hate and the fear stirred up since '68."

Earlier that same day I had got the opposite view from a Provo supporter. "Things had to get worse before they could really get better. We couldn't wait forever while O'Neill was pussy-footin' about tryin' to keep Paisley calm. He was a fool of a Prime Minister. Brave enough though, I'll say that for him. There was a time back in the sixties when a whole crowd of his own lot were itchin' to bump him. But he stuck with his principles, for all the good they were to anyone. Too much namby-pamby Eton carry-on. That kinda crap's no good in Belfast. He always went on like he was in London. Paisley could knock him flat with a look—and often did. He's bad news, Paisley. But at least he's a real Irishman."

Cycling through Belfast's slums, I often thought about Lord O'Neill's celebrated speech on the BBC in 1969 when he made the following statement: "The basic fear of the Protestants in

Northern Ireland is that they will be outbred by the Roman Catholics. It is as simple as that. It is frightfully hard to explain to a Protestant that if you give Roman Catholics a good job and a good house they will live like Protestants, because they will see neighbours with cars and television sets. They will refuse to have eighteen children. But if the Roman Catholic is jobless and lives in a most ghastly hovel, he will rear eighteen children on National Assistance. It is impossible to explain this to a militant Protestant because he is so keen to deny civil rights to his Roman Catholic neighbours. He cannot understand, in fact, that if you treat Roman Catholics with due consideration and kindness they will live like Protestants in spite of the authoritative nature of their church."

Tony Gray described this speech as 'almost stupefying in its tone of condescension'. But as well as being grossly offensive, it is partly true. It is also an excellent illustration of how Orangeism marks a man for life. By all accounts Lord O'Neill is an intelligent, well-meaning and honourable man who felt so strongly about civil rights for Catholics that he sacrificed his political career in an attempt to secure them. And yet, so deeply ingrained are his Orange prejudices that he could speak thus of Catholics over the BBC while sincerely regarding himself as their champion.

It is of course unfair to scorn Lord O'Neill for his immortal howler. He, as much as any shipyard worker in East Belfast, is a victim of centuries of anti-Catholic propaganda. I have heard it argued that Eton and the Guards should have been able to counteract his Orange heritage; but this is to miss the point. These institutions did, obviously, counteract those parts of it which were accessible to outside influence. The fact that he was able to see (as the vast majority of Orangemen are not) how badly Catholics had been treated, and that as Prime Minister he struggled so hard to improve their position, is proof of that. But no school and no regiment could soak the Orange dye out of his emotions. His remarks betrayed that however sincere his dedication to the cause of justice for the minority—and nobody ever seriously questioned its sincerity—he simply cannot regard Catholics as fully paid-up members of the human race. Some whites feel the same about blacks and some Indians feel the same about other Indians and all Chinese used to feel the same about all non-Chinese (and perhaps still do). I believe this sort of prejudice cannot be eradicated by the individual, however good his intentions and clear his thinking. He may *act* contrary to his prejudices, as Lord O'Neill did, but he cannot *feel* contrary to them.

According to Lord O'Neill the correct policy is so to treat Roman Catholics that they *will live like Protestants*. One can read too much into a statement made on the wireless during a period of considerable political and personal stress. Nevertheless, it seems reasonable to ask how Lord O'Neill would react if Catholics were treated justly but chose *not* to live like Protestants. Under a system that guaranteed civil rights for all, Catholics would soon be able to challenge successfully the dominance of Protestants in every sphere of Northern life. In 1969 the proportion of Catholic children in Northern Ireland's schools was 51 per cent though Catholics form little more than a third of the entire population. No wonder, as Lord O'Neill said, "The basic fear of the Protestants in Northern Ireland is that they will be outbred by the Roman Catholics."

At intervals, Belfast's habitual sectarian violence is augmented by feuding within or between the various Orange or Green paramilitary groups. At the time of my first visit to the city the Provos and Stickies were indulging in gang warfare, with the Irps playing some part in the background which I could never understand. Not even the best-informed student of Belfast's underworld can fully unravel these quarrels. On the Orange side they are often a result of rivalry in the protection-racketeering business while amongst the Greens they are more likely to be caused by bitter ideological differences. And there are some strange anomalies. In the summer of 1975 the Stickies' newspaper printed an article said to be from the UVF and demanding the killing of all Irps. During the past few years sinister links seem to have been forged between some Stickies and some UVF members and nobody is sure what these portend—or even which element in the UVF is involved. These are the apparently trivial mysteries which can wear your nerves to bits if you happen to live in an area dominated by paramilitaries.

From the ghetto dwellers' point of view such feuds and un-
accountable alliances are far more demoralising than 'normal'
campaigns; there can be no clearly-defined refuge from the bullets and knives of fellow Catholics or fellow Protestants. And
after only a few days in Belfast I could appreciate what this
means.

My own rapid adaptation to tribal life both astonished and
irritated me. Against the Belfast background customary attitudes, principles and convictions mean little; what mattered
most was my Southern brogue by which I could instantly be
identified in an Orange area as an 'enemy' and in a Green area
as a 'friend'. I soon discovered that many in the Orange areas
kindly welcome Southerners—who in the Green areas may be
suspected of spying. Yet at an instinctive, animal level I felt
safe in Green territory and unsafe in Orange territory. I used
to watch the walls attentively and feel my nerves relaxing or
tensing according to whether I saw JOIN THE IRA, UP THE
PROVOS, or UVF RULE HERE, FTP—or any of the innumerable variations on these themes. Just once I saw a neutral inscription on a Green wall: DEAR TERRY IS DEAD. There was
a mildness and tenderness about this expression of grief, in the
midst of so many brutal and blasphemous slogans, that quite
devastated me.

On my second night in Belfast I went to a Provo Sinn Fein
meeting which was attended by several mothers who had recently lost sons in the Provo/Stickie feud. About thirty people
were present in a small room—from articulate girls and boys
in their teens to Old IRA veterans in their late seventies who
spoke vigorously against the Provos. Practically every male in
the room had been interned and only then did I begin to see
the unwisdom of indiscriminate internment. When it was first
introduced by Brian Faulkner in 1971 I had thought it a desperate remedy, but one that seemed justified. However, I was
wrong. The individuals in the Catholic community who could
most effectively have counteracted the Provos were the moder-
ates among the Old IRA, men of my own father's stamp and
generation who had been 'out' in 1918–21 and whose patriotism
nobody could question. To have interned such men was an indication of how little the Stormont–Westminster–Military Intel-

ligence combination understood the Northern Catholic scene. Of course there are many Old IRA veterans who support the Provos and have always done so. But to sort these out from the moderating influences should not have been beyond the resources of British Intelligence.

The Provo representative who addressed us—an intense young man, tall, slim and wavy-haired—was so enmeshed in his own obsessions that it was impossible to get any sense out of him. At the start he antagonised everybody—even those who were clearly pro-Provo—by announcing that he could easily talk above our heads but would be careful not to. Despite this claim, whenever anybody disagreed with Provo 'policies' his only reply was to accuse them of cynicism. He drivelled on interminably about the IRA's 'great and glorious past' but looked very annoyed when a forceful young man asked what exactly a Provo victory would mean in terms of the future. An equally forceful young woman then stood up and asked how it was proposed to run a state on ideals without money. She was curtly told to read the Provo Policy Document wherein is set out the Federal Solution. An Old IRA man at once demanded, "When, where and by whom was the Federal Solution voted on?" Another Old IRA man answered him by saying, "It was foisted on the cumann by the leaders! It doesn't represent the hopes or ambitions of anyone but a few crackpots." To those our speaker replied smoothly that, "A policy is only a short-term thing you're prepared to try out and if it doesn't work you try something else." When this definition provoked sardonic laughter he added that "Provisional Sinn Fein is not a political party working within the system—it's out to *destroy* the system!"

An elderly woman then observed, "What we need is a sort of cross between the Provos and Stickies and SDLP." Her husband agreed, remarking, "When all's said and done, most people want to be respectable. That's why you get thousands voting for the SDLP even though half their hearts is with the Provos." But the young woman beside me strenuously denied this. "*We* don't want to be respectable! Not if that means going along with some new Stormont substitute. We only vote SDLP because we're realists and there's no other way to get things done at the moment—no one else to help us deal with the authorities."

Several times our speaker was pulled up for using 'we' and 'us' when discussing the organisation of the Provisional People's Assembly. He was reminded that the Provos have no right whatever to regard themselves as representatives of Belfast's Catholics and there was much opposition to the idea of their taking over—or even helping to run—any of the existing community organisations.

The subject that aroused the strongest feeling, however, was the Provo-Stickie feud. In a corner sat two middle-aged women who had been friends and neighbours all their lives though in 1970 their husbands had 'split', one supporting the Provos, the other the Stickies. Not long before the meeting the Provo mother's son had been murdered by the Stickie mother's son— who within a few days had himself been killed. These two women stood up together and begged for a truce. "For God's sake—for our sons' sakes—can't you all agree!" I gathered that the feud was being carried on exclusively by the younger generation on both sides; it is almost unknown for their elders to attack each other, however bitterly they may disagree. When our speaker insisted that the Stickies were 'Stalin-dominated' and wanted the Brits to stay, and that in every organisation 'a few youths get out of control', he was shouted down by enraged and bereaved parents. "Nonsense! You're keeping it going on both sides with your filthy rags! You're urging each other on to kill—you've gone mad, the lot o' yous!" One man of about fifty called out, "I've just left the Stickies and I don't care who knows—when our sons are being riddled on the streets by each other we should cease to be Stickies or Provos and become Irishmen! All I want now is to stop this killing!" Listening to him, I wondered if he ever thought about the English and Welsh and Scottish parents whose sons have also been shot on the streets of Belfast.

During the evening I became accustomed to references to 'the war', made quite unselfconsciously, just as the British might refer to their world wars. There were also many references to 'dropping Brits'. This activity was plainly regarded as praiseworthy by most of the younger people present. It had been sug-

gested that I should attend this meeting to increase my understanding of Belfast Catholic attitudes but I left it doubting if
anybody would ever be able to understand them. The Catholics
themselves are in a massive muddle. Most of the younger people
seem to sympathise with the Provos in their war against the
security forces while fiercely resenting any Provo interference
in their own areas and not wishing to be associated with Provo
attacks on civilian targets. This means that their willingness to
give the Provos practical help is rather half-hearted. The day
after the meeting I visited another Catholic district where three
householders had been knee-capped within the previous year
for refusing to hand over their car keys to 'volunteers'. Now,
in that area, people do hand over car keys on demand—and
who can blame them?

After the meeting gigantic pots of tea appeared and several
people kindly gave me the sort of information they have learnt
keeps journalists happy. Thus I discovered that to get booze
into 'the Kesh' you dehydrate a whole grapefruit and then inject it with gin through a needle borrowed from your local
doctor if he's a good sort and stolen from your local clinic if
he isn't. I also learned that teen-age girl snipers are regarded
as the most accurate of all for long-distance work and that
'something off the lorry' means hi-jacked goods. I was given
the addresses of three seemingly deserted and boarded-up shops
which are very well-stocked behind their blank façades. In one
of them the best Bushmills was then going for £3 a bottle. But
devoted as I am to Bushmills, and parsimonious as is my nature,
I reckoned that life in Belfast was quite complicated enough
without getting myself into gaol as a receiver—or imbiber—
of stolen goods.

An unexpected complication of Belfast life caught up with
me at the end of that tea-party. It was 1.30 am on a still, balmy
midsummer night and in two hours more the dawn would
break. But meanwhile it was very dark. And suddenly I realised
that I was afraid to cycle the five miles to my friends' house
just off the Antrim Road, which had recently been nicknamed
'Murder Mile'. Fear of immediate danger I know all about;
what I am not accustomed to is fearing something that may
happen but probably won't. The sensation was as unfamiliar

as it was humiliating. But I was past being shamed into bravery. I was gut-frightened at the thought of cycling through a series of Orange and Green ghettos when I couldn't see the graffiti and wouldn't know to whom I was talking if I got lost—as I well might, in total darkness, only forty-eight hours after arriving in the city. So I cravenly accepted the offer of a lift home and had it not been offered I would have asked for it.

In retrospect, I found this experience interesting. When I tried to analyse my uncharacteristic timidity I came to the conclusion that what I had been suffering from was contagious mass-fear. This is not, I hope, mere self-justification. After all, you could drop me in the middle of the night onto an Ethiopian plateau or into a Himalayan valley and I would positively relish the experience; but then I would be alone and creating, as it were, my own atmosphere. In a city of 360,000 people, however—most of whom are all the time subconsciously slightly afraid—the atmosphere can be very odd, especially at night. Of course one eventually adjusts to it and when I had learned my way around I did occasionally cycle at night—though never without wishing that I were doing something else.

Many Belfast people claim not to notice the city's tensions but the staggering quantities of tranquillisers consumed annually tell another story. Also, most city-centre pubs are not crowded at lunch-time; and the manager of a bookshop told me that business is declining because so many country people have given up shopping in Belfast while regular customers tend not to browse. Again, a bus-driver who takes excursions to Dublin said that he could always pick out his passengers from a Southern crowd—"They seem so watchful and worn-looking, alongside the Dubliners." Yet despite their strained faces there is a gallant sort of cheerfulness about the Belfast people, a good-humoured acceptance of the manifold inconveniences of everyday life. Shopping within the city centre security zone is a most tedious ritual, especially in very hot weather. One pities the exhausted elderly folk and the young mothers surrounded by fretful children who can't understand why they are not allowed to walk through the barriers to the ice-cream man. Nor is midsummer pleasant for the traffic wardens, civilian searchers and RUC and army patrols; the check point shelters become like

glass-houses and the air seems an almost unbreathable con-
coction of dust, heat and diesel fumes. However, the challenge
of coping with a crisis seems to keep most people going though
by now the 'crisis' has become permanent.

Belfast today is often compared with London during the blitz.
But at least the Londoners were united against an identifiable
foreign foe and not exposed to the furtive exploits of members
of their own society. It is the unpredictability rather than the
frequency of Belfast's hazards that makes them so nerve-wrack-
ing; and the seemingly elaborate security arrangements are a
deterrent rather than a protection. The prim-looking young
woman ahead of you on the pavement carrying a plastic bag
just might be on her way to blow up Marks and Spencers. Or
the neatly dressed, respectable elderly man carrying a tidy
brown paper parcel just might be going to hide it in that pub
towards which you are heading. Can people really get used to
living with this sort of thing? After ten days I fancied that I
had become reasonably immune to it. Then one evening as I
was writing in a friend's empty house a door banged upstairs
and for the next five minutes I could scarcely breathe, so violently was my heart hammering. Yet in any other part of the
world I simply do not react to sudden loud noises.

The different social classes are exposed to different degrees
and sorts of tension. In the poorer Catholic areas, where army
harassment is commonest and paramilitary harassment (or involvement) is most widespread, tension is least. Things are
happening all the time, people are active, there is less time for
brooding and more awareness of solidarity with the neighbours.
At the other extreme is the Catholic middle-class, which must
be the smallest social group in Belfast. As a minority within
a minority its general feeling of insecurity is intense. Also, it
has the sort of pride which inhibits it from giving in to intimidation as promptly as most ghetto people do when seriously
threatened. Families with adolescent children, or university
students living at home, are especially vulnerable to intimidation from both sides. I stayed with one couple whose medical
student son had had to leave Belfast in 1972, half-way through
his training, because night after night the Provos had forced
him to attend to their wounded and his mother was afraid that

in the end they would shoot him as a 'security risk'. He had been told that if he refused to co-operate his father would be killed. And that is but one of many similar stories in my note-book.

I visited another family who live in what used to be a mixed street, running parallel to one of the ironically named 'Peace Lines'. (It seems inexpressibly degrading that within a city of the British Isles neighbours have to be kept apart by tangles of wire, sheets of tin, brick walls, concrete barricades and piles of burnt-out cars. This was an aspect of Belfast I never got used to; on my fifth visit it upset me as much as it had done the first time I saw it.) A Loyalist paramilitary group is anxious to gain control of this whole area and most of the Catholic families have by now been forced out, to the shame and grief of their Protestant neighbours who of course dare not protest at what is happening. Within the previous month my friends had received three threatening letters, several telephone calls and a warning spray of machine-gun bullets around their hall-door. They had complained to the police, who regretted their inability to help. Such experiences underline the extent to which law and order have broken down under paramilitary pressure, even in the more 'respectable' districts of Belfast. A few days before my visit that whole street had been shaken by an explosion just around the corner, when the house of another Catholic family who had ignored all warnings was blown up. I could not understand my friends' dogged determination to stay in their home; I would have been gone after the first letter. They explained that since all their children have grown up and emigrated they feel justified in joining the élite who defy intimi-dation—especially as the husband is due to retire in 1978 and they can then retreat without dishonour from the urban scene.

At the far end of that district I cycled up a once attractive street past nine empty semi-detached houses from which Cath-olic families had recently been driven. Workmen were busy around some of them and by now I daresay all are occupied by Loyalist paramilitary supporters. But one Catholic was standing fast—a widower, recently retired from his profession and resolved not to move whatever the paramilitaries might do. "I've lived here with it all my life," said he. "My father was shot dead by the Tans in '21 as he was standing in a city-centre pub having a pint. And I well remember going to school through holes in garden walls, from garden to garden, because the streets of Belfast were considered too dangerous for children. But y'know—maybe this will surprise you—I reckon we're over the worst. The modern world is going to be too much for Northern Ireland. What was acceptable in the twenties won't wash in the eighties. We just need a little more patience—we don't need to do anything. And I'll bet Britain sees this. The Brits may look stupid in Westminster but they've an awful lot of grey cells tucked away in Whitehall. If we all sit back and wait, the whole bigotry-based structure of Northern Ireland is bound to collapse. Simply because it's against European human nature towards the end of the twentieth century. Even in Spain, they wouldn't stand for it now. Moderation will overtake us whether we want it or not.''

My next middle-class Catholic was rather a special case, a senior civil servant who is a target for both Green and Orange paramilitaries. His home has several times been stoned by rioting mobs; the last one consisted of some forty Loyalist youths from a nearby housing estate. The RUC had not long before found the numbers of his own and his wife's car on a list of those due to be booby-trapped by the IRA, and a Loyalist assassination attempt was made during 1975 on the elder of his schoolboy sons. His house now has bullet-proof windows and all sorts of alarm devices which are set off so often by the cat that nobody pays any attention to them. He assured me that one gets used to it all—that he never feels afraid—that one has to be fatalistic. I can well believe that he never allows himself to feel afraid yet he is obviously living under great stress. Westminster has now abolished religious discrimination in the civil service; but will many Catholics choose a career that would expose them to the hatred of both Orange and Green extremists? And this unfortunate man's wife is another source of anxiety. In an attempt to bring down the sectarian barriers she does voluntary social work twice a week in a Catholic area and twice a week in a Protestant area. Those are the truly brave people and one can see the price of bravery written on their faces.

7

Belfast Pedalabouts—Mostly Orange

Before leaving home I had received a letter of advice from an experienced, much-travelled journalist who has often worked in Northern Ireland. It included these comments: 'Many of the Six County people are Calvinistic Scot and have never integrated. They are dour. In Belfast they live in grey little streets in mean little houses and are grey and mean to match.' This shocked me. I would have expected the writer to realise that in no situation does it help to throw a blanket of contempt over tens of thousands of individuals. Indeed, Northern Ireland's illness could be described as a compulsion to view people as homogeneous masses of 'types'.

As the UDA rightly points out, Protestant workers have been exploited not much less than Catholics by the old Orange/Unionist school of landowners and industrialists. Geoffrey Bell explains the system in *The Protestants of Ulster:* 'The lack of trade-union militancy is not due to general satisfaction with the standard of living: that is much lower than in Great Britain. Nor is it due to the lack of issues to fight on. . . . The explanation for the death of the spirit of 1907 lies elsewhere, and a clue is found in the following words of Brian Faulkner, uttered at a meeting of the Orange Order in 1963: "Many a company director has marched with his lodge today, shoulder to shoulder with wage-earners. This is a healthy state of affairs. This is the right grounds on which to build the soundest of industrial relations." That the Unionist alliance has been an all-class alliance, that through that alliance the Protestant workers have gained marginal privileges, that within the alliance the Orange Order, controlled by the Unionist establishment, provides a social service for the Protestant worker—all this not only helps to prevent the emergence of class consciousness, it also provides an alternative for the services normally associated with trade unions: a social life, a "brotherhood", a preservation of a labour aristocracy.... And if, on occasions, economic agitation has threatened to disrupt the pattern, the threat has never been carried out. The Unionist establishment has always neutralised it, as they did in 1932 by labelling it a Catholic plot and by promoting, nakedly, a policy of jobs for Protestants first.'

These unique 1932 riots were wistfully recalled to me by a few older people in both Green and Orange areas. It is unfashionable to remember them now yet they strengthen that faint hope felt whenever there are rumours of inter-paramilitary talks. Liam de Paor describes the riots—and their consequences—in *Divided Ulster*. 'In 1932, a hunger march of the unemployed was again banned, but crowds gathered in the working-class areas of central Belfast. Police baton-charged unemployed workers on the Falls Road, in the Catholic area, and then opened fire over their heads. The Protestant unemployed of the Shankill Road rioted in support of their Catholic fellows and yet again Belfast saw wrecking, burning, and killing: two men died of wounds. But it had not been a sectarian riot. From this point on the government itself began to join in sectarian rabble-rousing. In the hungry 1930s the incitement of sectarian fears was a proven weapon of division to counteract the dangerous tendency towards solidarity among the urban workers.... The resentment and bitterness of the unemployed Protestant workers was turned, not against the social and economic system which exploited them, but against their "disloyal" Catholic fellow workers in outbreaks of violence which were sporadic until 1935, when ... the parades sparked off three weeks of burning, wrecking, and killing in one of Belfast's worst outbreaks of sectarian rioting. This time the conflict was one-sided. The Catholics in their ghettos ... were the victims.... Twelve people were killed, and the city coroner, T. E. Alexander, in reporting his finding that the cause of death was gunshot wounds in each case, gave his view that inflammatory and provocative speeches from "so-called leaders of public opinion" were responsible.'

If Belfast's Protestant ghetto dwellers do look dour and grey they have every excuse; and who can blame them if they are easily provoked to fear-inspired violence? They have been reared on a diet of ignorance, aggression, suspicion, misunderstanding, superstition and dread—dread that the

Catholics will outbreed them, and get their jobs, and perhaps marry their children and turn their grandchildren into Papists. Scorning these people for their bigotry is about as reasonable as scorning a cat for killing birds.

Yet one must not forget the importance of that bigotry throughout Northern Ireland's history. In January 1969 a group of Queen's University Northern Ireland Civil Rights Association students marched from Belfast to Derry and were savaged by Paisley-incited Loyalists at Burntollet, some seven miles from Derry. At first the police tried—not very strenuously—to protect the marchers, but by nightfall they had joined the Protestant mobs who were attacking the Bogside. The British government's Cameron Commission of Inquiry, set up a few days later, found 'that on the night of 4th/5th January a number of policemen were guilty of misconduct which involved assault and battery, malicious damage to property in streets in the predominantly Catholic Bogside area ... and the use of provocative sectarian and political slogans. ... We fully realise that the police had been working without adequate relief or rest for long hours, and were under great stress ... but for such conduct among members of a disciplined and well-led force there can be no acceptable justification or excuse.'

In elections the following month the Protestant working-class withdrew much of its support from Terence O'Neill, who had to be replaced by James Chichester-Clark—Chi-Chi to the masses. In August 1969 the new Prime Minister felt too weak to resist Loyalist pressure so he allowed the annual Apprentice Boys' March to take place in Derry against the advice of Sir Arthur Young, who had been imported from London to run the RUC. Then the British army had to be imported, and quickly, to control the violence that followed. Because of the part played by the B Special police (all Orangemen) in attacks on Derry's Catholic ghettos, London decided to disband them. This so infuriated the Protestant ghetto folk that the first shots fired at the British army came from Loyalist guns on the Shankill Road. In March 1971 Chi-Chi had to go, because the Loyalists fiercely resented his not introducing more British troops to smash the increasingly violent Provo campaign. And five months later Brian Faulkner's calamitous decision to introduce internment was made partly because it seemed likely to soothe his Loyalist opponents—which it did, but not for long. Another five months later Paisley and his devotees announced that they would intervene if the army were not used to stop the illegal anti-internment demonstration planned for Derry on 30 January 1972. The army was used, and ignored the advice of the local RUC chief, and Bloody Sunday happened. Six weeks later came the suspension—generally recognised as the *de facto* abolition—of Stormont. In due course it was replaced by the Assembly in which Brian Faulkner proved himself capable of the non-Northern virtue of compromise by co-operating with the Catholic SDLP. After the formation of the power-sharing Northern Ireland Executive the Loyalist Ulster Workers' Council organised a General Strike which demolished both the Assembly and the Executive. Paddy Devlin, in *The Fall of the Northern Ireland Executive*, has summed up the consequences: 'By the stoppage succeeding so completely the UWC have produced a crushing veto to any political initiative of which they do not approve. Thus, nothing moves unless it is favourable to their views on the type of society they want.'

The preceding pages sound distinctly anti-Loyalist but before describing my own encounters with Belfast's Protestant working-class I wanted to make clear both its power and its narrowness. Until the ingrained mistrusts of this class have been sorted out there can be no peace in Northern Ireland. To grant civil rights to the Catholics is easy but to persuade Loyalists that Catholics should be granted civil rights is at present almost impossible.

During early July I spent much of my time in the Protestant ghettos with families to whom I had been given introductions by community workers. These families had been selected for two reasons; because they were brave enough to admit me to their homes—though Protestants have been murdered before now in those areas for associating with Catholics or apparent Catholics—and because they were people to whom I could talk, in tactfully chosen phrases, about every aspect of the Northern problem. Yet I felt not entirely at ease in areas where it would never have occurred to the inhabitants that someone with a Southern brogue might be a non-Catholic. However, many individuals to whom I had no introduction were spontaneously generous and helpful. One very hot day I got a puncture just off the Shankill Road. An unemployed factory-hand, out painting his door for The Twelfth, at once offered to repair the tube while his wife invited me in for 'a wee cup of tea'. Little incidents like that—of which there were quite a number—made the slight strain of ghetto-exploring seem well worth-while. (Roz was punctured almost daily because of Belfast's abnormal quota of broken glass.)

Despite their pathetic fantasy about being a master-race, and the real advantages they enjoyed for so long over their Catholic neighbours, the Loyalists appear to need, at present, even more sympathy than the Green ghetto dwellers. The latter can derive a certain amount of consolation from having recently been shown to the world as Northern Ireland's underdogs; but the corollary of this is that the Protestants have been cast in the role of bully. This grieves, bewilders and embitters them—and has made some of them even more aggressibly intractable than usual.

A century ago *Punch* enquired,

> Loyal to whom, to what?
> to power, to pelf,
> to place, to privilege, in a word to self.
> Those who assume, absorb, control, enjoy all
> must find it vastly pleasant to be loyal.

Ever since, people have been asking the same question—"To whom, to what?" Repeatedly the Loyalists have proved that they are not loyal, in any accepted sense of the word, to the Crown as represented by Her Majesty's Government. The strength of anti-British feeling in Loyalist circles astonished me and I was many times told "They don't understand us". Often the interesting implication was that I, as a Southerner, could understand what would always remain an enigma to the British. But this message was conveyed quite unconsciously and much indignation would have been expressed had I registered receiving it. Yet the snide joke about the Loyalists being loyal only to the half-crown does not, I feel, do them justice—though it obviously applies to some of their political leaders. In every country it is easy to find a clique who are in politics for what they can get out of it; the difference in Northern Ireland is that the Unionist politicians have always been more brazen than is usual about their ambitions and methods. They could afford to be brazen because they were never threatened by those democractic processes through which their colleagues else-where on the British Isles may be removed from office. But the ordinary Loyalist certainly believes himself to be loyal to some-thing less ignoble than his pocket. However distasteful his obses-sions and techniques of self-assertion may seem, one must give him credit for this. Also, one must remember that his obsessions have been shamelessly manipulated. To blame him alone for the more uncivilized manifestations of his bigotry is not fair. Just once in Northern Ireland I nearly lost my temper; that was when a rich, well-educated Unionist smugly condemned the excesses of the Protestant lower orders in Belfast—though he himself, as a politician, had encouraged the attitudes that inspire such excesses.

Another extenuating circumstance is the extraordinary isola-tion—mental and emotional—of the ghettos. None of the work-ing-class Loyalist families with whom I spoke had ever before met anybody from the South. And while their welcome could not have been warmer their minds remained firmly closed to any new ways of looking at anything. Television is said to have done a lot to give insular Irish Catholics a more balanced view of the world. Amongst Loyalists, however, programmes which contradict their ideology are usually dismissed as the work of some hidden enemy of True Protestantism. In October 1968 television cameras recorded vicious police brutality in Derry during a Northern Ireland Civil Rights Association march. This was when the withholding of civil rights from Catholics, in a region of the United Kingdom, first became an inter-national scandal. Yet by now it is part of the Loyalist myth that somehow those cameras were used by God's enemies to give a totally false picture of Northern Irish life.

The Loyalist is blindly loyal to his own distorted view of Christianity—which fifty years ago would not have seemed all that distorted to millions in Britain. He would also like to be loyal to Queen Elizabeth II but is finding this increasingly difficult. From my conversations with Loyalist men and women, of all ages, it emerged that one of the main causes of their present instability and unhappiness is a realisation that Her Majesty would go to no great lengths to defend the Orange adaptation of Christianity. She is not a patch on William of Orange—has more in common with James II—seems to have been fatally infected, along with the whole Church of England, by ecumenism. To the average Northern Irish Protestant the changes that have taken place within Christendom since 1962 are catastrophic. And they have made an important though largely disregarded contribution to the present conflict. By strengthening the Protestant fear of Rome they have aggravated the ever-present Orange–Green tension and given Paisley a sure-fire rabble-rousing theme.

After a few days I decided that to confine myself to 'selected' families—though clearly those I met were typical enough—might give me a slightly too rosy view of the Loyalist community. I felt I should also meet Belfast's Loyalists casually, which could only be done through visiting their pubs. By now the reader will appreciate that from a taste-buds point of view, as it were, I considered it no great hardship to have to sink pints along Sandy Row and up the Shankill. But the security aspect worried me slightly. Belfast today is a city of scaremongers; its inhabitants would be less (or more) than human if this were not so. People told me that on Sandy Row they like to take Catholics—or even suspected Catholics—around to the back of a pub and slit their throats. When I argued that such occurrences must be very infrequent the reply was that the arrival of a Catholic in a Sandy Row pub is very infrequent. Strangely enough, a few days after this argument an eighteen-year-old Catholic girl did have her throat—and other parts—slit behind a Sandy Row pub where she had been drinking with three Protestant friends. No doubt someone had suspected her of 'carrying on' with a Protestant and sexual relations between Protestants and Catholics are so abhorred by Loyalist extremists that they often lead to murder. A typical case concerned the SDLP Assembly member, Paddy Wilson, and Irene Andrews, a young Protestant woman. The most popular Loyalist community newspaper, *Loyalist News*, suggests possible assassination targets to its readers and in September 1972 it asked, 'What prominent member of the SDLP is keeping company with a Protestant female from Belfast's Crumlin Road?' Nine months later the couple were found together in Paddy Wilson's car; they had been stabbed to death. (The *Loyalist News* also prints veiled threats and cryptic hints to do with the whole murky underworld of discrimination, intimidation and protection racketeering. It is well worth studying as a reflection of the most diseased areas of the Northern Protestant mind. There is nothing comparable among the extremist Catholic community newspapers.)

However, scaremongering is yet another vicious circle, inevitable after the tragic polarisation of the past eight years and now steadily worsening it. The chances of my being murdered in a Belfast pub seemed sufficiently remote for the risk to be taken but I avoided pubs in the evening unless escorted. In fact I was never the victim of even an unkind word though I soon learned to accept suspicious looks as part of the day's work.

Most Loyalist pubs seem to be either heavily guarded or not (apparently) guarded at all. Where 'speak-first' devices have been installed I was never admitted until the security guard had carefully scrutinised both myself and Roz. Roz proved invaluable as an ice-breaker. She could not be left alone for an instant in any part of Belfast and it isn't every day a solitary Southern Irishwomen approaches a Loyalist bar counter wheeling a bicycle. But even with such an ally it often took a long time to get more than monosyllables out of my fellow drinkers. I particularly remember one pub where the air froze the moment my accent was recognised. There I had to wait an hour and twenty minutes for the thaw. After about half an hour I realised that the situation was familiar but for a moment I couldn't think why. Then I remembered being through it all before on the outskirts of a tiny settlement in the Simien Mountains of Ethiopia where I was the first white woman to have been seen by the locals. There was exactly the same sort of tension in the atmosphere, the same alarm, suspicion and curiosity on the part of the natives, the same faint apprehension and awareness of the need for patience on the part of the traveller.

The difference came when at last the air unfroze. Conversation in English—even Belfast English—is easier than in Amharic.

In Belfast, as throughout the North, I found Loyalists eager to talk once they had accepted that my interest in their attitudes was based on a wish to understand and was not merely a quest for sticks with which to beat them. I always explained that I am not a journalist (over the past decade the press has antagonised most sections of Northern society) but that I hoped to write a book giving all Northern viewpoints as fairly as possible. The concept of objectivity is not readily assimilated by either Republican or Loyalist minds but obviously many saw me as a possible means of putting across The Truth—i.e., their own viewpoint—to a world grievously misled by the media. It is sad to think that should this book be read by any of those extremists who trusted my goodwill, they are certain to feel betrayed.

Two things stood out, after all those hours of attentively listening in homes and pubs. One was the appalling extent to which Protestants suffer from intimidation and protection racketeering at the hands of their own extremists. The other was the fact that there is a far wider gulf between the Orange paramilitary and his community than between the Green paramilitary and his. Most Northern Protestants have an inborn respect for law and order which is not shared by the ghetto Catholics. The latter have grown up in an atmosphere at least tinged— and often soaked—with contempt for Stormont. Thus, when powered by patriotic fervour, they can break the law with a clear conscience or support—at least passively, by remaining dumb—those who do. This attitude was regularly used by Unionist politicians to justify job discrimination which in turn strengthened the Green feeling that there was no democratic government in Northern Ireland deserving of respect. Yet for all the endemic lawlessness of the Catholic ghettos their inhabitants have not descended as far into gangsterism as the Loyalists. Per head of population there seem to be more 'straight' (non-political) criminals operating from the Orange ghettos than from the Green. This is partly because Loyalists have in the past been able to count on certain elements in the RUC 'not noticing' their exploits. (A situation that is now being improved by pressure from London.) Catholics, on the other hand, have always been marked men in RUC eyes; therefore many who might have embarked on a life of conventional crime, had they been born Orange, lacked the courage to do so.

In times of stress Loyalist paramilitaries can easily rouse large mobs and lead them out of their ghettos on Taig-bashing expeditions. But those who occasionally indulge in burning down Catholic houses, or shooting or stabbing Catholics, are not necessarily habitual criminals. When the hysteria of the moment has ebbed, and their leaders have stopped reminding them that 'Taigs are made for killing', as one popular ballad has it, many Orange rioters revert to being sober, law-abiding citizens. Communal rioting has quite different roots from ordinary crime. If men have been persuaded to see an attack on a Catholic ghetto as a means of cleansing 'all the shit' from an area, then they can go about their violent business feeling that God Blesses the Work. (The interweaving of pious sentiments with four-letter words is one of the more bizarre features of Northern life.)

In one neat little East Belfast living-room—its walls covered with large photographs of the British Royal Family at various stages of development—I talked for over an hour to a one-eyed man of about thirty-five who had chanced to call while I was having tea with the family. After his departure, my host told me that he had lost an eye while burning Catholic houses in Bombay Street in August 1969. A young mother with a tiny baby under one arm had run back into her home and lunged at him with a carving knife as he poured petrol over the furniture. For some reason, that story sickened me more than any other I heard in Belfast. Possibly my reaction had something to do with the juxtaposition of a baby and a carving knife. In a dreadful way, that seemed to epitomise the peculiar horror of sectarian conflict—war fought literally on people's hearths, without rules or order or method or any motive but hate powered by fear. As for my one-eyed friend, he now has quite a good job, suited to his disability. He had been injured in a good cause and his brother Orangemen did not let him down. I may add that I found him very friendly and perfectly willing to help a Southerner named Murphy. In no way did he resemble the type one visualises when thinking of mobs savagely rioting.

There are about forty illegal Loyalist paramilitary groups of which the best-known are the Ulster Volunteer Force, the Ulster Freedom Fighters, the Red Hand Commandos, the Orange Volunteers, Tara, Protestant Action, The Ulster Citizens' Army, The Ulster Volunteer Service Corps and the Down Orange Welfare. However, the main Loyalist paramilitary force, the UDA, is not illegal though it has been responsible for many ghastly sectarian murders. On the whole it seems to be more realistic than either wing of the IRA. (Not that that is a great compliment.) It evolved in September 1971, out of about sixteen local vigilante groups or 'defence associations' which had been formed during the previous month when 7,000 Catholics and 2,000 Protestants were burned or intimidated out of their homes. As its motto it took *Cedenta Arma Togae* (Law before Violence), thus splendidly illustrating Loyalist doublethink. Its declared aim was 'to see law restored everywhere, including the No-Go areas' (i.e., the Green ghettos). Significantly, 'no MPs and no religious mentors' were to be allowed to join. However, by May 1977 this attitude had been sufficiently modified for the UDA to collaborate with the so-called Reverend Ian Paisley, MP, in the organising of an abortive General Workers' Strike.

On 12 August 1971 one of the founder-members of the UDA was among a group of UVF men who handed out an anonymous leaflet in the Protestant areas of Belfast. This is worth quoting in full as it sums up UDA thinking at the time of the organisations's founding. 'Being convinced that the enemies of the Faith and Freedom are determined to destroy the State of Northern Ireland and thereby enslave the people of God, we call on all members of our loyalist institutions, and other responsible citizens, to organise themselves *immediately* into Platoons of twenty under the command of someone capable of acting as Sergeant. Every effort must be made to arm these Platoons with whatever weapons are available. The first duty of each Platoon will be to formulate a plan for the defence of its own street or road in co-operation with Platoons in adjoining areas. A structure of Command is already in existence and the various Platoons will eventually be linked in a co-ordinated effort.

'Instructions: Under no circumstances must Platoons come into conflict with Her Majesty's Forces or the Police. If through wrong political direction Her Majesty's Forces are directed against loyalist people members of Platoons must do everything possible to prevent a confrontation. We are loyalists, we are Queen's men! Our enemies are the forces of Romanism and Communism which must be destroyed. Members of Platoons must act with the highest sense of responsibility and urgency in preparing our people for the full assault of the enemies within our Province and the forces of the Eire Government which will eventually be thrown against us. We must prepare now! This is total war!'

During the past six years the tone of the UDA has changed. It now has an anti-Orangeism element, many members are not so sure about being Queen's men and its outlook is much more socialistic. So what exactly does the organisation stand for? What are its present aims? 'Money and power,' reply the cynical—and by now there is an unhealthy amount of cynicism in the North. I prefer to hope. The Orange Order and the various groupings of old-style Unionist politicians are impervious to change and must be got out of the way before Northern Ireland can attain any civilised form of self-government. But the UDA is new and relatively flexible and may yet prove capable of developing into something useful.

Rumours proliferate about the UDA but facts are scarce. One can only say definitely that it is a well-armed and well-organised force of often ruthless men; and apart from being by far the biggest paramilitary organisation in Northern Ireland— which may explain why it has never been outlawed—it operates very efficient protection-rackets and is therefore rich enough to run its own 'welfare system'. In certain areas of Belfast house-holders give a small sum every week to their 'local treasurer'. Some are quite happy to do so, feeling that in a crisis the UDA would prove more dependable than the British army. Others bitterly resent being forced to contribute to an organisation of which they disapprove. But I met nobody who would have considered not paying. One Alliance Party ex-politician recalled that when he was canvassing in East Belfast the normal housewife's reaction, on finding a stranger at the door, was—"Wait till I fetch me purse!" Such situations can easily get out of control and the stranger at the door may well be a reckless young free-lancer. (Reckless because if detected by the UDA he would have reason to regret his enterprise.)

Judging by the typical verses I have already quoted from the UDA 1974 Songbook, and by their magazine, the *Ulster*, UDA members are scarcely less fanatical than Paisleyites. Yet this is not at all the feeling one gets at their headquarters on the Newtownards Road. It is a tall, severe, tidy building with a shop on the ground floor selling records, badges, flags and very fine craftwork done by Loyalist prisoners. I noticed every one of that morning's Irish newspapers neatly laid out on a table in the reception-room—but not a single British paper. It was a strange setting in which to see the *Irish Press*. Everyone was very welcoming and Roz was tenderly wheeled away to the safety of a back room while I went upstairs. On the way up I passed a young man on a landing engaged in carefully removing the Crown symbol from the huge Ulster flag on the wall. He smiled and nodded at me but said nothing. His task, however, said a lot.

When I left that building, seven hours later, I had received few facts but one very strong impression. The UDA, unlike every other political or paramilitary organisation in the North, are not talking about how or why or when or where to get power. They have it and they are using it. And having listened to so much impractical word-spinning since my arrival in Belfast, I found their realism refreshing. One representative explained that the organisation's present leadership accepts the inevitability of polarisation for decades to come, while both communities outgrow their bigotry. Talk of Reconciliation Here and Now he dismissed as 'a load of sentimental crap', encouraged by the fascist Alliance Party and woolly-minded clergy. I protested that to strive towards reconciliation every day and every hour of every day seems the only right course in Northern Ireland now—and obviously *is* the only right course, on an ethical level. But I had to admit that it is unrealistic to dream of major reconciliation successes during the twentieth century. Therefore such strivings will not of themselves solve the urgent political problem and are in fact likely to be more fruitful if made without undue haste.

I was told that if the UDA gained power—or seized it, as would be more likely—they would try to establish an independent state on the Dutch model with everything separate for Protestants and Catholics: schools, hospitals, cinemas, newspapers, wireless and television programmes. A repulsive idea at first glance, yet with a streak of grim common sense running through it. In theory there would then be no sectarian friction as everybody could feel loyal to the new state and the minority would be granted a fair proportion of the national wealth. And according to one view, there need be no economic obstacle to UDI if all Northern Irish industrialists were 'persuaded' (how?) to withdraw their capital from Britain and invest it at home. Are these theories quite dotty or have the UDA got onto a bandwagon that will one day begin to roll? Certainly UDI, with a UDA-run government, is a popular solution in the more hard-line Loyalist areas. And it is not as completely rejected as one would expect in Catholic areas, whereas the Provo plan for an autonomous Protestant enclave within a thirty-two county Republic is generally detested by Loyalists.

In Orange districts a few brave UDA members told me, behind closed doors, that they hoped the organisation would eventually become a genuinely socialist and non-sectarian political party. Then bigotry could be overcome not by wishy-washy Christians singing hymns together but by working-class unity which would automatically lead to power-sharing. This is perilous talk in Loyalist circles. Two UDA leaders who indulged in it were killed by their own followers, Duke Elliott in December 1972 and Tommy Heron in September 1973. Tommy Heron several times met representatives of the Official (Marxist) IRA in an effort to weld the North's workers together. His rewards were 2,480 votes out of a possible 80,000 when he stood for the Assembly elections—and then death.

Most of my UDA friends argued that since the Northern Irish will continue to vote along sectarian lines for generations to come there must always be a Protestant government in power after any democratic election. But many also emphasised that, given special power-sharing arrangements between the workers, this need not mean reverting to domination by well-heeled Unionists. Reasonably enough, a Catholic willingness to scrap the *Ne Temere* decree is seen as a fair exchange for a Protestant willingness to share power with the minority.

To the UDA, Unionist politicians are almost as abhorrent as Provos. A heartening number, however, are able to distinguish between Provos and the rest of the Catholic population—a rare ability among Loyalists—and unlike most Unionists are willing to admit that Catholics have been discriminated against and that there can be no peace until such discrimination is ended—not merely formally, by the passing of laws, but within people's minds.

Mr Cosgrave's government gained much admiration in UDA circles for its tough anti-IRA attitude. "They've shown more guts than London, or than us up here," was a common remark. In the Green ghettos Mr Cosgrave is often described as a Quisling; his hard-line policy increased support for the IRA at a time when they had been losing it because of the evident futility of their campaign—"You can't desert a man when he's in gaol." And at present you can't win in the Irish political game, North or South.

In the North, Mr Cosgrave's unyielding anti-IRA-ism mattered a lot more than his rigidly orthodox Catholic views on contraception and divorce. These were sometimes used by Orange leaders to prove that Home Rule is indeed Rome Rule, but not as often as one might expect. Northern Protestant standards of sexual morality are far closer to Southern Catholic standards than to British 'permissiveness'. A nice example of this concord appeared one day in *The Irish Times* under the heading—'Fermanagh Councillors are United Against "Sin".' (The Fermanagh Council then consisted of ten Republicans and ten Loyalists.) I quote: 'The meeting ended with the councillors unanimously opposing the introduction in the North of laws on abortion and homosexuality similar to those in force in Britain. A former chairman of the council, Mr William Elliott of the Official Unionist Party, said that the North had

had enough troubles over the last seven years without "bringing the curse of God upon us as a people by bringing in this legislation". Mr Thomas Scott, of the Democratic Unionist Party, said he believed that any right-thinking Christian people that believe in God would oppose such legislation. He said homosexuality and abortion had not been legalised in even Sodom or Gomorrah; however, at Westminster the British government had legalised them. It would be a sin to foist such legislation on the Northern Ireland people. "I hate to think of the filth of it—especially abortion, which is premeditated murder in the sight of God." Mr Scott and Mr Elliott were supported unanimously by the other members of the council.'

UDA supporters tend to be more aware than most Loyalists of the Republic's constitutional claim to the territory of Northern Ireland. They are emphatic that until our constitution has been emended there can be no mutally-respecting co-operation between North and South and I sympathise with this viewpoint. There is a mad Celtic illogic about expecting friendly co-operation between two states—or a state and half a state—when the government of one claims the territory of the other. Some say that a referendum on this issue in the Republic could only lead to a dangerous re-opening of old wounds. But perhaps that is to underestimate the commonsense of the younger generation of voters—and every generation's longing for peace.

UDA members often refer to the British army as the military arm of fascism, keeping the poor in their place. And several boasted to me that if it ever came to the crunch—if, for instance, there were another general strike and the army tried to intervene—the UDA could win because their deficiency in equipment would be balanced by their devotion to Ulster. I thought this belief rather unrealistic, though a resolute Northern Protestant is a formidable thing. Mercifully it was not tested during the abortive general strike a few months later.

The various reactions to that curious exercise in May 1977 were revealing. Most commentators seemed convinced that Ian Paisley was being used by the UDA, and some SDLP and Alliance Party politicians described the efforts of this improbable team as a *putsch*. They may well have been right, though other politicians—Unionist and British—scorned the idea, at least in public. However, during the strike Mr James Molyneaux, hardline leader of the Official Unionists, announced at a press conference, "There is evidence that some people on the action council have a provisional government in mind and are moving in that direction. . . . The strike is a 'two-stage' operation, first disruption, then a move towards independence. . . . The issue is not now over security or devolved government, it is a straight issue for or against the Union."

During a wireless interview at that time I heard Andy Tyrie, chairman of the UDA, being reassuring about the fate of Catholics in any future UDA-governed state. His assurances were received with predictable scepticism and throughout the rest of the programme there was an unusual anti-UDA closing of the political ranks on the part of men—Orange and Green—who normally cannot abide one another. This was all very right and proper, in defence of a state that was being threatened by an organisation which does not scruple to bomb, burn, intimidate and kill in pursuit of ill-defined but unmistakably revolutionary objectives. Yet I remain convinced that somewhere, amidst the disordered speculations which are all one can see of UDA thinking, there are seeds of sincerity and constructive originality that should be searched for and tended. Everybody complains all the time about the 'refusal to change' of most Northern politicians. But the UDA has changed, for the better, since it was founded—and is still changing. It is almost certainly true that at present, if a civil war broke out, neither Mr Tyrie nor any other 'moderate' UDA leader could control a rank and file thirsty for the blood of Taigs. But this does not justify dismissing as hypocrisy their wish to do so. We are back to mistrust; we never get very far away from it. There can be no progress towards peace until the Northern Irish have replaced their ancient custom of instant mutual condemnation with the habit of pausing to wonder if there might not now be some grounds for trusting even the most unlikely people. The North's political problem is so extraordinary that perhaps its solution will have to be equally extraordinary.

The day after my visit to UDA headquarters I spent a few hours with an eminent Orange religious leader whose name, to many Catholics, has a sinister ring. He seemed a suitable

person with whom to bring up one of the root causes of the
Northern problem, the failure of Protestants and Catholics,
even when their families have been friends for generations, to
discuss religion and politics. As Professor Beckett has written
somewhere, 'They mingle with a consciousness of the differences between them' and, he might have added, with a determination to avoid mentioning those differences. But the
Reverend X— commended this polite evasiveness, though he
is an intelligent man. He said, "If members of a family disagree
on certain subjects, then when they all meet together it's their
duty to avoid any talk that might start a quarrel." Yet half
an hour earlier he had been deploring the absurdities believed
by Catholics about the Orange Order.

On both sides in the North many believe that 'the others'
practise weirdly unpleasant rites, verging on Black Magic. In
Co Tyrone a young Catholic woman recalled being friendly
as a child with the neighbouring Protestant farmer's daughter
and one day bribing her with sixpence (two weeks' pocket
money) to reveal what she was taught at Sunday School. When
the little Protestant solemnly recited the Lord's Prayer my
friend felt so cheated that she burst into tears. I told this story
to the Reverend X— and suggested that an awareness of the
prayers they said in common could only do good to the population of Northern Ireland. That same young woman was in her
twenties before she discovered that there are differences
between the Anglican and Presbyterian churches.

The Reverend X— agreed with me that one million Protestants would be very useful in a united Ireland to curb the
power of the Catholic hierarchy. But his fears of and prejudices
against Roman Catholicism-cum-Irish Nationalism went as
deep as any that I had encountered in the most ill-educated
homes of the Loyalist ghettos. Yet within the past few years
this particular leader has mellowed quite a lot. He would never
now take up in public the attitudes that came naturally to him
a decade ago; or if he did, it would be under pressures which
he dared not resist. Intimidation of their leaders by the Orange
ghetto mobs causes a lot of frustration. By now a few Protestant
religious and political leaders have reached a 'post-bigotry'
stage in their thinking, but too often they dare not try to pass

on to their followers—who initially have been inflamed by those leaders themselves—the benefit of their own increasing wisdom.

Leaving the Reverend X—, I was aware of having been in the presence of a good man. His brand of religion does not appeal to me—and aspects of it might not appeal much to Christ. But somehow its total genuineness outweighed its limitations. Frequently people condemn the hypocrisy of Orange clergymen and this particular clergyman has attracted more criticism than most. Yet there was an impressive quality about him that nobody could miss, after two and a half hours of serious conversation. Towards the end of that time he said, "If you are in love you don't hide it and I don't hide my relationship with God." Only people who are utterly sincere and unaffected can make such a remark without sounding sanctimonious.

That evening I wrote in my diary: 'So now I've been with the IRA, the UDA, the Orangemen—and where are all the ogres? The evil influences, the brutal thugs? They must be somewhere but I've not met them. (Tho' I have seen a few really frightening faces.) Yet here an evil situation exists— almost one could say has been created by good men who inherited hate and fear. But can this be? Can evil be perpetuated by good men? How can one disentangle it all? My friends here obviously think I'm naïve and sentimental because I see good in all sorts of people who are supposed to be bad. But I'm sure it's there. One of the worst diseases of this tormented society is the determination of so many not to see it, always to stress the other fellow's faults and question his motives. Looking for unworthy motives seems to have become a compulsion, even amongst the most balanced—so how can they expect to find peace? I suppose this acute distrust is inseparable from the use of labels. When people are thought of only as Prods or Taigs, Unionists or Republicans, Orangemen or Papists, then it must become impossible to judge them on their individual merits as human beings.'

Next day, I at last found one of the evil influences—and there was no mistaking it when it appeared.

Ian Paisley's Martyrs' Memorial Free Presbyterian Church on the Ravenhill Road is the third most expensive ecclesiastical edifice to have been built in the British Isles since the Second World War. It cost £175,000; only the Anglican Cathedral at Coventry and the Catholic Cathedral at Liverpool cost more. Presumably most of this money came from bible-belts in the US and Canada. Despite the amount of publicity he attracts, and the amount of damage he does, Mr Paisley's acknowledged following in Northern Ireland is not great. In 1971 the Free Presbyterian Church of Ulster had only 7,337 members, or about 0·5 per cent of the population. Obviously one cannot measure by a head count the power of any man with his flair for and training in communication. But it is consoling to know that so few people are exposed to the peculiar kind of venom he exudes in his church. (It needs to be emphasised that Mr Paisley founded his own sect which has no connection whatever with the Presbyterian Church in Ireland.)

I entered the building one very hot Sunday morning in July, perfectly prepared to find that Mr Paisley, too, has a good side—reserved for his congregation, so that I hadn't been able to see it before. Yet when I left the place an hour and a half later I knew that I had been in the presence of pure evil.

St Peter's, Ravenhill, as some Taigs facetiously call it, is attractive in a simple, dignified way. As I cycled up the Ravenhill Road prosperous, shining cars were pulling into a large car park and family parties of prosperous, shining Free Presbyterians were happily greeting each other—the women in garden-party hats and bright dresses, the men in summery, not-too-sober suits, the many children in apparently brand-new Marks and Sparks outfits. The average age was noticeably lower than in most present-day congregations, with a remarkable number of adolescents and several couples encumbered by tiny babies. Friendly, nice, ordinary citizens they all looked. Despite my rudimentary mode of transport and inelegant attire, little notice was taken of me as I chained Roz to the car park railings; security is unobtrusive but strict in the church grounds and it seemed a safe assumption that there at least nobody would abduct her. Inside the building my hand was shaken and I was told how welcome strangers are; I was afraid even to mutter "Thank you" lest someone with an aversion to Southern strangers might be within earshot.

The huge church was scarcely half-full when Paisley stage-managed himself into the pulpit to begin the service. The theme of his sermon was 'The Biblical Call to Arms' and the violence of his imagery was extreme. When he and the congregation had read alternate verses of Genesis 3 he picked on the fifteenth verse—'And I will put enmity between thy seed and her seed; it shall bruise thy head and thou shalt bruise his heel'—and these words were used to 'prove' that the present state of Northern Ireland has been willed by God because until the Anti-Christ has been vanquished there can be no peace. We got the 'sharp two-edged sword' from Revelation and also Revelation 2, 9, 10, 23, 26, 27. Verse 10, I suppose, was intended to console those present who had paramilitary connections in gaol. And also, perhaps, to remind the audience that their beloved preacher had himself been cast into prison by the devil, disguised as Her Majesty's government. Jesus evicting the money-changers from the temple came next and was used to emphasise Christ's violence. "Christ was not a man of peace! Don't you believe it! Christ was not a namby-pamby sentimentalist! He was no softie! Christ was a *violent* man! Violent for good! Violent to stamp out wickedness, violent for God's sake! Our battle is not against a *system*—it is against the people who uphold that system! And *we* must be violent for God's sake! We must attack the people who uphold rottenness—as Christ attacked the money-changers! Remember—it's not the system we must attack but the *people*—the people who represent the Anti-Christ in our midst! Be violent for Christ's sake, to defend that faith which he himself defended with his fists!"

As I transcribe these words from my diary, where I wrote them within moments of leaving the church, I realise that some readers will have difficulty in believing that a man who pretends to be a Christian, and sits as an MP in the House of Commons, could say such things to a gathering of Belfast citizens in the year 1976.

Paisley's pulpit is in fact a small stage and while preaching he strides up and down, gesticulating, shouting, grimacing—and, on this Sunday, waving a huge Bible above his head and declaiming, "This is not a book of peace! This is a book of war! War against Christ's enemies, against the deceits of the devil, against the snares of ecumenism! We must listen to the call to arms and not be afraid! And Christ will fight with us, as he overturned those tables, and will be proud to see us as we go forth bravely to attack for him!"

I was aware of blasphemy being committed as this demented creature paced from end to end of his pulpit-stage, flourishing the Bible and repetitively—almost hypnotically—insisting on the need to defend, to fight, to do battle, to vanquish, to conquer, to assert, to unsheath the sword, to show no mercy to the enemies of God. . . . The cunning with which he used an aggressive, militaristic phraseology—all culled from the Bible—was literally blood-chilling. At a certain point it brought me out in gooseflesh though Belfast was in the middle of a heat wave. I longed then to get away, somehow to escape from this man's powerful emanations of evil. But I was afraid to move lest I might be pursued by some young man anxious to secure his salvation by putting a bullet in my irreverent back. Meanwhile everyone else was listening, rapt, and many fervent murmurs of approval greeted the various climactic exhortations. Hellfire was guaranteed for all who disregard Paisley's version of the word of God and very skilfully he presented himself as prophet, hero, saint and martyr. Occasionally there was an attempt at light relief—"*We* don't need to run jumble-sales and coffee-mornings and dandelion teas and pea-soup dinners! The Lord is providing for his chosen! Last Sunday what did the Lord provide? He provided £724.61! And for the Manse Fund an anonymous £50! And for the World Congress Chorale £566!" (These figures were also printed on the programme under the heading 'The Lord's Treasury'.) Later there was a reference to so many joints in so many ovens becoming burnt offerings if he didn't stop soon—an indication of kindly, homely humanity which had the audience in raptures. Before stopping, he told us that at 3.30 he would be preaching at Portglenone Independent Orange Service (the official Orange Order and the Free Presbyterians parted company about fifteen years ago) and that anyone who cared to attend would be most welcome. In any event, he hoped to see us all again at 7.30 pm when he would be back in the Martyrs' Memorial. And he announced the text for his evening sermon: 'If the Trumpet

Give an Uncertain Sound, Who Shall Prepare Himself to the Battle?'

This whole horrible travesty of a Christian church service was diabolically clever. And I mean diabolically. Paisley might not convert an atheist to a belief in God but he has certainly converted me to a belief in the devil—which after all comes to the same thing. I find it hard to accept that unaided human nature has the capacity to be so evil. Although I gave up church-going twenty-five years ago I felt a strong urge, as I left that building, to exorcise or cleanse myself by attending some—any—really religious service, whether Christian, Hindu or Muslim. But of course it was by then the wrong time of day; even in Belfast they knock off for Sunday lunch. In any case I had at once to find a quiet corner and make the necessary notes. But the fact that my reaction to that experience was so hysterical is a measure of Paisley's power to throw people.

Later in the summer, a rural Presbyterian minister told me about a parishioner of his—a good-natured young farm-labourer—who went to Belfast for a week-end and was taken to the Martyrs' Memorial by a friend. On his return home he told his minister that for an hour after leaving the church he felt that he would enjoy nothing more than throttling a Roman Catholic. I was also told, by a Catholic that his son, while a student at Queen's, once went to the Martyrs' Memorial out of curiosity and half way through the sermon felt that he wanted to cheer Mr Paisley. Afterwards, he tried to explain his reaction and described it as 'a cross between being mesmerised and smoking pot'. His father, a scientist, has a theory that performers like Paisley can, by the psychic grip they take on a personality, temporarily alter the chemistry of some bodies and make people feel and behave in ways altogether alien to their nature.

How much does Paisley's sort of preaching really matter in Belfast? The Moderator of the Free Presbyterian Church of Ulster merely amuses some outsiders and he can also be viewed as a well-trained con-man, a theological freak, a slippery politician or a caricature of a seventeenth-century Covenanter. Bored visitors frequent the Martyrs' Memorial for laughs, seeing it as Belfast's only amusement centre to open on a Sunday—

and this would indeed be the most healthy reaction if Paisley were operating in London or Dublin. But he is operating in a city where at present some people need very little encouragement to kill other people. It is true that his audiences, and their forbears, have been reared on anti-popery tub-thumping and presumably have inherited or acquired a certain immunity to it. Remembering the individuals present at that service— devoutly going through the motions of a normal Christian congregation—it is hard to picture most of them in less edifying roles. Yet their preacher was reminding them that as good Protestants, threatened from every side by Devil-guided conspiracies, they should be engaged in violence. And there were many young men in that congregation with access to guns, who listened intently to Paisley as few of their generation elsewhere in Europe would listen to a long sermon on a cloudless summer Sunday. One young man, sitting on my left in the next seat, twisted his folded hands until his knuckles cracked at each exhortation to go forth and attack the anti-Christ.

People often ask why Paisley is not picked up under the Incitement to Hatred Act. The snag is that although his sermons are undisguised 'incitements to hatred' it is never possible to prove that a particular crime was committed as a direct result of something he said and that it was his intention to provoke that crime. Even if it were possible, it is doubtful if the authorities dare arrest him again. His followers may be few in numbers but in aggression and fanaticism they are probably worth several regiments. Moreover, he is immensely popular as an MP and has a reputation for working hard to help his constituents— both Catholic and Protestant, which astonished me. An Alliance Party politician, observing my surprise, dryly likened Paisley's concern for his Catholic constituents to the kindness of a nineteenth-century Tory landowner who set up soup kitchens for his starving tenants while opposing every move towards social reform.

Many suspect deep-laid Machiavellian plots behind Paisley's inconsistencies; others see them as symptoms of some incurable mental disease. Having founded the Democratic Unionist Party, Paisley announced that he wanted it to have no connection with the Orange Order and condemned the Order's link with the Unionist Party as 'undemocratic'. Yet he zealously supports the Rhodesian and South African régimes, chiefly— it is said—because of their Calvinistic bases. However, the files of the *Protestant Telegraph* indicate that he disapproves neither of dictatorship (by God's Elected, of course) nor of racism. Another inconsistency was Paisley's opposition to internment, which the vast majority of Protestants enthusiastically supported until the army began to 'lift' Loyalists.

Someone who has known this frightening man for twenty-five years described him to me as a four-faced personality with the ability to switch on whichever face is appropriate to the moment. One face is for the Martyrs' Memorial and visits to his parishioners. One is for the House of Commons and visits to his constituents. Another is for the media and the fourth is for social and personal relationships. When wearing that last face he can, according to many people, seem sympathetic and congenial. If this four-faced theory is correct he must be considered completely in control of himself and so entirely to blame for his rabble-rousing. Others sum him up as a born fascist suffering from extreme personal insecurity, a massive social chip and an overwhelming obsession about his public image. But however people may disagree in their analyses of Paisley the man, everybody recognises the danger of Paisleyism the cult.

One is often told that Paisleyism is as old as Protestant Ulster, or as Scottish Calvinism. But nowadays its effects are more harmful than ever before. In its Free Presbyterian manifestation, the emphasis is as much on anti-ecumenism as on anti-popery; and Paisley's determination to maintain Northern Ireland's traditional level of bigotry and discrimination has so far proved the strongest single force on the Northern political scene. Throughout his career he has fostered an atmosphere in which authority is belittled and mob-law becomes possible. The psychological effects of his successful campaign in 1967, to block the then Anglican Bishop of Ripon's visit to Belfast, have proved long-lasting. Letting Paisley have his way during the sixties was one of Stormont's worst mistakes. If Yorkshire were threatened by cholera the government would not hesitate to enforce laws against the spread of infection, even if the liberty of the indivi-

dual had in some cases to be curtailed. Why are similar precautions not taken against infectious emotional diseases?

It is generally believed in Belfast that Paisley's zenith has
passed. The observations I took in the Martyrs' Memorial over
the next year showed a steady decline in attendance and one
shrewd Belfast shopkeeper summed it up thus: "His own people
are turning against him because violence is spreading in all the
Protestant areas. It was OK before—sectarian killing was confined to the slums and only poor nameless Taigs were being
thrown in the Lagan. But now that the Provos are retaliating,
and the violence is extending to the businesses and homes and
lives of middle-class Protestants, the picture is changing." However, there remains a vast reservoir of hate in the Orange
ghettos—and can that terrible accumulation somehow be
rendered harmless or will it be like those indestructable deposits
of nuclear waste that threaten future generations? I put this
question to an elderly Protestant woman who runs a little café
and in her spare time does voluntary work for the Alliance
Party. "Cheer up, love," she said, "and listen to this one! Mrs
Paisley was getting into bed when she stubbed her toe hard and
cried out 'Oh God!' So Paisley says, 'It's all right, dear, you
don't have to call me that when we're alone.'"

It is impossible to be gloomy for long in Belfast. I was feeling
rather depressed one afternoon when I turned a corner and saw
on a gable-end the familiar NO POPE HERE. And underneath,
in different coloured paint, LUCKY OLD POPE!

8

The War of the Myths

I met Bill in the post-office-cum-general store of a Co Antrim village and he invited me home for a cup of tea. He is a British army pensioner who lives with his wife and half-a-dozen dogs in a little council house. Their only daughter is married to a policeman now stationed in Belfast; their only son went across the water the day after he left school—"We didn't want him hanging around getting mixed up in things." Before the first world war Bill's Catholic father migrated from Cavan to Enniskillen, joined the British army, married a Church of Ireland girl and became a Protestant. He had wished to become an Orangeman but could not though his conversion was no matter of convenience but absolutely sincere. Only very occasionally are converts admitted to the Order and this man was thought to have too many Papist relatives. However, Bill himself was allowed to join his Junior Orange Lodge at the age of eight and thus he became a full Orangeman at seventeen instead of eighteen (the normal age for being initiated). He explained, "Discrimination against Catholics just doesn't look like discrimination to the average Orangeman. It looks like defending the state against the enemy within the gates—people who have been working to destroy it every way they know how since it was founded—see?"

I did see, but I asked, "How long can you expect a state to survive when one-third of its population is opposed to its very existence?"

Bill sighed and slowly shook his head. "The pity is the Redmondites couldn't win before there was any UVF or any 1916." We shook hands on that and two beautiful collies wagged their tails delightedly, apparently being Home Rulers too.

On either side of the living-room hearth were bookshelves loaded with volumes on Irish, English and European history—Bill's hobby. He left school at fourteen, just as I did, and like

many self-educated people who lack congenial companionship
in their own circle he frequently writes to the newspapers and
proudly showed me his file of cuttings on an astonishing variety
of subjects. He also showed me his most treasured possession,
a hand-written letter from Brian Faulkner thanking him for his
help—when he lived in another area—during an election campaign. His devotion to the ex-leader of the moderate Unionists
verged on hero-worship and he assured me that had Brian
Faulkner not been opposed so relentlessly by Paisley the North
would now be prospering under the power-sharing Executive.
Although to outsiders Brian Faulkner seemed such an uninspir-
ing character he aroused tremendous admiration among those
who worked with him and deep affection among his constituents.

Bill admitted that the way things are now he wouldn't fancy
crossing the border—except of course into Donegal, which no
Northerner seems to regard as Republican or Romish though
it probably contains more Provo supporters than any other
county in Ireland. Having spent many years abroad with his
regiment, which included scores of Southern Irishmen, he feels
strongly that Northern Irish Protestants have much more in
common with the 'Fenians' than with anyone else though their
myth forbids them to recognise this affinity. Despite his army
background, he distrusts and dislikes the British. A lot of the
trouble, he said, is being caused by their failure to study the
Northern Ireland situation closely enough. "They don't really
know what's going on, or why—and they don't realise that the
'Why' is even more important than the 'What'. They keep on
and on about 'restoring law and order'. But the UDR—a
British army regiment, don't forget—openly helps the UDA
with training and equipment. And sometimes the UVF, too.
And that's been going on for several years. Then the UDA uses
its British army weapons to intimidate Her Majesty's Protestant
subjects and get money out of them—how's that for a way to
restore law and order? The UVF just fix a night to go and raid
a barracks and nobody happens to notice. Mind you, I prefer
them to the UDA. I know they're illegal—and quite right too—
but they're *idealists*, like the Provos. The UDA are just a bunch of
thugs. D'you know who was sitting in B. . . . . Town Hall during

the '74 Workers' Strike, controlling everything and handling out chits and permits to everybody? The UDA candidate in the last election—and he'd got 346 votes out of 28,000! How's that for democracy and law and order? Do you wonder I'm anti-British?"

In a town not far from Bill's village I had my first experience of intimidation, if that is not too strong a word for a tiny incident. Going into a Catholic pub at noon I joined five customers who were drinking at the bar and noticed in a corner by the door a bearded, stalwart young man sitting alone with a large whiskey and the *Irish News*. The cheerful barman—the publican's son—was not long finding out all that his customers wanted to know about me, including my destination for that day.

On the previous evening a local policeman had been badly wounded by a Provo sniper and when this topic was introduced the atmosphere became charged with conspiratorial approval and many cryptic (to me) remarks were made about the ambush. In such a place I should have remained non-committal on all delicate subjects; instead, I replied truthfully when asked for my views on the future of Northern Ireland. It was a pity, I said, that the Provos had no intelligent leaders to help them change their tack. At which point the barman—then sitting opposite me at a little table, having a drink himself—trod heavily on my toes, frowned and rolled his eyes in the direction of the bearded young man. Soon after I went upstairs to the 'Ladies' and on coming out found the barman waiting in the corridor. He advised me, with a dead-pan face, to look at my map again when I got back to the bar and announce that I had changed my mind and was not going to my original destination. Just for a moment I felt a ridiculous twinge of fear, followed by a rush of impatient resentment. Then I meekly said "Thank you" and returned to the bar to take his advice. In the North today the dividing line between absurdity and danger is not always clear.

That evening, on a Catholic farm in Co Tyrone, my young host and hostess were able to identify the silent bearded figure. A well-known character, they said, who had been interned without trial for four years and become very unbalanced. Joe was scathing about my indiscretion. "You've been around the Six Counties now for nearly three months," he said. "Isn't that long enough to teach you sense?"

I tried, rather feebly, to defend my rashness. "It's partly not wanting to go along with the violent way of life—I'm used to living in a country where anyone can say what they like about anything. And partly it's an inability to take it all seriously, even after three months. Everything seems so normal on the surface, outside of Belfast and Derry...."

"But you know it *isn't*," said Joe. "Mind you, that lad in the pub wasn't a normal hazard. I've known him all my life and he was *not* in the Provos, or any other illegal organisation, when they lifted him. And he never had been. But he'd an uncle out in '58 and that seemed a good enough reason to put him inside. By the time they let him out he *was* a Provo. He did a few jobs but then they chucked him—too unstable. Being interned four years without trial, for no reason, has eaten away at him. He's gone very violent lately and you just wouldn't know how he'd react to anything. It's now he should be put away, poor devil."

Joe and his wife Phil are in their late twenties and The Troubles have been part of their entire adult lives. They both wistfully recollected their adolescence when it seemed that Terence O'Neill might peacefully end Orange domination. "Things were so relaxed then,' said Joe. "We lived on this farm here—my parents and myself and three older sisters. It's mostly Protestant round here so we always had a Protestant maid and Protestant farm-lads. When we were small the lassie came with us to Bundoran for a fortnight every summer and took us to Mass with no quibble. You wouldn't get that happening now. You notice the polarisation in all sorts of little ways. My father used to give me double pocket money for the Twelfth and he'd insist on me going to watch the marching for fear he'd be accused of holding me back. It was dead boring but worth it for the extra money. Nowadays round here Catholic kids would be afraid to go outside their front doors for days before and after the Twelfth."

Phil, however, had slightly less rosy memories of childhood on a Co Fermanagh farm. She recalled going to a neighbour's birthday party and being reprimanded for walking on the lawn by her nine-year-old hostess, the daughter of a B Special. When she pointed out that other children were playing on the grass she was told, "Do as I say! We're more important than you because we're Protestants and if we want we can take your land!" At once Phil burst into tears and rushed home. Never having heard anti-Protestant talk within her own family she had been unprepared for this introduction to sectarianism. Then, as she grew up, her mother admitted that she dreaded going to Protestant social gatherings because of the silence that fell when a Papist entered the room. "But the point is that she *was* invited to those gatherings," said Joe. "I doubt if she would be now."

Joe's parents have emigrated to live in Canada with a married daughter. "They couldn't stand another moment of it here,' explained Joe. "Not after a Protestant neighbour was shot dead in his cowshed and the local UVF tried to put it about we sheltered the killer. And before that my mother's first cousin had her legs blown off in Belfast and my youngest sister was beaten up by a vigilante patrol. Some people can go on and on taking it but my mum's not like that. She went to bits altogether after the murder. And I was happy to stay—I'd hate to be away across the water in a city. People think we're brave, especially since Paisley built one of his new churches just down the road. But I reckon round here everyone's safe enough if they see and hear nothing and keep stuck in their work."

On the following Sunday I girded my loins and went forth to sample rural Paisleyism. The small Free Presbyterian church on the edge of the town was most attractive; whatever else may be said about Mr Paisley, he certainly encourages an agreeable style of modern architecture. When I entered the building a young woman wearing a pink dress and wide golden hat with flowing pink ribbons was playing the harmonium in one corner and the waiting congregation was cheerfully humming a hymn. As in Belfast, all the women were dressed to kill. And the many little girls, with shiny ringlets, frilly frocks and wide-brimmed hats, looked like illustrations from the sort of Victorian storybook that utterly repelled me as a child. The church was about two-thirds full and again the congregation included a remarkable number of young people. Beside me sat an elderly woman, with a kindly, gentle face, and a small grandson who throughout the service silently chewed toffees non-stop, neatly tucking the folded papers into the tops of his white nylon knee-socks. My neighbour, realising that I was a novice church-goer, helped me to find the hymns and shared with me her Bible which had many verses—non-violent—underlined in biro. The preacher was a visiting minister of about fifty, clad in conventional clerical black. He was very professional yet not unpleasantly 'smooth' and had a harmless if rather rudimentary sense of humour. He told us that he came of a staunch Church of Ireland family and ten years ago had been in a good job, with excellent prospects, which he left when God called him through Ian Paisley. His not to reason why and we must not either when the Lord calleth. . . . He spoke of his Church of Ireland relatives in Tipperary and Wexford who are very, very anti-ecumenism and are beginning to take a serious interest in Free Presbyterianism. He visibly tingled with joy as he foretold that in the near future the new faith—which was really the oldest and only form of Christianity, rescued for us by the Reverend Dr Paisley—would sweep the 'Free State' leaving a devastated Church of Ireland in its wake. This would serve the Church of Ireland right; its faithful members had been properly taught to regard the Mass as an evil deceit but now were expected to applaud their clergy actually *attending Mass*. He described the new Prayer Book as 'an annual event, in different covers every year like a children's Annual at Christmas time'. This was a symbol of the indecision, instability and weakness of present-day Anglicanism. His sermon was based on Jeremiah 6—'follow the old paths'—and we were repeatedly reminded that all supporters of ecumenism will unfailingly go to hell.

This might seem fairly uncouth stuff if one weren't comparing it with Paisley's evil invective. I particularly enjoyed an aside telling us that though there are many good things in the 'Free State' its signposts are not among them. There was something disarming about this innocuous sop to the anti-State sentiments of the congregation; and a neat metaphor quickly followed, deploring the fact that so many down South could not find 'the old paths'. But what chiefly impressed me was the

emphasis on avoiding something quaintly termed 'carnal violence'. The only weapons of Free Presbyterianism should be
spiritual—preaching and prayer—and our preacher made
plain his disapproval of 'certain people, even within Free Presbyterianism', who seem to think otherwise. This warning so
fascinated me that I decided to investigate rural Paisleyism in
greater depth—not a difficult task, according to the notices,
because this sect is particularly lavish with its services and even
provides a sort of dawn chorus at 6.0 am on weekdays.

There was nothing 'silent' about the collection here; only one
note lay on the plate which reached me and ten pence seemed
to be the average offering. As we left, the minister, standing
in the porch, shook hands with each individual. When I
appeared, clad in slacks and a hooded anorak, he looked embarrassed. Part of his sermon had been a denunciation of what he
called 'he-shes'—women who wear slacks and short hair and
men who wear colourful clothes and long hair. However, he
quickly recovered himself and assured me that all are welcome
to hear the word of God and seek the old paths. Outside the
church my Bible-sharing neighbour shook my hand and said,
"I can tell by your clothes you're not saved, but would you
like to know how I got saved?" There is only one polite answer
to such a question and I was therefore invited to tea at 5.30—
the meal had to be early on Sundays, Mrs T— explained, so
that nobody would be late for prayer-time at 7.0, to be followed
by the Evening Service at 7.30.

At 3.20 I pursued my researches by cycling to the crossroads
on the edge of the town where about quarter of the morning's
congregation had dutifully gathered to support a fat little lay-
preacher with a croaky voice who was trying to save the sort
of person not given to church-going. But the only non-church-
goers in sight were a group of tough-looking youths who hung
about briefly, chewing gum and looking cynical, while we were
being exhorted to beware of weak clerics who would lead their
followers astray to Rome. The preacher made straight for me
at the end, obviously seeing me as the most promising fruit of
his afternoon's labour. While I wheeled Roz he walked back
to the town centre beside me, desperately begging me to cast
off sin—by which I imagine he meant my trousers. His sort of

religion has such an unfortunate effect on me that I was almost tempted to take them off then and there in the Diamond.

Mrs T— and her family were awed to hear that I had actually sat at Paisley's feet in the Martyrs' Memorial. None of them has ever seen the building because since 1969 they haven't risked going to Belfast. I wondered then if Paisley preaches Belfast-style throughout the countryside; it is hard to imagine the gentle Mrs T—listening with any enthusiasm to such rabble-rousing. But possibly she and her like are too overcome by their Founder's personality to analyse the drift of his 'sermons'.

Mrs T—'s twenty-two-year-old son and his nineteen-year-old bride explained to me that they find the 'no-change' attitude of Free Presbyterianism very reassuring. One can well understand its having this effect—at least in its rural manifestations—on youngsters who since childhood have known so much tension and violence, not to mention social and political changes of the most unsettling sort. All my subsequent observations convinced me that rural Paisleyism attracts many people who are not particularly fanatical but only want to retreat into the security of the familiar. They don't want to have to think about what part they could play in a changing society and usually they haven't in any case got very much with which to think. Yet what they may lack in intelligence they often make up in good-nature and sincerity.

By the end of the following fortnight I felt that I had earned the right to pontificate on Paisleyism, having attended eight full-length Free Presbyterian services. Apart from their paralysing boredom no one could take exception to any of those sermons. Three out of the eight preachers condemned violence of any sort, used for any reason, and not one of them even obliquely encouraged it. In all these little churches Free Presbyterianism appeared merely as a dreary sterotyped fundamentalism. Admittedly it contributes nothing to the cause of Reconciliation Between Christians. But neither does it deter its followers from showing strangers a great deal of warm friendliness.

Towards the end of September, when Ian Paisley was in Canada, I checked on the Martyrs' Memorial to see how Belfast Paisleyism fares in the absence of its founder. The church was scarcely one-sixth full and Mr Paisley's stand-in was a rather feeble preacher. But the amplifiers were so skilfully manipulated that the hymn-singing gave the impression of a huge throng—an important point since cassettes of the day's proceedings are sold in the porch after each service. The programme exhorted us to 'Continue to pray for Dr Paisley as he preaches at the old-time Gospel Campaign in Toronto'. It also urged us to 'Make sure to order a copy of Dr Paisley's 30th Anniversay volume. Order forms in the porches of the church.' And it revealed that in the Chief's absence the 'Lord's Treasury' had dropped the previous Sunday to £484.89. What interested me, however, was the complete inoffensiveness of the sermon, without even a side-kick at Rome or Canterbury. This cheered me enormously. At least Paisley does not have, as I had feared he might, a large team of mini-Paisleys echoing his message throughout Northern Ireland.

At the end of August I briefly returned home, to get my daughter back to school, but early one September morning I was again crossing the border, just after dawn—this time into Co Armagh. I remember a wonderful pink-streaked sky and a silent, hilly landscape that looked strangely un-Irish after the long, hot summer; all golden-brown and fawn, with dry, colourless leaves falling prematurely and glowing bunches of rowan berries like lanterns in the woods. Honeysuckle and convolvulus draped dusty hedges and then I was cycling above the shores of a wide lake dotted with wooded islets. Soon after, on my right, another lake appeared. It was small, round, still and black, with two swans floating on their own reflections. And all morning the traffic consisted only of cows being driven back to their parched fields after milking.

I reckoned afterwards, when studying the map, that I had crossed the border seven times within a few hours—usually without realising it—while making my way north-west from Carrickmacross. Only one of these crossings was on an 'approved' road where, south of the border, a tiny prefab hut contained a solitary, yawning customs officer sitting beside a hideously wailing 'trannie'. A little way up the road were some fifty overturned, burnt-out car wrecks, rusty memorials to those days when the border was regularly blocked. And half-a-mile further on I passed a large, heavily fortified British army post.

By a happy coincidence I free-wheeled into a little border town at 11.30 am, just as the pubs were opening. But at first it was not easy to discern a pub. That IRA stronghold has seen so much shooting and bombing, that its pubs are now fortified—not professionally, as in Belfast, with wire mesh and special locks, but clumsily, with boarded-up windows and barricaded side-doors. The pub I eventually detected was packed by noon and I stood at the bar beside the only other woman customer; she was small, sallow, voluble and wearing an inappropriate winter overcoat. "The men round here have nothin' to do but drink," she informed me. "It's crool, the unemployment."

"And what about yourself, Molly?" said a weatherbeaten young man with enormous ears. "Haven't you somethin' else to do, with the wains comin' home for their dinner?"

"They don't come home," retorted Molly. "They has it at school." Two vodkas later she was telling me about her husband who had gone across the water in '71, when the RUC were after him, and never got in touch with her since. At that point Big-ears dug his elbow into her ribs, winked at me and said, "But now there's many more get in touch with you, isn't that right, Molly?"

Molly looked tearfully into her vodka. "'Tisn't the same," she said.

A teenage girl hurried in then and tapped Molly on the shoulder. "D'you know who's watchin', Moll?"

Molly swung around and stared through the open door. On the opposite pavement stood an elderly woman wearing a headscarf and carrying a shopping basket. She was certainly looking in our direction but in rather a vague way. "Jaysus!" said Molly. "The bitch! She's at it again!"

"She looks fairly harmless," I observed.

Molly groaned. "Now she'll be away to tell himself on me!"

"Himself?" I asked.

"The priest above," said Molly irritably. "The Parish Priest—and by this evenin' he'll be at me again over drinkin' the wains' money." She slammed her empty glass down on the counter and turned to go. "But isn't it me own business what I does with me own money? I'm not asking' him for nothin'!"

"Nobody could possibly see into the pub from across the street, in this bright sun," I pointed out. Molly laughed sardonically. "Don't you believe it! That witch could see through reinforced concrete!"

I marvelled afterwards at how exactly all this measured up to the Orange concept of Fenian mores. The shiftless deserted wife—of doubtful virtue—drinking at noon, leaving her wains to fend for themselves; and the Parish Priest's housekeeper spying on behalf of her master, who would promptly mete out some ghastly secret punishment in the name of Rome. Being over-dependent on pub contacts puts one in danger of getting lopsided impressions. For every Molly-type in that little town, there must be a hundred respectable, conscientious wives and mothers never met by wandering cyclists.

The following evening I camped in very beautiful countryside on the edge of a tiny village which at first appeared to be publess. Panic-stricken, I cycled up and down the deserted street—actually half a street, since there were houses on only one side—and then saw a British army Land-Rover pulling up outside the minute shop. Six weapon-laden youths jumped out and for a moment I thought I was at last going to witness some drama. But no, they had simply stopped to buy ice-creams. As they stood around their vehicle, licking, I approached to ask if they knew where the nearest pub was. The sergeant grinned and nodded towards what looked like a private house on a corner. "Knock on the side window and you might get someone at home," he said. I was lucky; the young Church of Ireland farmer who runs the part-time pub had just returned from his harvesting.

George was articulate and outspoken, with firm principles but without bigotry. He represented a Protestant type one meets often but hears too little about so much more 'newsworthy' are the Loyalist paramilitaries and the Orange politicians. Soon we were joined by an old man named Pat, a neighbouring Catholic farmer in for his regular six o'clock "half-pint and a short". He and George were in complete agreement about how The Troubles have affected their area. When

I remarked on its beauty and apparent tranquillity both shook their heads and Pat said, "Easily known you don't live here!"

"It's not like Belfast or Derry," explained George, "with gunmen fighting the Brits or each other and sectarian assassinations every week. We've had our share of that—one of my best friends was murdered in '72, aged twenty. But now it's mostly plain crime, not even disguised as any sort of patriotism. Too many youngsters have guns. And not a worry about using them. I've an eighteen-year-old cousin—he was eleven when it started and he accepts violence as normal. Last month he robbed £528 from a post office and was caught immediately because he hasn't really the temperament for crime. But his parents will never get over the disgrace. It's shaken a lot of us to watch this process among the youngsters. There's not much parents can do to protect kids from the violence in the air. People think this is mostly an urban problem but they're wrong. Round here, the amount of robbery with violence is just desperate. Ten years ago we wouldn't have believed it could ever be like this. It's not Protestant versus Catholic now—it's Young Thugs versus The Rest. We never know who the next victim will be. Except that it'll surely be someone defenceless. And the security forces aren't even pretending to cope. Maybe they can't. Maybe they've to concentrate all they've got on the Provos." He nodded towards the window. "See yon 'phone box outside? A few nights ago at 1.30 two young lads were trying to get some sense out of the nearest RUC barracks. Local lads. I know them well. They'd just been roughed up by a Loyalist vigilante patrol—so-called—and they'd guts enough to report this. But the RUC didn't want to know. They wouldn't listen. They told the young lads to belt up and go home to bed. And I'm asking—what's the good of the authorities begging us to co-operate with the security forces if the security forces won't co-operate with us?"

"Mebbe they were afraid, above in the barracks," suggested Pat. "Wouldn't you be, if you were expected to get out after that lot in the darkness of the night?"

"Then they should be in another job," said George shortly. When Catholics make similar complaints against the RUC one tends to take them with a grain of salt; but George was a staunch Unionist.

"I'd settle for Direct Rule indefinitely," he went on, "if only it *was* rule and not this kind of sham. The solution may be everyone getting so worn down by violence it flickers out. That's happening already in some places. A lot who supported the extremists at first are just fed up now."

Pat shook his head. "I'm eighty next month," he said, "and I can tell you that 'everyone getting worn down by violence' is no solution. When partition came, I was the one age with George there. A few years after that, we were all worn down, too—worse than now, a lot, because there was no social security to keep us fed and our bodies were worn as well as our souls. So the violence stopped. For a while. If it stops again now, it'll only be for another while. Unless there's been a *real* solution worked out somewhere, by someone."

We changed the subject then, by a sort of Pavlov reaction. Perhaps because of 'outsider participation' we had ventured much closer than is normal to those areas where Protestants and Catholics fear to tread together.

Before I left George said, "Remember this—it may be something a stranger doesn't notice but it's *true*. Everybody in Northern Ireland—*everybody*—has been branded by our experiences since '69. If you meet people who tell you The Troubles have never bothered them, they're liars. Maybe some of us needed to be branded. Maybe all of us did. You don't have to be damaged when you're branded. But we've all been painfully changed, us and our country. We'll never be the same again".

"It's not really about religion or jobs or power," said the young university lecturer. "Maybe once it was, but not now. Now it's all about identity. Who's what? If everybody in Northern Ireland could answer that question, *without* hesitation, we'd be more than half-way to a solution."

"What are you?" I asked.

Andrew hesitated. And then we both laughed, a little wryly.

According to himself, Andrew is the fervently agnostic son of orthodox Presbyterian parents. He votes Alliance, is married to a Dublin Catholic and hopes soon to get a job in Britain.

No wonder he hesitated. However he described himself—whether as an Ulsterman, an Irishman or British—he would, in these confused times, have an uneasy feeling that he was not being quite precise enough, that someone or something was somehow being 'let down'. He knows exactly when his forefathers came from Scotland to help colonise Co Armagh. They came in 1618, two years before the *Mayflower* sailed. And many centuries earlier, their forefathers may well have migrated from the north-east of Ulster to help colonise Scotland.

"Trouble is," I said, "you colonists went too easy on us natives. What sort of mess would the US be in now, if the Indians hadn't been properly tidied away?"

"Trouble is," replied Andrew, "that we weren't all the same religion. Can you imagine a family which moved from Scotland to England 358 years ago not regarding itself as English? And if my parents go to Scotland for a holiday they don't feel they're going home the way colonists from Rhodesia might. Of course they don't feel they're abroad either. But they admit if they meet a Southerner in London they feel they've more in common with him than with all the Prod Londoners. Yet they won't go South for a holiday any more because they reckon it's a foreign state with designs on *their* territory. Do you wonder a lot of us are in agony at the moment, with the horns of our dilemma so sharp?"

"But a few moments ago you said it wasn't about religion!" I protested.

"Of course it was, originally—religion *plus* land-ownership. I meant it isn't any more. The hang-up's identity, now."

"But," I said, "to the outsider you Northerners already seem to have a special and very distinct identity. It exists. It's not something new or artificial you're trying to find or make. Surely the hang-up is about *recognising* what you have in common, instead of fiercely denying it?"

Andrew suddenly became impatient with himself—or with me, or with Northern Ireland. "Personally," he said, "I've had all this waffling about looking for a new identity for Ulster. Why should one and a half million of us in this little corner of a little island have any special identity? In global terms, aren't we all first cousins if not half-brothers and sisters on these islands? And aren't we all in the EEC and moving towards the twenty-first century? Why can't we just get on with being Europeans?"

When people are deeply unsure of themselves, when their past has to be constantly invoked to explain or excuse their present and when nothing about their future is known or can be safely predicted, a sort of intellectual ferment starts; and not merely, or even chiefly, in academic or literary circles. All over Northern Ireland ordinary people are trying to think their own way through The Problem and this personal sorting-out process marks one of the most obvious differences between North and South. The Northern Irish do not just passively endure their regional tragedy. Many are questioning and probing and doubting and the result is immensely stimulating for a visitor from the lazy-minded South. The combinations and permutations are endless as individuals half-fearfully look at themselves in relation to their homeland, and to Britain and the Republic, and grope towards something new. Something as yet nameless and formless and not—at least on the Protestant side—greatly desired, but now dimly seen as inevitable. I remember a young-ish Catholic mountainy farmer in Co Derry debating UDI with his cronies and attempting to work out a basis for it that could be acceptable to Catholics. And a middle-class Protestant housewife in Co Down entertaining me in her kitchen while she did the wash-up and remarking that she would never have believed, a few years ago, how little the British public know or care about Unionist feelings. Then she asked, very sadly, "Has loyalty any meaning if nobody wants it?" And in Co Antrim a Presbyterian minister filled me with potato cakes and said of course a united Ireland was coming but the good stock would never stay to be ruled from Dublin. "So in the end the IRA will have its way and we'll all go back where we came from—or at least, the best of us will. And I wish Dublin joy, trying to cope with the rump that's left." There is nothing very startling about any of these remarks, except as indications that people who ten years ago would never have stopped to think about their myths now feel compelled to do so. Recently, out-siders have begun to comment on Northern Ireland's apathy; but this disease is largely confined to frustrated and disgruntled politicians. Although the Northern Irish may have their defects apathy of any sort is not—in my experience—among them.

In general the country-folk seem more flexible than the city-folk; there is a basic pragmatism in farming communities that contradicts the notion one has of cautious, conservative peasants. Life on the land teaches people to make do with what's available and to adapt to the dictates of wind and weather—to forces beyond their control. And The Troubles are a force beyond control. They have blighted Stormont, dried up the sympathy of the Great British Public for Unionist aspirations and made Orangeism an object of scorn. The average rural Unionist, given civilised leadership, might slowly be led on from here to an acceptance of such horrors as power-sharing with Catholics—not initially because he saw the justice of it but because it has become inevitable, as it might be inevitable, one year, to sell calves for a pound apiece. The tragedy is that such leadership is nowhere in sight. This is one of the reasons why there is unlikely to be any Great Leap Forward into the 1970s as the rest of Europe knows them.

Many of those with whom I discussed the future spoke in terms that would have appalled their fathers, Orange or Green, but often they seemed unaware of having budged from their inherited position. And if I betrayed that I had detected a deviation they tended to explain hastily that they never meant *that*—they weren't giving in on anything—they were only talking *generally*. . . . The modification of Northern attitudes is going to be like the movement of a glacier, imperceptible to the onlooker though with effects which change the face of the land.

Andrew had complained about the sharp horns of the Orange dilemma and the horns of the Green dilemma, though quite differently shaped, are no less uncomfortable. (As a child, I used to picture a dilemma as something between the Great Irish Elk and the rhinoceros.)

All Northern Catholics unequivocally describe themselves as Irish; they hesitate—if they do—only when asked, "To which government do you owe your allegiance?" Most now see four alternative governments, two existing and two hypothetical; Westminster, the Dail, some future power-sharing Stormont substitute—possibly associated on a federal basis with Britain and the Republic—or some future semi-autonomous nine-county Ulster Parliament ('Dail Uladh') forming part of a thirty-two county Republic. That last is a Provos' 'solution'; not even they imagine that Northern Ireland could be brought into an All-Ireland Republic without 'special arrangements' having been made for the one million Protestants. (I am leaving Official IRA ambitions out of this. As Marxists, the Stickies have few followers at present. But they advocate a genuinely secular state, and as thinkers are far better equipped than the Provos, so they may well prove more important in the end.)

Extreme Republicans swear fealty to Dail Uladh, ignoring the fact that it is very unlikely ever to exist. Indeed, in an hallucinatory sort of way they regard themselves *as* Dail Uladh. When asked on whose authority they are fighting their 'war' they claim, in all seriousness, to be the only legal government of the Irish Republic. This fantasy is not laughable; it has brought too much grief and suffering to too many for its comic element to be any longer visible.

What most surprised me, however, was the number of moderate Catholics who admitted—often with elaborate, apologetic explanations—that in a changed atmosphere, which did not make them feel inferior, they would willingly forget about a united Ireland and be faithful to a power-sharing Stormont-substitute if it did not insist on ritual affirmations of loyalty to the Crown. A significant number of non-extremist under-fifties either belong to this group or are being pushed towards it by the South's increasingly explicit loss of interest in reunification. There are of course other moderate Catholics who still regard the Dail as their 'natural' government though they may dislike the particular régime that happens to be in power in Dublin. But this group, too, has been forced, over the past few years, to acknowledge the impracticality of its preference. Its members seem now to be moving either towards the Provos—seeing Dail Uladh as the only acceptable substitute for a Dail Eireann which has betrayed them—or towards those who are hoping for some more durable version of the Northern Ireland Executive, minus that Council of Ireland which so infuriated the Loyalists. After the Executive had been sabotaged in May 1974, the Dublin Government—according to one popular

Green interpretation—kicked the Catholics while they were down by suggesting that the most realistic policy for the future would be to slaughter the sacred Green cow of a united Ireland, in the hopes that eventually the Unionists might respond by slaughtering the sacred Orange cow of 'a Protestant Parliament for a Protestant people'. This blasphemy did to some Catholics what had been done to some Protestants by Britain's declaration that Westminster would not oppose a united Ireland should the majority of Northerners ever vote for it. They could scarcely credit Dublin's perfidy. And yet, harsh as this may sound, they needed some such shock to dislodge them from the myth to which they had been clinging for so long. Neither the British nor the Irish government was being unreasonable when their adherents were 'betrayed'. The British were politely expressing their longing to be honourably free of a problem that has haunted them at irregular intervals since 1886, when Lord Randolph Churchill decided—for his own political ends—that 'the Orange card is the one to play'. And the Irish government was being realistic at last when it admitted that for the foreseeable future it will be not merely futile but irresponsible for any Dublin administration to advocate a united Ireland. To recognise this fact is not to feel happy about it. And those Northern Catholics who bitterly accuse the South of selfishness and cowardice—of trying to disengage because we are terrified of becoming involved in a full-scale war with the Loyalists—are missing the point. For many years we have indeed shown an I'm-all-right-Paddy indifference towards Northern problems. But the fact that few of us would wish to see our army crossing the border to fight Loyalist paramilitaries is a mark of maturity rather than cowardice. Such a war could not possibly benefit anyone in any way. If another 'pogrom' situation did arise—which to me seems unlikely—it would make more sense to welcome half a million refugees into the Republic and made some sacrifices to look after them there rather than to send 12,000 troops over the border to defend them on their own territory.

Apart from new Green hesitations about loyalty, the physical fear which exists throughout both communities is much greater on the Catholic side. A report published by the Northern

Ireland Community Relations Commission states that between
1969 and 1972 Northern Ireland experienced the most widespread forced movement of populations to take place in Western Europe since the second world war. And of the 60,000 who
had to leave their homes during that period 80 per cent were
Catholics. Moreover, moderate Catholics are very aware of the
increasing danger from Loyalist paramilitaries to which continuing Provo violence exposes them. Paddy Devlin has pointed
out one sad result of this in *The Fall of the N.I. Executive*,
published in 1975. 'The current rate of enquiries at the emigration offices in Belfast indicates that the number of families interested in moving abroad is nearly five times what it was a few
years ago. It is significant that the families making enquiries
are almost all of the Catholic faith; are of the professional
classes; have been living outside the ghettos and would be ideal
types to blaze the trail towards integration across the frontiers
of the sectarian divide.'

Paddy Devlin's own career provides a good example of the
sort of horns a Green dilemma can have. Born in 1925 into a
Belfast ghetto, he joined Na Fianna (the junior IRA) at the
age of eleven. Six years later, as a full member of the IRA, he
was interned in Crumlin Road gaol. In 1950 he left the IRA
because it seemed to him badly-led and politically aimless. He
then became involved in the Trade Union movement and in
local politics and in 1958 he joined the NILP, hoping through
it to be able to improve the lot of the ghetto dwellers, both
Orange and Green. His election to Stormont as a NILP candidate took place early in 1969, after he had helped to found
NICRA. In 1970 he became one of the founders of the SDLP
and when the power-sharing Executive was established in
January 1974 he was appointed Minister of Health and Social
Services. I have never met Mr Devlin—or any other 'reigning'
Northern politician—but he is praised even by Orangemen as
the best Minister of Health the North ever had. His book certainly reveals a typically forthright Northern character, tough-
talking, tender-hearted and quick-witted, with a no-nonsense
approach to 'delicate' problems and a fierce loyalty to—the
North. The spontaneous, white-hot fury with which he defends
the Loyalists (his deadliest political enemies) against Wilson's

infamous 'spongers' sneer is amongst the most cheering things to be found in any recently published book on Northern Ireland. Yet for all his sensible willingness to serve the Northern Irish as one of her Majesty's Ministers, and for all his clear thinking on social issues, he is obviously in a hopeless emotional muddle about 'Who's What?' He writes, 'The [Northern Catholic] minority realise that identification with the Southern Irish people and loyalty to the idea of a full Irish State is their only real hope of survival. . . . A mounting measure of despair is enveloping them for they recognise the chilly isolation of their position. They see themselves as being in a strait-jacket surrounded by a growing circle of enemies. Not all of them [the enemies] are inspired by hatred of Catholics. . . . Nonetheless, they are with the enemies of the Northern minority just the same. It is of little consolation to the minority that some of these politicians have a responsibility under the Irish Constitution to protect that part of the national majority that lives over the Border.' Reading those statements through Orange eyes, they provide ample justification for never trusting a Fenian—and for believing that one day, if Britain deserts the North, it will be invaded by the Irish army on the pretext of protecting 'that part of the national majority that lives over the Border'. Reading them through my own eyes, they strengthen my conviction that we would help all the Northerners to sort out 'Who's What?' by scrapping Articles 2 and 3 of our Constitution.

I met many Catholics who confessed that they had lost all faith in traditional Republicanism but not one Catholic who would even consider accepting full integration with Britain. Yet some expressed a grudging appreciation of Direct Rule, merely because it is so much less awful, from the Green point of view, than was Stormont. And those people often added, "Unless the Unionists are to be allowed to take over again, there's no alternative to Direct Rule for decades ahead." Meanwhile, of course, all citizens—even the most extreme Republicans—give *de facto* recognition to Westminster and make the best of a bad job by collecting as many government hand-outs as possible.

A carefully-planned campaign to re-teach history in Northern Ireland would be one of the most practical contributions the British government could make towards an eventual solution. I have been rather unkindly told that this suggestion is typical of the useless weeds that flourish in literary minds. What ghetto hard-liner, my critics ask, is going to sit down and read (or listen to) a version of history that will repeatedly diverge from the myths on which he or she has been nurtured? However, I am not now thinking of the ghetto folk but of the tens of thousands of other hard-liners, people who would be horrified to be so described though their brains have been as thoroughly washed as any ghetto dweller's. That section of the population might slowly be weaned off its myths, over the next few generations, by a change of historical diet. Many people are, in a sense, waiting for it now; their reluctant half-admissions that there must be a new Northern Ireland—neither Orange nor Green—shows this.

At the very least, the present policy of handling the 'official' Orange myths with kid gloves could be discouraged. In one large town I talked to a Protestant secondary school teacher who the previous winter had been invited by the local Council to give a series of historical lectures as part of an adult education course. He saw this as a wonderful opportunity to eliminate some popular misconceptions and expended much time and energy on producing six lectures as unbiassed as he could make them. But so many in the class objected to the first of the series that the remainder were heavily censored by semi-literate Loyalist members of the Council. Again, I heard several people, including two history professors, complaining about a recently-held History Exhibition in Belfast which apparently leaped from St Patrick to 1914 in one disingenuous bound. And—though here we move from the secular to the religious authorities—one of the saddest examples of a responsible institution unconsciously distorting history is *Loyalism in Ireland*.

This little pamphlet of thirty-six pages is a report prepared by the Committee of the General Assembly of the Presbyterian Church in Ireland and presented to the General Assembly in June 1975. It is competently written and the authors have obviously tried hard to be fair. But their heritage proved too much for them. The nearer we get to the present day the more misleading is their choice of words. The start of the troubles in 1968 is described thus: 'A campaign for Civil Rights mushroomed, professedly not concerned with the issues of "Irish unity", but with compelling the Northern Ireland Government into internal reforms by mass demonstrations and "direct action" rather than by parliamentary processes. A university-based marxist-inspired "People's Democracy" movement helped to increase the confrontations and defiances of authorities and their exercise of public order. On the loyalist side a similar extra-parliamentary campaign was mounted.' Only a Loyalist could see any 'similarity' between the People's Democracy Movement and the numerous Paisleyite gangs, armed with nail-studded cudgels and newly-sharpened scythes, which roamed the countryside in November 1968 to harass the unarmed Civil Rights marchers as they attempted to use a police-approved route. The pamphlet goes on to explain that 'Two foci for defiance of the elected Government and its law enforcement authorities were in the Roman Catholic strongholds in parts of Londonderry and Belfast. During the summer of 1969 these more than once came to each other's aid with fresh riots (including the start of petrol bombing) when the other seemed hard pressed. In Belfast more particularly this provoked violent reaction from loyalists, who were no longer prepared to stand by and see such developments apparently reviving a conspiracy to defy and destroy the State which they supported. Punitive raids were accordingly launched into the heart of Catholic areas.' Here the use of the word 'punitive' conveys that those against whom the raids were launched deserved to be punished. There is no direct attempt to defend the behaviour of the Loyalist mobs; but an uninformed reader could be left feeling that their anger and violence were easily excusable—even laudable in intent, though ill-judged in deed. Which is not at all the impression given by that popular Loyalist ballad dealing with the same events around Bombay Street which I have already quoted.

On the next page we are invited to view the Unionist Party through Orange spectacles. 'While the Unionist Party may always have had an uncompromising appearance in its defence of loyalist interests, its reality has been otherwise as its history of adjustments shows. Considerable readiness was shown to accept the need for reforms and to begin their implementation. This was not to accept that the faults had all been on one side; so that the failure of the minority to match such changes but, instead, continually to increase their demands, produced its own reaction. This failure lent strength to those among the loyalists who criticised too ready a yielding to demands, which they saw as tending not just to healthy administrative and political reform, but to the undermining of the State itself, and the democratic will and processes.'

These quotations reveal the compulsively dishonest thinking of men whose personal integrity is, one can be certain, above reproach. To some, all this may seem like nit-picking; political propaganda and slanted reporting are common in every free society. However, in Northern Ireland, where British tolerance is virtually unknown, distorted history and slanted stories can and do endanger lives.

Had I read *Loyalism in Ireland* before visiting Northern Ireland I would have dismissed it as contemptibly tendentious; now I can exactly picture the types likely to write such a thing. Studious, upright, God-fearing characters who would never deliberately harm anybody, who uphold job-discrimination and never employ Catholics but in other ways would go to great lengths to help a needy Catholic because that is their Christian duty; and who firmly believe that the Vatican is rooting away in the background for a form of Irish unity that will destroy Irish Protestantism. A closed mind is repellent on paper but it does not necessarily imply either a cold heart or a feeble intellect. While talking to the sort of Presbyterian who might have written that pamphlet, I was often reminded of my own father. He had exactly the same sort of closed mind, except that his bigotry was not religious/political but pure political. He was almost (not quite!) as blinkered about Britain and the British as Orangemen are about Rome and the Pope. But that did not prevent him from being, in other ways, a perfectly reasonable and civilised man.

Loyalism in Ireland scores a valid point in relation to the Green myth-makers: 'Demonstrations in support of the will of the majority, whether by loyalist parties or Orangemen and others, have been automatically labelled "provocative", while far

more defiant and disorderly demonstrations by the minority
have not; and any casualties arising have been simply blamed
on the authorities and in no way on the lawbreakers, e.g. in
the tragic "Bloody Sunday" shootings in Londonderry.'

As Henry Kelly has pointed out in *How Stormont Fell*, 'In
Northern Ireland the fact that appearances are more important
than reality is a running tragedy. The state lives . . . on "ghosts".
And it lives on myths that don't need to have originated in 1690
or 1916. A day is generally long enough.' The Bloody Sunday
myth has become so valuable a weapon against the Brits that
anyone seeking to blunt its cutting edge will not be popular.
Indisputably, none of the thirteen civilians shot dead by British
paratroopers in Derry was handling a gun or bomb when shot.
Equally indisputably—and by now this is common knowledge—the Provos had made a careful plan to attack the
William Street barricade; two senior volunteers were armed
and waiting in a house to shoot at the army; and the paratroopers saw an armed group racing out of Glenfaddagh Park,
where the Provos had parked a car containing guns. The 'myth'
version of the tragedy does not include these details. If the
Provos wanted to make sure that no innocent civilians were shot
during that illegal march they should have kept themselves and
their weapons out of the way.

In my ignorance, I used to feel that discussing the role of
the myth in Northern Ireland was a way of being comfortably
abstract about the whole problem and evading the real issues.
I have learned a lot since then. Now I feel that the single most
important issue is the extent to which ordinary people live in
an extraordinary miasma of untruth. The average Northern
Ireland citizen is born either Orange or Green. His whole
personality is conditioned by myth and he is bred to live
the sort of life that will reinforce and protect that myth for trans-
mission to future generations. Moreover, those myths are
used daily to justify distrust and resentment of 'the other
side'.

Quite apart from the effects which this way of life is having
on Northern society at present, it is a personal disaster for the
individuals concerned. It retards their development as free
human beings, which is no less of a tragedy than having a limb

blown off by a bomb. No individual is free who cannot evolve beyond the confines of the mental world into which he was born. And in Northern Ireland most people are inhibited, by the atmospheric pressures of their mythology, from maturing and mellowing in the way that is normal for twentieth-century Europeans. At least, in the South, we are now free in this sense. Someone born into a Catholic or Protestant, or Fianna Fail or Fine Gael family can decide to change sides without their whole world collapsing around them—or any of their neighbours deciding that they should be shot. Not many of us, as yet, use this freedom; but that is owing to mental laziness rather than to irresistable forces thwarting our natural development. The Southern myths, based on Catholicism and Republicanism, have never, even at their most potent, been as restrictive as the Northern myths. Churchmen and politicians may have wished them to be so but some inherent flexibility has always saved us from the worst consequences of our own myth-making.

According to Malinowski, 'The function of myth is to strengthen tradition and endow it with a greater value and prestige by tracing it back to a higher, better, more supernatural reality of ancient events.' (Though in Northern Ireland recent events will do, as Henry Kelly has noted.) But are there any living traditions left within the Orange and Green myths? Or are they mere empty shells, continuing to exist after the creature inside has died?

The Irish Republican tradition can trace its spiritual origins far beyond the French Revolution, which is usually quoted as its first inspiration. Under our ancient Gaelic law the land belonged to the people, who were free, following the death of a provincial King or chieftain, to choose a new ruler from among the dead man's heirs. In 1170, when a Norman army landed at Waterford under Strongbow, there began a slow conquest that was to replace the Brehon Laws by a system under which all land belonged to the King and nobody could possess it except by Royal Grant. One can therefore understand how the Republican ideal, when first presented to the Irish in the 1790s, sounded echoes within their racial memory even after six hundred years. France's newfangled Republicanism might not have too much in common with the Brehon Laws but at

least it was a step away from England's system of government
which had come to be associated, after the Reformation, with
rulers who hated the religion of Ireland's majority.

By now, however, extreme Republicanism might more
accurately be described as a militant anti-British tradition. If
a full-blooded Gaelic king could be conjured up tomorrow
morning, and if he made the right anti-British noises, I am convinced that most of our extreme Irish Republicans would
promptly become fanatic monarchists. In the 1790s Wolfe Tone
wrote, 'To subvert the tyranny of our execrable government,
to break the connection with England, the never failing source
of all our political evils, and to assert the independence of my
country—these were my objects . . .' And in the 1970s Seamus
Loughran of Provisional Sinn Fein, when asked what he meant
by 'British withdrawal', said, "We want to get rid of the British
way of life." The same sentiment is expressed even more succinctly on many walls in Northern Ireland and on some walls
in the South: BRITS OUT. Yet sociologists have come up with
statistics to prove that in the Republic we prefer the English
to any other foreigners; a fact ascertainable without benefit of
statistics if one happens to live in the South. And about one
and a half million Irish people are settled in Britain (as many
as live in Northern Ireland) and seem to find the English
way of life entirely agreeable and a good deal more lucrative
than the Irish way of life. At this point any student of the
Irish scene might be forgiven for losing his way in the mists of
humbug. One cannot even argue that the Irish living in Britain
are not subscribers to the Republican myth; many of them
are.

Happily, the militant, anti-British tradition within the Green
myth is now dying fast, of its own absurdity, in both Northern
and Southern Ireland. Yet it remains stirring enough to lure
easily-roused youngsters and the ineffectiveness of the Provo
campaign is a positive asset to its guardians. As J. Bowyer Bell
remarks in *The Secret Army*, 'No tradition runs deeper in Irish
politics than to turn physical defeat into spiritual victory, the
slain rebel into patriot.' Many ballads, often execrable in both
their moral and literary content, commemorate Republican
martyrs from 1798 to 1977. A typical sample was written in

1957, after the killing of two young IRA volunteers during a raid on Brookeborough Police Barracks.

> My name is O'Hanlon, I'm just gone sixteen
> My home is in Monaghan, there I was weaned.
> I learned all my life, cruel England to blame
> And so I'm a part of the Patriot Game.
>
> I don't mind a bit if I shoot down police
> They are lackeys of war, never guardians of peace.
> But at deserters I'll never let aim
> The rebels who sold out the Patriot Game.

One is immediately struck by the unwitting accuracy of that phrase 'the Patriot Game'. By now militant Republicanism has become just that: a macabre bit of make-believe in which grown men and women behave like six-year-olds earnestly enacting their fantasies. Incidentally, the 'rebels' referred to in the last line are the Southern politicians who accepted partition.

Some people see the IRA's lack of animosity towards Protestants *qua* Protestants as a sign of almost saintly magnanimity. But it is not quite like that. Undoubtedly, as I have already pointed out, most Northern Catholics (though not their clerical leaders) are more tolerant religiously than most Northern Protestants. But sometimes there is an element of fantasy in their tolerance; on analysis it is seen to be part of the Green myth. Since the Northern Protestants are Irish it would be totally against Republican tradition to oppose them *as non-Catholics*. When the Provos kill a policeman, or a Belfast business man, or a UDR man, they are attacking these people not as fellow-Irishmen with whom they disagree on religious matters or domestic politics, but as pro-British Quislings. Of course they hate the UVF, the UFF and the various other Loyalist para-military groups which have been responsible for the random murders of so many innocent Catholics; in 1973 an article on the UFF in a Provo newspaper was headed THIS UGLY CREATURE MUST BE DESTROYED. Yet the main Provo aim is to convert the Protestants—not religiously, pace Orange fears, but politically. A few years ago they produced a pamphlet entitled *Freedom Struggle* in which they urged the Northern Protestants to see the light. 'The Provisionals ask the majority in the North to unite with them in making a new nation, an old country. Six counties is but a fraction of Ireland; the Protestant and Presbyterian peoples of the North have as much birthright to the twenty-six as have any Catholic. It is our dearest wish that they would claim that birthright now and having claimed it that they then proceed to enrich and cultivate it with the industry for which they are renowned.' The fatuity of this plea is staggering when one remembers that it was written on behalf of an organisation which is engaged in a ruthless attempt to destroy the Protestants' beloved 'Ulster'. There could be no clearer proof of the extent to which the Green myth isolates the Provos from reality. And yet this plea is curiously moving, too, because it is utterly sincere; and the viciousness of the Provo campaign is partly a result of their frustration at not being able to convince the Protestants of its sincerity.

The Orange myth similarly isolates Unionists/Loyalists from—I am tempted to write, not merely reality, but sanity. The Orange tradition, too, is dying at the moment, but very slowly. The allegedly canny, unimaginative Protestants seem to be finding it even harder than the allegedly impractical, romantic Catholics to abandon the technicoloured past and face the black and white present. In September 1971 Billy Hull of the Loyalist Association of Workers revealed the panic-stricken tangle of post-1969 Orange emotions. To a huge Loyalist rally in Belfast he announced, "The age of the rubber bullet is over. It's lead bullets from now on. ... We are British to the core but we won't hesitate to take on even the British if they attempt to sell our country down the river." Orange mental confusion also seethes through an anonymous pamphlet entitled *Security in Northern Ireland* and produced a few years ago by the United Ulster Unionist Coalition (now defunct). In the second paragraph we read, 'It may be assumed that the ultimate aim of both the British Government and the UUUP is the same: that is to see a permanent end to violence in the Province. Where they differ is that the British Government does not really mind whether this is achieved within the UK or within a United

Ireland, whereas the Unionists are determined that it shall be within the UK.' This is very lucid yet the rest of the pamphlet shows no awareness of the imbecility of persisting in frenzied protestations of loyalty to a UK that is at best, on this anonymous writer's own admission, indifferent as to whether it receives Northern Irish loyalty or not. The Northern Protestant has always prided himself on his independence. Yet he is now reduced to forcing unwanted attentions on a Britannia who would much prefer not to know him and may one day rap him over the knuckles with her trident and tell him it is time he took his loyalty elsewhere. But where? Plainly the present generation of Loyalists would prefer to starve on the streets of Belfast rather than to be linked, however loosely, with the Republic. Even if they believed that nobody in a United Ireland would discriminate against them, they would still—like the white Rhodesians—detest the prospect of being a minority with only a share of power surrounded by a majority whom they see as inherently inferior to themselves. For the Republic to alter its laws to accommodate the Protestant ethic would not be enough. The Loyalists would also need to be educated to feel that we Southerners are 'equal' enough to share statehood with them.

'Which Majority?' is an integral part of the 'Who's What?' dilemma. Our anonymous guide to Unionist thinking gives one sort of answer: 'Westminster seems to have accepted that the basic cause of all the trouble is partition itself.... Such a view is contrary to the principal (*sic*) of self-determination as laid down in the Atlantic Charter, something which has been tested by plebiscite with an overwhelming result. The idea that such a plebiscite should have been taken by the whole of Ireland or the whole of the UK is not self-determination at all. This kind of plebiscite would have allowed Hitler legally to absorb all his smaller neighbours and enable, for instance, the British Isles to vote back the Irish Republic into the UK if it wished. The existence of Northern Ireland as a Province of the UK cannot therefore be challenged.' But how and why did Northern Ireland first become a 'Province' of the UK? In 1920 the Unionists were granted those six counties of Ulster which had the largest Protestant populations; but in Fermanagh and Tyrone

Catholics were in the majority and were appalled to find themselves thus abandoned to Orange domination. Had these two
counties been allowed 'self-determination' at that time they
would without hesitation have voted themselves out of Northern Ireland. Neither were the Unionists too pleased, since they
wanted not Home Rule but a maintainence of their position
within the UK. However, as Professor Beckett explains in *The
Making of Modern Ireland*, 'They were won over by the fact that,
in the six counties left to them, they would be in a permanent
majority'. It is often forgotten nowadays that the Government
of Ireland Act (1920) was not intended to partition Ireland permanently. It made provision for the setting up of a Council of
Ireland, 'With a view to the eventual establishment of a Parliament for the whole of Ireland, and to bringing about har-
monious action between the Parliaments and governments of
Southern Ireland and Northern Ireland ...' It even mentioned
reserving to Westminster postal and other services 'until the
date of Irish union'. Fifty-two years later all this was echoed
in Mr Whitelaw's Green Paper which declared that 'No UK
government for many years has had any wish to impede the
realisation of Irish unity, if it were to come about by genuine
and freely given mutual agreement.... Whatever arrangements are made for the future administration of Northern Ireland they must take account of the province's relationship with
the Republic of Ireland; and to the extent that this is done,
there is an obligation upon the Republic to reciprocate. Both
the economy and the security of the two areas are to some considerable extent interdependent, and the same is true of both
in their relationship with Great Britain.'

Now, however, the Northern Protestants are more determined than ever to resist absorption into an overtly Catholic
Republic which they are quite convinced has been energetically
supporting the Provo campaign since 1970. But for how long
more can the dying Orange tradition linger on? It is very much
a wary, close-the-ranks tradition, always suspecting threats,
plots, betrayals, conspiracies, always on the look-out for
danger—from Rome, from a Canterbury corrupted by ecumenism, from the US, from Dublin, from Moscow, even from
some surrealist alliance between all those 'enemies'. As a social

force it is as negative and destructive as the Republican hatred of England, as an expression of Christianity it is as perverse as Irish Catholicism (how much have these bitterly antagonistic parodies of Christianity influenced each other?). Yet Northern Protestantism—especially the Presbyterian version—has produced many individuals whose profound religious faith can be oddly consoling, even to an agnostic, amidst that tortured chaos to which the churches, as arrogant institutions, have contributed more than their share. Shorn of its neuroses, it could become a very valuable asset to the Ireland of the future.

I attended my first Peace March in Coleraine; because of domestic commitments I had missed the earlier, historic marches in Belfast and Derry. People warned me that this would be a mini-march—"The Coleraine folk are too bourgeoisie and buttoned-up, they'd never let themselves go like your lot from Shankill and the Falls!" By the standards of those early marches it was indeed a small, subdued turnout of perhaps 2,000 (in a town with a population of 15,000). The majority of marchers were female and looked 'middle-aged, middle-class and middle-brow'. Yet there were also quite a few young couples with infants in push-chairs or on Dad's shoulders and several pairs of clergymen—Protestant and Catholic—pointedly walking together. I wondered what were the attitudes of the many impassive onlookers and passers-by who were not taking part. Surprisingly few policemen seemed to be around and there was no counter-demonstration such as had been organised by the Provos in Derry.

In the shadow of the handsome Town Hall we recited the Peace Declaration fervently, and sang a few hymns, rather tentatively, and mumbled a few prayers, rather vaguely. Then everybody marched down hill to cross the fine stone bridge over the Bann. On the other side we followed the river upstream for a quarter of a mile before turning off to pass through a working-class district with UVF RULE HERE daubed in black paint on several walls. Outside the Orange Hall we were silently observed by a group of hard-faced men (the UVF reps, mayhap?). One small boy, sitting astride a high wall, yelled, "Fuck the lot o' yous!" and the chatty woman beside me—wearing pale blue hair and a pale pink sweater—said apologetically, "Don't be shocked, dear. You have to make allowances for them—it's the way they're brought up." I assured her that I was not shocked.

Afterwards in a crowded pub I sat among several young women who were refreshing junior marchers with odious fizzy liquids. When an elderly woman came to sit beside me I asked her if she had been marching. She looked scandalised and said fiercely, "I'm a Unionist, see. I wouldn't have anything to do with these Peace People. It's all organised from Andersonstown, so it is." (Andersonstown is one of Belfast's Catholic strong-holds.) Two friends of hers at the next table added grimly and rather cryptically—"It's too late now!" Yet the four of us had soon settled down to a mild booze-up and those hard-liners could not have been kinder to me. They were the type—very common in the North—who have hermetically sealed com-partments in their minds. With the contents of the ideological compartment they hate Fenians and anything that might be suspected of having a Fenian taint; with the contents of the 'human' compartment they are spontaneously warm and wel-coming to the individual 'Fenian' who happens to come their way.

Wherever I went, during this period, I heard people arguing about who should march with the Peace People. To outsiders it must seem that every sane person should have supported them, everybody who for seven long years had felt frustrated because there seemed to be nothing the ordinary citizen could *do.* . . . But of course no Northern situation has been as simple as that for centuries past. In some areas I found that the most ardent peace-lovers had chosen not to march because they felt it was wiser to avoid giving the Movement a 'gentry-image'. In other areas it was argued that no clergy should march as it would be fatal to give the Movement a 'church-image'. Else-where it was judged a mistake for the families of ex-servicemen to march as this could give the Movement a 'government-image'. And these various reactions were not as neurotic as they may sound. Behind the scenes at that time, in both the Orange and Green wings, many stood poised to seize on any scrap of 'evidence' to 'prove' to their gullible followers that the Peace

People were somebody's tools. On the Orange side it was easy to discredit them by stressing their Catholicism, as Paisley did on the front page of his *Protestant Telegraph* on 18 September 1976. There he reminded his readers that the Peace Campaign was 'commenced in St John's Chapel, encouraged by Roman Catholic priests and perpetuated by such as Miss Corrigan and Mrs Williams'. Really nothing more was needed to turn thousands of fundamentalist ghetto dwellers against the Movement. However, to reinforce their antagonism five 'anti-peace' biblical quotations were provided on the same page. For instance, 'Draw me not away with the wicked, and with the workers of iniquity, which speak peace to their neighbours, but mischief is in their hearts (Ps. 28.3).'

It is tempting to condemn those who are so readily swayed by Mr Paisley. But the Loyalists to whom I talked in the ghettos of East Belfast, when I returned there in mid-September, did not seem blameworthy. To them there is a war on and they feel for the Peace People that scorn which the average stout-hearted Englishman or woman felt for pacifists during the world wars. I particularly remember one small neat parlour where Queen Elizabeth and Ian Paisley were grotesquely improbable companions on top of the television set. A pale little woman with lank black hair, whose UVF husband had been 'in' for the past two years, told me that a friend had urged her to march—'for the sake of the children, to try to stop it all before they grow up'. But how could she betray her husband—he who was doing time to preserve Ulster for the Queen!—by 'walking in the street with papist harpies and viragos?' (A verbatim quote.) To this woman, as to thousands of her neighbours, Fenians represent a threat to *their* state, *their* jobs, *their* religion. So they are easily persuaded that to support a movement which opposes all violence, including anti-Fenian violence, is treachery. Mr Paisley's party proclaims itself interested only in Peace through Victory, by which it means a return to pre-1969 days with the Protestant majority firmly in control and no nonsense talked about power-sharing.

Green anti-Peace Movement propaganda paralleled the Orange version. It portrayed the Peace People as cowardly Quislings who were prepared to betray to the Brits those gallant lads who have sacrificed so much to win justice for the minority. This sounded plausible in those districts which for years now have been suffering daily and nightly at the hands of British soldiers who torment both the innocent and the guilty as they go about their business.

However, all the world knows that during the autumn of 1976 very many thousands ignored the propaganda of their hard-line leaders and were brave enough to march with 'the other side'. When I returned to Belfast on 15 September it was over two months since I had left the city and I at once became aware that the eruption of the Peace Movement, during August, had dramatically changed the atmosphere. It is very difficult to describe such changes. I can only say that there was new hope on people's faces and in their voices—even people who themselves had never marched, for one reason or another, and were sceptical about the Movement's long-term prospects.

The other momentous event to have happened in Ireland during those months was the assassination of the British Ambassador to the Republic near Dublin. Throughout the Northern countryside that tragedy—so shattering and humiliating for us in the South—seemed to have made extraordinarily little impression. Where the murders of friends and acquaintances are comparatively common the blowing up of one more unknown person is evidently not very memorable. In Belfast, however, I did notice an unpleasant 'undercurrent' after-effect. Among extremists of both communities disappointment was frequently revealed at the failure of the assassination to damage Anglo-Irish relations. There was an almost childish sulkiness involved. Catholics commented sourly that after the grovelling public speeches of various Irish cabinet ministers, both on the day of the murder and at the memorial service, the 'Free State' might as well rejoin the UK. And Loyalists commented, equally sourly, that Britain had lost a wonderful opportunity to show the world what she really thought of those Fenian bastards. One man added, "See how well the IRA propaganda machine works? Even when an ambassador is murdered London can't see through the hypocrisy in Dublin. But *we* won't be listened to! In London they'd listen forever to Fenian propaganda, like it was the gospel, but never to us."

Several Loyalists insisted that the ambassador's death was just one more bloody stupid Fenian mistake and that the intended victim was a top Northern Ireland Office official who was travelling in the next car. When I aired this theory in Provo circles it was naturally denied. But whether a mistake or not, Mr Ewart-Bigg's murder is already being woven into the Green myth as the great and glorious exploit of a selfless patriot-hero. And of course there is a ballad....

The Northern Ireland Problem repeatedly provokes such ghastliness that it has come to be seen from outside almost as a Morality Play featuring allegorical figures impossible to think of as people like us; the figures of Anger, Pride, Greed, Revenge—or (rather less conspicuously) Temperance, Humility, Forgiveness. After eight years of terror and horror the mental gulf separating the North from the rest of the British Isles is immense. Even before 1969 it was wide enough because of Northern Ireland's chronic introversion. For historical reasons the region has always been inward-looking and during its half century of self-government it 'got lost', as far as the rest of the world was concerned, and simmered unhealthily in its own mythological juices. Then it was found again, but in circumstances that emphasised its isolation by making it seem—to the uninformed outsider—physically unapproachable, economically unreliable, morally undesirable and generally not nice to know. (Or at best, to the more charitable, an object of exasperated pity.) If this disdain is not tinged with guilt it should be. The Republic is guilty for having until quite recently encouraged Northern Catholics to adhere to the Green myth; and Britain is guilty for having ignored the dire influences of the Orange myth on the administration of one area of the UK.

A prolonged crisis becomes distorted in the public view when known only through the media. Tragedy, violence, drama, destruction, suspense—day after day and year after year the abnormal is stressed. And the ordinary individual, trying to lead as normal a life as possible, is quite forgotten. In an effort to restore the balance sentimentalists sometimes assert that only a tiny minority of the Northern Irish are responsible for The Troubles, the rest being innocent victims. I myself used

to try to believe this but within weeks of crossing the border
I had realised that it is nonsense. No society could get itself into
such a mess without a majority of its population being involved—not through their deeds but through words and attitudes that create an atmosphere conducive to hatred, suspicion
and revenge. It would be dishonest and ultimately unhelpful
to ignore this harsh fact.

9

Back to Belfast

At 6.30 am on 15 September I left Corrymeela on its stormy
clifftop and crossed Torr Head with a gale behind me. To the
north-east, just above a turbulent sea, the blue-green sky was
scattered with pinkish shreds. Higher, shafts of golden light
came streaming towards the water from between vast, torn
masses of grey and purple cloud-banks—a wild and lonely sky
it was, as restless as the sea. I thought, as I sweated up Torr
Head, of the Children of Lir, changed into swans by their
father's jealous second wife, and swimming for centuries on the
waves of the Moyle, awaiting the first ringing of a Christian bell.
When they heard that sound they again became children—and
died. Maybe Christianity never brought much luck in this part
of the world.

My father remembered speaking a version of Scots Gaelic
hereabouts, during the first world war, to the people of the
Glens. From the road above the Head I could see Scotland
clearly, less than thirteen miles away. Always the people of
north-east Ulster have felt closer to Scotland than to the rest
of Ireland. Before the coast road was built the locals brought
many of their more cumbersome necessities by boat from Duna-
verty, on the Scottish coast, instead of struggling overland from
Carrickfergus.

At 9.0 am I got to Cushendall, feeling very ready for breakfast, but the entire village seemed still asleep. When I finally
succeeded in rousing a hotel the astonished-looking proprietress
said breakfast was never served before 9.30. Plainly north-east
Ulster *is* in Ireland, however many affinities it may have with
Scotland.

One of the loveliest roads in Europe follows the coast from
Cushendall to Larne and nowadays it is almost traffic-free.
With the wind helping I sped along effortlessly. The sun was
bright and noisy waves leaped at the nearby rocks, drenching

me with spray; and away beyond the sparkling and glinting of the blue-green sea Scotland lay clear on the horizon. During such interludes the North's tragedy seems merely a nightmare and its beauty the only reality.

In Larne I chose to have my pint in the town's poshest hotel. I had by then become an expert on where and how to meet whom and Larne seemed a promising hunting-ground for Protestant businessmen. This ploy was only too successful. I was made to feel very welcome by a group of moderate Unionists, immoderate Orangemen and disgruntled ex-local government officials. The pint became countless pints and the afternoon slipped away. It was dark when I wavered into Belfast in a happy haze.

One of my drinking companions—Henry, a senior Ulsterbus official—told me that on the previous day his company had lost £54,000 worth of buses. These had been burned by the UDA who that week were running a campaign of violence to protest against the ending of 'special category' status for political prisoners. When I asked why the UDA has not been made illegal Henry shrugged and said, "How can you outlaw the most powerful organisation in a state? It may be psychologically desirable but it's physically impossible."

In fact outlawing the UDA would seem 'psychologically undesirable' to many within the Protestant community. Most of my Larne friends would resent it were the organisation made illegal, despite what one elderly businessman described as its 'occasional regrettable excesses'. To the Protestant mind, the fact that the largest of the Protestant paramilitary organisations remains legal, no matter how subversive its activities, is a comforting (if confused and confusing) proof that the Protestant majority is still recognised by Britain as the rightful power in the land.

That night I stayed in Belfast with Catholic friends in what used to be a mixed middle-class area. A few years ago fifteen Catholic families lived on their road, now only four remain. The UDA decided to have 'a clearance' and a Protestant neighbour—a widow, living alone—told my friends that an armed man had called on her some months previously and ordered her never again to speak to any of the remaining

Catholics. "We don't want any publicity around here," he said. "We've got rid of most of them and we'll just shift the rest quietly, one by one." Very bravely, the widow reported this to the RUC and along came two plain clothes policemen and a representative of the Housing Authority. These men investigated in a ritualistic sort of way and then announced that there was really nothing they could do. So the widow it was that moved, to a country town. My friends showed me a letter in which she had written: 'It is a great relief to be able to speak to anyone I like without being threatened by gunmen.' The ambiguous role of the police is one of the most disconcerting features of the Northern scene.

Community workers often comment on the extraordinary capacity for self-discipline shown within No-Go areas from which the police have been completely excluded for years. A good example is the orderliness of many Republican drinking clubs. (There are also, of course, disorderly shebeens where fighting and heavy gambling are common.) I was taken one night to a newly-built Green club which from the street looked not unlike a Khyber Pass fortress. The security check at the door was one of the most thorough in my experience—even our matchboxes were opened by a smiling, chatty, gimlet-eyed woman—yet within it was all very ordinary. Just a large, crowded luxurious pub with colour television in one corner— the volume up full, but nobody listening—and groups of non-sinister looking men (and a few women) sitting around talking relaxedly. The drinks were blissfully cheap, presumably because they had come 'off the lorry'. Soon after our arrival the double-doors swung open to admit a children's fife and drum band, very smartly turned out in green kilts and white shirts. None of the children was over twelve and all their Provo fathers were 'inside'. The television sound was turned off while they played traditional airs very professionally indeed and collected a handsome sum for 'P. O. W.' comforts.

Then our table was approached by a man of about fifty, poorly dressed and very unwashed but perfectly sober. Fastening on to me, as a stranger, he began to air all the old obsessions; e.g., we should refer to the 'Free State' and never to the Republic of Ireland because there can be no Republic till the thirty-two counties are free. Tossing back his greasy grey locks he glared at me and announced, "But I don't want reunification with those rats you have below in the Dail! When we've got the Brits out the twenty-six counties can join *us*!" He pulled up a chair and sat beside me. "I'm not anti-Protestant—all those buggers who say this is a fuckin' religious war are *wrong*! In a thirty-two county Irish republic the Protestants could have all the religious freedom they want, and every other sort of freedom too. Mind you, I'm not for the Provo methods and I don't care who hears me say it"—he stared defiantly around and a tall young man with black hair and chestnut side-burns yelled from the bar, "Fuck off, Gerry! You're on'y too old! You didn't mind the methods in '58!"*

"Little youse can tell about '58!" retorted Gerry. "Still in your stinkin' nappies! If I was out then 'twas because we were fightin' a decent clean war and killin' on'y the Queen's men—not blowin' up women an' babies an' anythin' else that happens to be around. A bit o' discipline we had then and real officers and a bit o'humanity. I don't hold with the present carry-on and I'll say so anywhere to anyone!" He turned to me again. "Don't get me wrong," he said, suddenly anxious. "We're *all* for Provo aims, even if we don't fancy the way this lot is goin' about the job. Brits out! That's what we all want. Fifteen times I've been lifted by the troops—*fifteen* times! And nothin' could they ever pin on me. I'm just lifted, and me and me family tormented, because of '58. Eight hundred years' torment from the Brits—small wonder we're mad to see their backsides. All the best land they took off of us and that we must get back, which or whether. I could tell you where the land that was ours is, away below in the Co Down—and rich planters gettin' fatter on it every day and talkin' all the time about the lazy Taigs who wouldn't work for a livin' but go drinkin' on the dole!"

"But isn't it time," I suggested tritely, "to get on with living our own lives, instead of wrangling about our ancestors' misdeeds or misfortunes?" It was, however, quite impossible to unhook Gerry from the past; he seemed to need his grievance, to have built his whole personality around it. (Just as many in the Orange ghettos have built their personalities around an

* In 1958 the IRA were running an anti-Brit campaign in the border areas.

hysterical fear of Rome.) When he first began to talk I had felt only a mixture of exasperation and amusement. Then I began to feel pity and despair; and some fear, too. The combination of so much resentment—generations of resentment, forming the very marrow of the soul—the combination of that with the white-hot pseudo-patriotism cultivated by extreme Irish Republicanism prevents any glimmer of rationality getting through to the afflicted mind. When I asked Gerry how he proposed taking back 'his' land from the planters, while at the same time giving the Protestants 'every sort of freedom' he turned on me angrily and said, "'Tis easily known where you come from! Youse down South don't know the way we've suffered up here—and youse don't care! With a cabinet full of Creepin' Jaysuses grovellin' and whinin' around Westminster...."

"Pack it up, Gerry," interrupted my companion. "We know. We've got the message. You don't love the Dublin Government...."

"Does anybody?" asked a new voice. It was very indistinct, the difficulties of a strong Belfast accent being compounded by a prodigiously thick, bright-red beard through which words came as though the speaker were far away in a forest. But there was nothing unclear about his views. He hated the Dublin and London governments, all the Christian Churches and every form of Communism. He believed only in Irish Republicanism and saw it being threatened on the one hand by Christianity and on the other by Communism, with a third force called 'American materialism' waiting to finish it off if the others couldn't. But he was less clear about how Irish Republicanism might be made to work in an All-Ireland Republic containing a 25 per cent minority who abhorred it.

The next visitor to our table was a young man with shoulder-length hair, a pale, broad, handsome face and large dark eyes that were brilliant and mad. ("Charles II's double," observed my companion.) He came and knelt before me on one knee and clasped my right hand in both his hands as though he were about to swear that he would love me forever. Then he said, "The only way is to kill. Kill! Kill! Kill! Always in human history there was no justice without death. Good-bye." Quickly he stood up, and went. I looked at my companion. "An act he always puts on for journalists?" I suggested hopefully. "Or was he just plain drunk?" Tom shook his head. "Neither—he meant every word of it." I wondered then if being born into an unnaturally tense society drives some people mad who might otherwise have led relatively normal lives.

Next day I saw my first bomb explosion. At lunch-time I was sitting on the grass in front of the City Hall, eating a cheese sandwich and talking to two young shop-assistants from the British Home Stores. Then suddenly fire-engines began to arrive and the street opposite was cleared and the barrier at our end closed. Two elderly women who had been on their way to the shop next door to the bomb-target came to sit near us, fuming against the slackness of the security arrangements. One suggested that armies of unemployed should be recruited as searchers but her companion quickly pointed out that this would never do. "You've to be able to trust security officers and you wouldn't know what sort a dole crowd might be. Provos themselves, most likely." It is not really surprising that bombs can still be smuggled into the supposedly closely-guarded city centre. Trade would soon be crippled if the main shopping areas of a city of 360,000 people were effectively guarded.

The bomb went off with a loud bang which shook me ridiculously though I had been waiting for it. But there were no 'earth-tremors'. 'A controlled explosion', one of the shop girls explained knowledgeably.

I moved to the barrier then and watched the small fire being fought while corporation workmen quickly and efficiently swept up buckets full of broken glass. The assistants who worked in the damaged shop were patiently awaiting permission to re-enter the premises where business would at once be resumed in as much of the place as was left. The men and women of the security forces stood around looking benevolent and relaxed and an increasing crowd gathered at the barrier, waiting for it to open so that they could get on with their shopping. To me this seemed an extraordinary scene yet to those around me it was all part of the day's work. Passers-by, or newcomers join-ing the crowd, asked anxiously, "Anyone hurt?" Then, having been reassured, they went on their way or settled down to read their newspapers. Of course professional grumblers operate in Belfast as elsewhere. One woman remarked to her husband, "No other country would put up with it. We've had seven years of it now. Who could live with it?" Her spouse did not reply. He had, I imagine, heard these remarks before.

A tall, middle-aged, pale-faced man came to stand beside me; he was out for his lunch-break from a City Hall office. "You'd wonder sometimes", he said, "how much of it is terrorism and how much sheer psychosis. Just think—the bomber could be anywhere in this crowd, watching and enjoying the turmoil he's caused. The physical, visible destruction, the inconvenience to thousands of citizens, the cash-loss—all that stock gone up in flames—and the cost of paying all those extra security forces and firemen and corporation workers. And probably it's all been caused by one or two cool teenagers who known their way about. Imagine the satisfaction it could give some nut-case with a lust for power, or a personal grudge against society, or just a craving for excitement."

By this time an immense queue had formed at the barrier and in response to the urgings of two mothers with crying babies one of a group of soldiers opened the entry gate on his own initiative. As shoppers began to stream though a senior RUC officer swung around and sharply ordered the soldier to turn back the crowd and keep the barrier sealed. Spewing obscenities, the youngster violently kicked the gate until it clicked shut. Then he glared at the RUC inspector's back with what seemed to me an altogether disproportionate degree of hatred. I could imagine how he would behave, while in that sort of mood, to someone even suspected of terrorism. Yet the incident had been occasioned by his soft-hearted response to the pleas of two harassed young mothers. Another mother with three small children was standing beside me. "He's mad for being caught in the wrong," she observed. "They can't stand each other, the army and the RUC. Always tryin' to catch each other out."

Later that day, near Queen's University, I paused to watch a huge blaze destroying an antique shop and the three-storey dwelling above it. The few onlookers were remarking to each other that this was what you got if you stopped paying 'the rates'. The shop had recently been bought by a devout Presby-

terian from North Antrim who had told 'them' that it was
against his conscience to pay protection-money. In this case
'they' were Loyalist paramilitaries. "It's not sensible to argue
with them," said one sad little man. "You're better off paying
quiet and regular and never mind your conscience. Isn't it
worse a lot to see all you've got in ruins?"

His companion nodded. "'Tis on'y a fool won't pay.
Nobody's ashamed no more to give in."

At dusk, as I was returning to North Belfast, I noticed an
unusual number of UDR and RUC men lining the Upper
Crumlin Road. In my favourite off-licence the owner's wife
announced, "There's more trouble coming. It's in the air."
That off-licence has been blown up twice within the past four
years and a few months ago the owner's nearby home was badly
damaged when a car-bomb went off outside the hall door.
Opposite the shop all the fire-engines from the local station were
leaving for the city centre where yet another cloud of smoke
was rising high.

It is now safer to live in a ghetto rather than in a mixed area
which makes the task of the paramilitary 'Housing Authorities'
much easier. So I was told when I visited Brendan and Bernie,
a Catholic couple in their fifties who live in a still mixed street
of working-class houses. For security reasons this couple share
a bedroom with their four teenage children and every night
draw a four-foot-wide wardrobe across the door. Many other
families along the street do likewise. Within the past two and
a half years there have been four assassinations in this small
area. Last year, a few days before Christmas, the widower in
the house opposite—a Protestant electrician, who often worked
for government departments—was shot by the Provos in his
hall-way and died in Bernie's arms while Brendan was
telephoning for an ambulance. Nine months later, Bernie had
not fully recovered from this experience. We tend to forget how
many people are involved in the North's violence, apart from
the victim and his or her immediate family. Every death spreads
its ripples of fear, grief and hate throughout a whole neighbour-
hood.

Brendan—a community worker—told me that one of his
major problems is getting children's social centres organised in

such a way that they can remain social centres. Such places commonly start off well, getting government grants for structural alterations and attracting lots of youngsters. But they are often taken over by Orange or Green paramilitary groups who either close the doors completely to children and turn the place into a drinking club or use the centre as a recruiting agency. A few days previously I had met the Chairman of one Youth Club who was so badly beaten up eight months ago, when he tried to protect his centre from the local paramilitaries, that he is still on crutches.

Another of Brendan's worries is how best to occupy schoolchildren during the summer holidays. After several years experience he has decided that it is not a good idea to send selected groups abroad for a few weeks. The majority find it hard to settle down when they get home and some, having tasted luxurious living, give their parents hell on finding themselves back in ghetto-land. Some of his colleagues, however, believe that those disadvantages are worth enduring for the sake of broadening the minds of the next generation. Most community workers encourage inter-denominational holiday schemes in Ireland, even if these are only day trips to the sea. One brave young Protestant, who works in a Catholic community centre where one of his colleagues was shot dead beside him last year, expressed the general attitude. "They may outwardly revert to type before they're five minutes back in their home districts, but having shared ordinary childhood experiences will have sown the seeds of an inner recognition of the other side's humanity. And *inner changes* are what we have to work for." That same young man told me that many of the teenagers in his club can remember playing with 'the Oranges' when they were small. And they wish those days were back, if only because they then had so much more freedom of movement.

When I first heard Belfast experts pessimistically discussing the long-term effects of violence on young people, I wondered if they were not underestimating the resilience of youth. By September I knew better. Almost every day I had met a child or adolescent who had been adversely affected by the poisonous atmosphere of the past seven years. For a time I tried to keep things in perspective by telling myself that the situation could be much worse, that after all Northern Ireland is not enduring a real war with hundreds being killed in a day. But I am no longer sure that a full-scale war would be worse than this long-drawn-out agony of communal tension and suspicion, and suppurating resentment and revengefulness. Physically a 'real' war would of course be much more dreadful while it lasted—and much more obvious to the outside world and therefore bad for Britain's image as 'the referee'. But nothing could be more spiritually destructive than the present situation.

Resilience is one thing—all the Northern Irish seem to have more than their share of it—but the young are very vulnerable to fear. In a quiet-seeming suburban home I met a mother who described what is by now a typical experience of Belfast parents. This educated sensible woman has done all in her power to give her three daughters a calm and happy home-life. Yet when the family went to London for a holiday the twelve-year-old became mysteriously ill and after a few days her elder sister discovered that she was terrified of having to walk past so many parked cars to get anywhere. Although she is an intelligent child it was impossible to reason her out of her terror, so profoundly has the car-bomb campaign affected her.

One of Brendan's neighbours told me that when she took her teenage daughter and son to Dublin for a few days their greatest treat was stolling up and down O'Connell Street after dark, feeling free to go into any café for a hamburger or a coke. At least these two were able to relish their freedom; other parents told me that their youngsters, when taken on holidays, were too nonplussed by liberty to enjoy it. The understandable restrictions imposed on many middle-class children must do almost as much harm—of a different sort—as that freedom to vandalise which is so common in ghetto areas.

There are some 10,000 vandalised empty houses in Belfast, according to an official Housing Authority estimate. On a few occasions I have watched the ghetto vandals at work. Most of them are in the eight to thirteen age group, old enough to have considerable physical strength but too young to be in any paramilitary gang. They hunt in packs, armed with a variety of tools, and swarm all over a building taking a wild delight in demolishing it. They smash windows, break down doors, rip walls asunder, chop up staircases, shatter bathroom fittings, pull down ceilings and pull up floors. They pay not the slightest attention to anyone who tries to stop them and their parents, if aware of what the wains are up to, often choose either not to notice or to abuse any outsider who may have attempted to intervene. This is among the most harrowing of Belfast's many vicious circles. All these youngsters need help, yet as things are it is virtually impossible to reach them either physically or emotionally. A lot could be done if an army of social workers were to replace the soldiers on the streets; but for that to happen the British would have to adopt a new philosophical approach to the whole problem.

There is nothing fundamentally amiss with such vandals. They are ordinary children who have been born into extraordinary circumstances. Watching them being mindlessly destructive, it is easy to forget this and to feel outraged by their deeds rather than by the society which has bred them.

One afternoon, in the grimmest of the Catholic ghettos, I was cautiously cycling along a glass-strewn street when I noticed smoke pouring through the smashed windows of a comparatively new but thoroughly vandalised two-storey house. Squeals of childish laughter came from inside, inspiring a ghastly vision of tiny charred corpses being found a few hours later. I went to the gap where once a hall-door had been and peered through the smoke. Amidst the rubble, ten six-to-eight-year-olds (including three girls) had made a bonfire of doors already chopped up by slightly older vandals. They recognised 'the lady with the bike'—I had been that way before—and greeted me delightedly. One little girl offered me a squashed and dust-impregnated peppermint cream and politely invited me to sit on the floor. When I suggested that the whole building—and the occupied houses on either side—might soon go up in smoke, everybody giggled happily at the prospect. Then suddenly they lost interest in their bonfire and spontaneously followed me outside to talk. Their questions—of a sort with which, as the mother of an eight-year-old, I am only too familiar—revealed a pathetic ignorance and an even more pathetic longing to learn. In that group there was only one dull child; the rest had nimble, eager, hungry little minds. And it is significant that the moment an outsider arrived, to provide some mental stimulus, they lost interest in their destructive play. This is the age at which they need to be rescued from their circumstances. Within three or four years they will be confirmed, professional vandals, proud of an anti-social life-style and scornful of attempts to change it. What better breeding-ground could there be for the paramilitaries of 1990?

We had been sitting chatting on the broken pavement for about half an hour when one little boy begged to be allowed to ride on Roz. He was much too small to reach the pedals from the saddle but none the less went happily whizzing off around the block. When he returned everyone else had to have a go and until I had firmly laid down the law there was some dissension about whose turn it was next. Then all went well until a tough-looking fourteen-year-old joined us. (His father, I afterwards discovered, is serving a life-sentence for killing a policeman.) This lad wanted a ride *at once* and ignored my protests that the little ones must first have their turn. When the seven-year-old who had just taken over Roz tried to pedal away, the newcomer knocked him to the ground and then picked him up by the shoulders and before I could intervene had cracked his head three times, hard, on the road. Four other adolescents then arrived and the largest of them—he could have been seventeen—attacked the fourteen-year-old with his fists before himself taking off on Roz.

As I cuddled the whimpering seven-year-old I realised what a sheltered life I lead. Presumably this sort of thing goes on all over the world in urban slums but my travels do not normally take me into such places. So now I was trembling in reaction to the sheer brutality of these boys' behaviour. It was not at all like the usual sort of male adolescent horseplay; afterwards, trying to analyse the difference, I decided that it lay in the purposefulness of this ghetto violence. For these boys, there is only one way to get what you want—through force. Restraint and negotiation are so foreign to them that they are not prepared to wait five minutes for anything. And outsiders feel shaken by such scenes because they are reminders of how close violence is to the surface of human nature—everybody's nature. When one has been brought up in an environment which inhibits physical violence almost from the moment of birth, it is easy to forget this.

Some ten minutes had passed before it occurred to me that I might never see Roz, or my luggage, again. My luggage consisted of a sponge-bag, a beloved flea-bag which by now has acquired mascot-status and several expensive new books. However, Roz was my main worry; you can get an artificial leg or a new bicycle but it's not the same thing.... For the first time I *felt* the full implications of a No-Go area. Apart from his inherent honesty, there was no reason that I could see why that boy should return my property. (When I remarked on this later to a ghetto friend he said dryly, "People have been knee-capped for less. We may be a No-Go area but we're not lawless. Those lads all know what they would get if they stole from a visitor." A comment that reminded me of Afghanistan.) For whatever reason, Roz was safely restored to me after half an hour. Whereupon I decided that enough was enough and left my young friends stirring up the embers of their fire.

On the following morning I had my only personal encounter with paramilitary violence. The UDA were still running their protest campaign, against the abolition of special category status for political prisoners, and as I was cycling towards West Belfast I saw a road-block some hundred yards ahead of me. To have taken an alternative route would have made me late for an important appointment and punctuality is among my few virtues. A solitary RUC man stood at the junction where I had paused to consider the situation; he was diverting all the traffic to avoid confrontations between angry motorists and the UDA. When I asked his advice he said, "They'll probably let a cyclist through." So I continued towards the line of apparently unarmed 'volunteers' who were turning back those cars and taxis which had approached them through streets where no police were on duty. Most of the taxis were packed with women, small children and push-chairs; it was a Saturday morning, when many go into the city centre to do their weekly 'big shop'. In that area the victims would have been mainly Protestant and as they were ordered to leave the taxis and walk home they did not hesitate to tell the UDA what they thought of them, often in terms not fit for the ears of small children.

As I approached the 'volunteers' I was waved back and a man shouted angrily, "Can't you fuckin' see this is a road-block?" At that point I should have wordlessly vanished. But suddenly an obsessional punctuality was reinforced by an indignant impulse to assert my right to use the Queen's highway. Although assert is much too strong a word; I merely asked politely if I might go around the edge as I had a very important appointment nearby.

The moment he heard my accent the leader switched his attention from a taxi, pointed to the spot where I stood and said curtly, "You stay right there. We'll have to think what to do about you." To emphasise his order, he stepped forward and kicked Roz's front wheel with a large boot, breaking five spokes. He looked ridiculously like what one would have expected him to look like—a short chunky man with coarse features and small bloodshot eyes.

For the next twenty-three minutes—I was very time-con-scious that morning—I stood in the middle of the road being pornographically insulted at intervals by those thirty men. This was an extraordinarily effective method of mental torture. It eventually reduced me to tears of humiliation though by normal standards I am a tough old boot. I would have far pre-ferred a beating-up. As it was, I knew that if I did or said nothing provocative I was in no danger. The anti-censorship advo-cates of 'porn for all' might profitably reflect on such examples of the connection between porn and violence—something I had often heard about without ever expecting to observe it.

Altogether this was an enormously instructive incident. I recognised one of the 'volunteers' as a man with whom I had spent two hours drinking pints a few days previously. He gave no indication of ever having seen me before; indeed, he was one of the most foul-mouthed of the gang. In a devious way, this consoled me when I thought about it afterwards. Here 'gang' or 'herd' is the key word. As an individual, this man is not evil. He is not even truly bigoted or he would never have talked to me as he did in that pub. But he is a man of low intelli-gence and minimal education and therefore he is susceptible to every sort of social and moral infection. He, too, is a victim—as who, in Northern Ireland, is not?

Other victims were nearby, as I stood waiting for my ordeal to end. Twenty yards beyond the UDA were six armed policemen who could hear some of the obscenities that were being shouted at me. And thirty yards beyond them a military patrol stood around near their armoured vehicles. But nobody dared move forward to interfere; had they done so—I was later informed by a local Protestant clergyman—they would have been surrounded within minutes by hundreds of well-armed UDA members.

When the 'volunteers' became bored they contemptuously signalled to me to pass their barrier; why they did not then turn me back is just another of the many minor mysteries of Belfast life. I paused by a policemen, nodded towards the UDA and asked, "What do they think they are doing?" The sergeant, his eyes narrowed with rage, glared at the road-block and said, "They're trying to be big boys—and succeeding. Because we can't lay hands on them to break their fuckin' necks!" (It was only afterwards that I appreciated this anatomical inexactitude.) Approaching the army patrol, I realised that the young lieutenant had been observing my experience through binoculars. He looked embarrassed and apologetic and offered advice about the nearest bicycle shop. His men looked tense and angry. No wonder the security forces so often misbehave. They have too much frustration in their lives to be able to exercise the sort of ideal self-control required by the situation. If youngsters are armed and trained to fight, and then are curbed hard in situations that would seem to call for action, naturally they become more and more aggressive. And so violence spirals, every day drawing newcomers into its savage vortex.

Only by transposing the Northern Ireland security situation to Britain can one appreciate its 'through the looking-glass' quality. Imagine a Hampshire regiment helping The Angry Brigade to acquire arms and military training—covertly, yet with the tacit approval of large sections of the population. Then imagine that organisation regularly obtaining protection money from thousands of helpless citizens, and occasionally setting up road-blocks throughout the Home Counties, and hijacking and burning dozens of London Transport buses as a protest against those of their members who were in gaol being treated as common criminals. Next, imagine that Brigade telling the police and army—as the UDA did in September 1976— that they would call off their campaign of disruption and destruction *if* none of their members was arrested. Finally, imagine this bargaining being effective, though the police knew exactly who had planned and directed the havoc. One simply cannot imagine such things happening in Britain. Yet in theory Belfast is just another city of the UK where Her Majesty's subjects are no less entitled to the blessings of democracy than the inhabitants of Manchester or York.

On a late September day as hot as mid-summer, I boarded a Protestant 'Peace Ladies' bus. The young Presbyterian minister—dark-suited and dog-collared—welcomed me warmly but distractedly; five of his ladies were missing and it was almost time to leave for a distant town. His colleague, if that is not being over-ecumenical, was an even younger Church of Ireland curate in a T-shirt and jeans. Much later, when my Presbyterian neighbour and I were on first name terms, she confided her dislike of clergy who look like Teddy-boys. (A quaint term, yet somehow not surprising from an elderly Belfast lady.) Everybody had a picnic basket and was in an 'outing' mood to match the weather. Halfway to our destination we stopped for lunch on a wide verge of yellowed grass. When other Peace buses passed, their labels telling us from which Belfast district they came, we waved and cheered and clapped; and the cheering was that much louder for a Catholic bus. Long before we got to the rallying point a tremendous atmosphere of unity and hope had been generated. It was a very happy feeling. Even on sweet thermos-flask tea my spirits rose.

Among my companions there was much predictable anti-Paisley talk and some less predictable criticism of the Reverend Martin Smyth who had recently abandoned 'exploratory' talks with the SDLP. Nobody was impressed when I suggested that Mr Smyth might not be personally responsible for the breakdown—that he has to cater for the mob behind him and cannot be considered his own master, even if he is Grand Master of the Orange Order. "They're all rotten, them politicians!" said one young woman with a thin, lined face. That evening, when she and I were on our own, searching for the right bus, she told me that her UVF husband got a ten-year sentence in 1973. Their four children hardly know him. "I went to see him yesterday and he told me, so he did, 'If I was out of this place I'd be Peace Marching with yous.' But he can't say that where he is. He'd be beat up if he did."

There were an estimated 20,000 Peace People at that rally and it was very moving, as we marched through a largely Catholic town, to hear many of the local onlookers cheering especially loudly as Protestant groups passed by. (Each group marched behind its own enormous banner.) Of course other onlookers did not cheer but merely stared impassively. And there were a few small boys and pimply youths who treated us to obscene gestures and Provo slogans. These youngsters provoked several minor scuffles, one of which I witnessed. It started after the march, during the hymn-singing and praying. Three Provos on a high grassy embankment just behind me began to shout abuse which the crowd drowned by chanting . "We want Peace! We want Peace!" Then one Provo recognised an Andersonstown woman beside me and yelled—"You fuckin' bitch!" while giving what is I believe now known as the Harvey Smith sign. (An odd way of achieving immortality, when one comes to think of it.) At once the woman's adolescent son hurled himself on the Provo and in the ensuing mêlée three old ladies were knocked to the ground. A nearby television reporter was busy filming the scene and one woman put her headscarf over the camera and begged him not to show violence. He swiftly removed the scarf, saying coldly, "Our editor will decide what to use." All around me, as young men were tussling with the Provos, women exclaimed, "They're not well—be easy on them!" "Leave them alone—they can't help it!" "Don't call the police!" Then a girl-friend of one of the Provos, who had been among the marchers, abandoned her fellow-Peace Women to try to defend her boy-friend. As he broke away from—or was released by—his opponent she flung her arms around him and he quickly kissed her. Together they scrambled a little way up the embankment before turning to face the crowd. Still clinging to each other, they flung hysterical defiance at us—and then burst into tears. They were very young.

"She came on the March because she wanted to get him outa the Provos," explained the woman beside me who had known both since they were in push-chairs. "But now he's got her feelin' ashamed for desertin' so instead of him leavin' the lads I suppose she'll be joinin' them." At that point, I felt my euphoria evaorating. It is too easy for the uninvolved to be Peace Marchers, publicly proclaiming their abhorrence of violence. For the people of the ghettos, life is not so simple.

During the march we had heard a mighty explosion in the direction of the nearby border and seen a huge pillar of smoke against the cloudless sky. As we dispersed, to look for our buses, word spread that an oil-truck had been hi-jacked at the border, loaded with a bomb and the driver ordered to take it to a depot where it went up according to plan. What must that driver's feelings have been as he wondered how accurate was the timing-device?

After the rally, the town suddenly seemed full of army vehicles and foot-patrols in combat dress with weapons at the ready and camouflaged faces. Soon my spirits were rising again; never before had I seen troops looking relaxed in Northern Ireland. Instead of being surrounded, as they usually are in Catholic areas, by a public which likes to show how much it hates them, they were moving through throngs of Peace People who smiled at them kindly. For me their response was the most memorable feature of that day. Instead of the hostile expressions they so often (and so understandably) wear, their black-streaked faces were split by delighted white grins as they returned the Peace People's friendly greetings. At one stage a girl from a Catholic ghetto was walking with me. As we passed a tall young soldier she smiled at him and said, "We'll soon have yous out of a job!" The soldier smiled back. "I hope so!" he said—with a depth of feeling which gave those three syllables an extraordinary eloquence. Had that girl dared in her home district to treat a Brit as another human being she would have been 'suitably punished'. I felt then that the Peace Movement was worthwhile, even if it never achieved anything more than these small gleams of humanity through the clouds.

Not many hours later this sentimentality—if such it was—was being scorned by a clinically cool mind in Belfast. "Did you not notice," said Susan (originally from Dublin), "that most of your fellow-marchers were not *real* grass-roots but the next layer up?" (I had noticed.) "Of course you can be more optimistic about it all after you've been out feeling benign with 20,000 others. But don't forget that for many a Peace Rally has become something to do on an otherwise humdrum Saturday afternoon."

We tried then to imagine the Peace Ladies at home, urging their local paramilitaries to pack up the guns and 'go political'. Susan agreed that being aware of the moral support of so many others might give some people more courage for this task. But we both had to admit that we found it hard to imagine any paramilitary paying the slightest attention to such advice. And without anything to show for their efforts, could the Peace People be expected to sustain their enthusiasm?

"I'm afraid it's no good," said Susan. "If Peace is to be anything more than a symptom of exhaustion, it must be preceded, or at least accompanied, by other things. Like justice, as the Provos so rightly say."

Susan has been living in Belfast since before The Troubles began and I asked her if she thought belonging to the Peace Movement would make it easier for people to co-operate with the security forces. "Already there's more co-operation," she said, "but I don't think it can ever be enough to make a great difference. Bowing to intimidation has become a mental habit with most people, even when there's not much risk. They feel superstitious about informing, as though it must inevitably draw bad luck on them. And often they feel dependent on the paramilitaries—a feeling that's going to get stronger the longer we're left without our own government. In Protestant areas you've people who hate and fear the UVF or whatever and will march their shoes off for peace every week—and yet won't inform because they believe they may yet need their paras for protection. This is especially so in East Belfast. The RUC have a very bad name there for thieving and looting after a fire or a bomb. And of course you get the same feeling in Catholic areas."

Next day I met a government-employed psychiatrist who explained a further convolution of the informing issue. As a government servant he feels doubly bound to pass on any information that comes his way yet as a social worker it would be almost impossible for him to achieve anything without the co-operation and trust of the local paramilitaries. By now, he said, there is a vast No-Man's-Land between the legal and illegal worlds of Northern Ireland. Anybody who works in that region has to forget his 'obligation to society' and keep his mouth shut.

This dedicated man looked as though he had long since lost the knack of relaxing. He mentioned having recently attended a football match in England to study crowd behaviour. "The difference there," he said, "was that when a gang turned rough the crowd withdrew, isolating them for police attention. Here it would have advanced to join them. That's what we're up against. And even if some wizard found a political solution in the morning we'd have that sort of problem on our plate for generations to come. But at least if less was being spent on security more would be available for rehabilitation."

10

The Special Case of South Armagh

Two days after Christmas, on a bright icy afternoon, I crossed the border on foot and turned west away from the main Dublin–Belfast road. (Sadly, on this fortnight's mid-winter return to the North I was without Roz because of the time-factor.) As usual, I could not be sure precisely where I had crossed the border. On the bus from Dundalk my fellow-passengers had been talking about a young man who was charged in the local court with driving an uninsured car. The case was dismissed after it had been proved that when the gardai stopped him his car's off-wheels were in the Republic while its near-wheels were in Northern Ireland.

An eight-man military foot-patrol was the first indication that I had arrived back North. Their faces had been blackened to hinder identification and render them less conspicuous as they lurked in ditches; and coming on them thus, ten minutes after leaving the normality of the Republic, gave me a mild culture-shock. Crossing the border into South Armagh is not at all like crossing into Co Fermanagh, or even Derry. Then suddenly I discerned an element of grotesque comedy in the situation. It seemed ludicrous, on the outskirts of a quiet Irish village, to have these eight young Englishmen, in full combat-kit and armed to the teeth, moving cautiously—as though in some Burmese or Malayan jungle—between rows of neat little cottages and new bungalows where children were playing with Christmas toys in small front gardens. Then I found myself wishing irritably that all concerned would stop being so child-ish, that the Gaels would drop their demented posturing about an unattainable united Ireland and the Brits their provocative deploying of troops all over a quiet countryside.

Beneath their camouflage these Brits looked pleasantly surprised when I wished them a Happy New Year and the lieuten-ant—he had a gentle, unmilitary voice—went to a lot of trouble to explain exactly how I could find the crossroads pub I was seeking.

Half-a-mile further on, beyond the village, I saw a solitary two-storey house with an inscription in huge white letters on the gable-end facing me: YOU ARE NOW IN PROVOLAND. Beside the inscription was an accurate painting of a rifle, three times life-size, that seemed to be pointing towards me. Round the next corner I came on another inscription, carefully painted right across the narrow road in three lines of letters two feet high. It said—THE ONLY GOOD BRITISH SOLDIER IS A DEAD ONE. The letters are so large, I was told later by one of the artists, because the message is intended to reach the helicopter crews who patrol the border and the foot-patrols who are transported from point to point by helicopter because the Provos have made it far too dangerous to move them on the ground. I looked up from the road and across the still, frost-bound, hilly terrain—poor land for farmers (which is why the population is almost entirely Catholic) but good land for fugitives. And I thought of those eight youths on patrol, who probably know nothing whatever about The Irish Problem. How do they feel, when they first come across such inscriptions? They have been sent to Northern Ireland, they often believe, to prevent the Irish from killing each other, burning each other's houses, blowing each other up. They have not come to conquer new territory, subdue the natives or do any of those old-fashioned, imperialistic, military things. But however neutral they may feel on arrival towards the North's various factions, so many taunting flourishes on walls and roads cannot fail to provoke a Paddy-bashing mentality—which in turn further alienates the Catholic population. In certain areas the Provos are now able to recruit from traditionally 'moderate' Catholic families whose sons—and daughters—would not for an instant have considered joining the IRA in 1968. Numerically the Provos have undoubtedly lost support among ordinary folk but the continuing presence of the army has ensured them a steady flow of (not always very suitable) replacements for active service campaigns.

Walking on, I reflected that it had been silly of me to feel impatient about the foot-patrol's melodramatic progress through a quiet village. For the Brits, life in South Armagh has to be melodramatic. And it can be tragic. Not half-a-mile from where I paused to read that inscription, Captain Nairac was to be kidnapped—and apparently killed—by the IRA five months later. He had been gathering intelligence and it seems nobody warned him that his regular drinking in civvies with the locals in their pubs was literally suicidal.

In the pub, when eventually I found it, half-a-dozen men were sitting around a huge log fire recovering from Christmas. I roused suspicion at first by speaking Irish. Innocently, I had assumed that this would prove to the South Armagh people that I was not an English spy feigning a Southern brogue. But when my 'contact' had joined me it was explained that the Special Air Service personnel posted to South Armagh are believed to include some Southern Irishmen who speak fluent Irish. The Brits are also believed to employ Southern Irishwomen to collect information (nobody in South Armagh cares to use the word 'spy'). So much for my little attempt to be linguistically diplomatic.

Visitors to South Armagh are comparatively rare in midwinter—or at any other season, for that matter. I was therefore welcomed as a novelty and also, when it emerged that I was writing about Northern Ireland, as a possible mouthpiece for the Republican cause. (This is not necessarily the same thing as the Provo cause; some of those men were very anti-Provo.) But my companions found it hard to believe that an English publisher would bring out a book not loaded in favour of the Brits. And they considered my ponderings and probings a gratuitous complicating of a perfectly simple situation. They had the answer: BRITS OUT! TROUBLE OVER!

A grey-faced man of about fifty sat in a corner saying very little; he was introduced to me as the father of two boys, aged fourteen and sixteen, who had been killed not long before by a booby-trap bomb left near their home—for the benefit of the Brits—in a wrecked car. The boys had been trying to remove a door-handle when the bomb went off instantly killing both. Their father, however, seemed to feel no bitterness against the Provos; or if he did he was prudently concealing it. He blamed himself, he said, for not having sufficiently warned the lads to keep away from wrecked cars, abandoned refrigerators or cookers and inexplicable milk-churns. To the company in general those two boys were war casualties, not victims of terrorism. Had they been looking for someone to blame they would certainly have chosen the Brits, arguing that only their presence makes it necessary to plant bombs around the countryside.

Tentatively, I confessed to feeling a certain amount of sympathy for the ordinary British soldier, who is only doing his job by patrolling the fields and air-spaces of South Armagh. At once three men replied simultaneously that the Brits are legitimate targets. They are volunteers, not conscripts, and when they join the British army they know they will be sent to Northern Ireland where there is a war on and they may be killed. From the point of view of the speaker, to whom the Provos are a morally defensible army fighting for a just cause, this was sound reasoning. The whole concept of an 'illegal organisation' is utterly meaningless in certain areas under certain circumstances. To the people of South Armagh the Brits are the illegal army, occupying their territory against the will of virtually the entire population.

Another massive log was thrown on the fire, more pints were pulled, and outside, the last of the light drained away beyond Slieve Gullion. A helicopter snarled past overhead, very low, stopping our conversation. Then it returned, and returned again. When it had finally moved off the man beside me shrugged. "Annoying," he said, "but not as annoying as when they do it for an hour non-stop in the middle of the night, over a row of houses where innocent people are trying to sleep." I stared into the fire, saying nothing but reflecting that from the British angle nobody is innocent in South Armagh.

When I steered the conversation towards the Peace Movement the reaction was predictable; and all over South Armagh, during the next few days, I found it echoed. The Peace People were condemned and derided as tools of the British. The fact that Mrs Ewart-Biggs, Lord Longford and John Biggs-Davidson shared the platform with them at the Trafalgar Square Rally at the end of November 1976, and that Queen Elizabeth mentioned them approvingly in her Christmas Day speech, completely antagonised those Catholics without whose support

the Movement can never hope to achieve anything very significant. The three founders, who all come of Belfast Catholic back-
grounds, have been criticised for failing to foresee this reaction.
But one has to remember that at the time they were totally
bemused by the world-wide publicity to which they had been
exposed. The Northern Ireland Office, however, should have
had the nous to muzzle quietly those well-meaning supporters
whose touch was death to the Movement's influence in Republican circles.

At about seven o'clock my 'contact' and I left the pub to
walk three miles to an isolated farmhouse where we were to
meet a young couple who would, I had been assured, give me
an insight into Provo thinking.

The air was hurtfully cold as we followed a narrow side-road
by starlight. Underfoot ice crackled, and overhead helicopters
swarmed noisily; usually at least three were visible. Regularly
their searchlights picked us out and held us for an instant in
a wavering beam. They obviously intended finding out exactly
where we were going and, probably, how long we would remain
there and where we would go next. Twice, machines with no
lights of any sort passed very close, hedge-hopping. These were
big troop carriers which can put forty men out in the fields.
"A fine file they must have on you by now," my companion
remarked conversationally, "you were around so long during
the summer." It is not pleasant to realise that in a part of the
British Isles one's movements are being closely scrutinised and
tucked away in a computer for future reference. The whole process gives off an unappetising and very un-British aroma.

Again, as we walked along that road, my rationality was
offended by the situation—the sheer lunacy of this tiny corner
of Northern Ireland absorbing so much of the British tax-
payers' money while the local people become daily more exasperated by and resolute against 'Brit coercion'. Perhaps the
local emotion was infectious; I suddenly found myself resenting
those busy machines with their snooping searchlights. When
I said as much to my companion he laughed and teased—"I
thought you were the one who felt sorry for the Brits!"

"I am sorry for them" I said, "but don't you ever feel two
contradictory emotions at the same time?"

"Never!" he replied. "I'm a plain simple Irishman and these days I only have room inside me for one emotion—and that's not sympathy for the Brits!"

The farm kitchen was not at all traditional, with its gas cooker, chromium sink, plastic table-cloth, strip lighting and Tintawn. But the young couple's conversation made up for that. They talked as though we were still living in 1916, a few months after the Rising. 'Provo thinking' is a misleading phrase. The Provos don't think; they inherit fixed attitudes and on the basis of those they feel deeply and act ruthlessly. They are equally impervious to reasoned argument and moral exhortation because they believe themselves to be wearing the armour of righteousness. In this respect they are much closer to the extreme Loyalists than to the bulk of the Catholic population of Northern Ireland.

Our host—we might as well call him Paddy—was a man in his early thirties with a strong square face, raven-black hair and dark brown eyes. He had a subtle sense of humour which, unfortunately, didn't function on the political plane; if it did, he could not be a paramilitary. Humour is no frivolous quality but the ingredient that keeps us sane.

Paddy believed that the Brits are determined never to leave Northern Ireland, whatever their politicians may imply publicly to the contrary—a common conviction in South Armagh. Some Armagh people, however, prefer to think that the British are longing to go but for strategic reasons the Americans won't let them. The thought of the once-mighty British being pushed around by the Yanks gives much satisfaction in this part of the world.

As we ate a late high-tea the too familiar Provo line was repeated several times—"There can be no peace till we drive the Brits out." After tea Paddy's wife handed him their six-months-old daughter, to be 'winded' while she was undressing their two-year-old son by the fire. "And what then?" I asked. "When the Brits have been driven out?"

Paddy looked rather annoyed but remained polite. "Haven't you read our plans? The Loyalists can run their own show in one corner—*we* don't want to dictate to them." The baby burped dutifully and Paddy beamed at her.

"But supposing they don't want to stay in one corner?"

Paddy laughed. "Leave them to us! If the British took away their support there isn't one Loyalist would dare come near a Republican area. They're a bunch of bullies and cowards. So long as they've 14,000 Brits between them and us they'll parade around with guns—but just watch them running when the Brits are gone! Have you noticed? Not one Catholic was assassinated in South Armagh this past year. You know why? Because we executed a busload of Loyalists last January!" He handed his daughter back to her mother and took his son on his knee for a bedtime cuddle, stroking back his hair and kissing his forehead.

I stared at Paddy in silence, lacking the courage to challenge his euphemism and wondering if he really believed that all Loyalists are cowards. Apparently he did; there was no trace of bluff in his manner. I remarked then that the Loyalists, too, remember 1916, when over 5,000 fearless Ulstermen died in the Battle of the Somme. Paddy, however, brushed that aside. One of the basic differences between Green and Orange paramilitaries is that the former live in a fantasy-world but the latter do not. They do not need to; if Britain withdrew and a civil war ensued and the Republic did not intervene the Oranges would win—and they know this. Some even feel that they would win despite the Republic's intervention. And given their numbers and equipment and fanaticism this seems sufficiently probable not to qualify as fantasy.

At midnight I stood up to go; my escort was staying at the farmhouse. Paddy, helping me on with my coat, asked, "Well— is South Armagh as bad as you thought?"

"Why should I have thought it bad?"

Paddy shrugged. "What about the propaganda? 'Bandit country' and all that.... Down south you listen like a lot of zombies to what the Brits tell you. That slandering is what we won't forgive in a hurry. It's one thing to have taken our land and persecuted us for 800 years—we'll forget that as soon as we've got the land back. But—'Reputation, reputation, reputation! O, I have lost my reputation! I have lost the immortal part of myself, and what remains is bestial!'"

"Isn't that unpatriotic?" I said. "Quoting a Brit?"

Paddy chuckled and opened the door. "He's not a Brit! He belongs to everyone!"

As I walked across the farmyard I thought what a congenial friend Paddy would make if only he could be 'defanaticised', as my mother used to say. More strongly than ever I felt that communication between individuals must be part of the answer to Northern Ireland's problem. Before going North myself I had quite lost sight of the Provos as human beings. They had become mere symbols of violence and unreason, sinister masked figures without pity or love. And one can grow to hate symbols. But few people, I believe, can hate individuals whom they know—however much they may disagree with, disapprove of or dislike them.

As a Provo Paddy is doomed never to talk to anybody but his own kind, apart from a few media characters and an occasional Southern tourist. He will never have a pint in a pub with a British tommy, or talk about fishing (his favourite hobby) with an Orangeman, or speculate about next year's harvest with an RUC man, or discuss The Troubles with the sort of moderate Catholic who might belong to the Alliance Party. If for any reason he goes to England his mental and emotional environment will not change. He will join a colony of kindred spirits in Kilburn, or some Irish ghetto in Liverpool or Birmingham, and together with his fellow-exiles will regularly bewail the events of those fictitious seven or eight hundred years during which the Ulster Gaels have been persecuted by the Brits. Yet a man who can quote Shakespeare with such relish and affection is surely not incapable—given the necessary stimulus—of moderation and change.

I had only been a few moments in my first Crossmaglen pub when I heard a cheerful Geordie accent which flatly contradicted my preconceptions about the bandit 'capital' of South Armagh. Looking around, I saw a burly youngish man standing with his pint among a row of locals and complaining that he had been 'deceived' the day before by a racehorse. Later, I discovered that ten years ago he had married a South Armagh girl in England and when her mother became an invalid the whole family moved to Crossmaglen. There this Protestant

Englishmen successfully runs his own little business and has been completely accepted by the local community. Moving on to the next pub on my agenda, I heard another English voice, this time belonging to the wife of a Crossmaglen man. That young woman has been happily living in South Armagh since 1970 when her husband inherited an uncle's farm and gave up his job in Leeds. It is important, I was told, to understand that when South Armagh people say they hate the Brits they mean not British civilians but anybody in a British uniform—which includes Northern Irish policemen and members of the UDR, whatever their religion. Like all true Irish Republicans the South Armagh folk pride themselves on having remained faithful, through all the sectarian vicissitudes of the past 180 years, to the original ideals of the United Irishmen. More than once they quoted to me Wolfe Tone's vision: "To unite the whole people of Ireland, to abolish the memory of all past dissensions, and to substitute the common name of Irishman in place of the denominations of Protestant, Catholic and Dissenter."

Unless the South Armagh people suspect a stranger of spying, they will make him warmly welcome whatever his race or creed. There is no reason why the area should not have a thriving tourist industry with military activities as an added attraction; Brit-watching could become a new spectator sport. And yet, when I rang a friend in Dublin and told her where I was she exclaimed, "Crossmaglen! The very name makes me shudder!" Thus, over the past few years, has this little Irish town become synonymous with treachery, cruelty and sudden death.

I myself had felt no great urge to explore South Armagh during the summer. Although I was nver gullible enough to think of it as 'bandit country'—the Brits' favourite description—it did seem a place where anything might happen at any time to blow anybody up. Yet within hours of arriving there my antennae told me that I had nothing to fear.

In no sense but the political does South Armagh belong to Northern Ireland. From time immemorial all its links—social, commercial, athletic, cultural—have been with Monaghan and Louth rather than with North Armagh. Its accent is similar to the Monaghan accent, its families have intermarried with Southerners for generations, its job opportunities (for those

interested in conventional earning) have been greater in Dundalk than in Newry. Its temperament is conspicuously Southern—lazy, generous, evasive—and always it has steadfastly
ignored Partition. Unlike many other Northern Catholics the
South Armagh folk are never going to resign themselves to their
constitutional fate as British subjects. No wonder, then, I felt
at ease in that area; I had not really left home.

I did not argue with my Dublin friend since no region of
Northern Ireland—least of all South Armagh—is amenable to
elucidation on the telephone. But it saddened me to see, over
the next few days, what British propaganda is doing to the ordinary folk of the area. Proud though they are, with a long history
of spiritual if not political independence, it seems they are now
being slightly embittered by the hostility and contempt so often
expressed against them through the media.

Repeatedly one hears of British soldiers being shot dead,
blown to bits or maimed for life in South Armagh. It has also
been the scene of several peculiarly vicious civilian assassinations—Paddy's bus-load of Loyalists is an example—and often
the killers, if Green, escape across the border into the Republic;
a quick sprint over a field or two and they are safe. (I do not
understand *why* they are then safe, despite close co-operation
between the British and Irish security forces. It has been suggested that just south of the border a considerable percentage
of the population remains strongly pro-IRA and that those who
fail to share that feeling are made to act as though they do.
According to my informant, the percentage is much higher than
in South Armagh itself, where daily life has been so disrupted
by Provo activity.) The fact that snipers can go to ground
within a rifle-shot of Crossmaglen's British army post partly
explains South Armagh's evil reputation. As one local women
said to me, "They come, they kill, they go—and we are left
to bear the brunt of it." She was of course over-simplifying.
It is true that most people in South Armagh have never in their
lives handled a gun and would not know how to begin making
a bomb. They are witty, amiable countryfolk who regard smuggling as an honourable profession; otherwise the local crime
rate is remarkably low. Yet it is also true that they have contributed more than their share of moral support to the Provos

because they passionately and unanimously desire a united Ireland *now*. Throughout the area one feels that everybody's hopes and dreams crystallised finally some sixty years ago. They cannot be changed, only destroyed. Which is sad, for those hopes and dreams are not evil in themselves though they have inspired so many evil deeds.

It is hard to disentangle South Armagh emotions for non-Irish readers; whenever a statement comes to the tip of my pen I at once see the need to qualify it half-a-dozen times. Take the very word 'Republican'. To an outsider it might seem that there is no difference between a Republican and a Provo but this is not the case. Almost everyone in South Armagh is a Republican but only a minority approve of Provo methods. Support for the Provos is largely a creation of the Brits; so fiercely is the army's presence resented that anybody who opposes them becomes to some extent acceptable. Those regional affinities mentioned above also explain why both the locals and outside observers feel less anti-Provo in South Armagh than elsewhere in Northern Ireland. There the Provos are not seeking to impose the will of a tiny group of extremists on an antagonistic population but are fighting to bring about what the local people most ardently desire. During the summer I had been assured by British army officers that the South Armagh people have been so terrorised by the Provos that they dare not help the security forces, even by using the confidential telephone. This is nonsense; there is no need for intimidation on the informing issue. For other reasons—usually fund-raising or refuge-seeking—it does of course occur. But few South Armagh people could ever bring themselves to inform on either branch of the IRA, any more than your average Englishman could have spied for the Germans during the world wars.

What infuriates many British onlookers is the fact that South Armagh Republicans avail themselves as much as possible (and often much more than is legal) of Her Majesty's lavish social security benefits, while insisting that Her Majesty's forces have no right to be in their territory. To the British taxpayer, this is unprincipled hypocrisy. "Why should they have it both ways?" he wonders. "Why should they live well on our money while refusing to acknowledge British courts, and openly and incessantly and often violently expressing disloyalty to Britain, and sometimes killing our young men?" The answer is that since Partition it has been a consistently followed policy, among Northern Republicans, to milk the British exchequer by every conceivable—and some inconceivable—means. This is seen as a way of hitting back at the government responsible for depriving the Ulster Gaels—some 350 years ago—of that land which had been theirs before history was written. And on a more mundane level the Provos find the dole very convenient. It leaves them free to concentrate on 'the war' without having to break off to earn a living.

I successfully hitch-hiked hither and thither in South Armagh, something that would be almost impossible elsewhere in Northern Ireland because of the public's fear of hijackers. No driver failed to stop; on these narrow, hilly, winding roads there is so little traffic that to refuse a lift would seem downright rude by local standards. Normally hitch-hiking encourages confidential exchanges but South Armagh does not allow the usual degree of anonymity. For security reasons I told everybody who and what I was the moment they picked me up. Nevertheless, a farmer or doctor or van-driver tends to talk more freely in his own vehicle than in a pub.

"I wouldn't mind them killing the Brits," explained the driver of a cattle-truck, "if it did any good. But I can't stomach the way innocent people get caught up in their carry-on. I'm away to Australia next year if I can shift the wife. This is no place to bring up kids. You could have them kicking a football around a field one minute and the next minute shot dead or blown to bits."

I flew my favourite kite again. "But aren't these young Brits innocent, too?"

"No," said the driver flatly. "They're soldiers and they know that soldiers get killed. If they want to make sure of staying alive they should be in another job not over here persecuting harmless people. Not that the lads [i.e. the Provos] are much better. But at least they're doing what they're doing for their own country."

"So are the Brits," I remarked provocatively.

"Balls!" said the driver. "They're doing it for money—if you'll excuse me, m'am."

"But aren't *they* on the make, too?" I persisted. (I had observed that in South Armagh one avoids using the word 'Provo' as though it were some sort of harmful *mantra*.)

The driver shook his head. "Maybe they are in Belfast, or other places. But all they get here is a tenner a week and a bullet in the knee if they're found with more money than they should have. There's no police in South Armagh—except maybe a few now and then skulking around in the back of an army vehicle. But there's hardly any crime, either. Somebody's looking after law and order." He paused to offer me a welcome swig from his pint bottle of Guinness. Then he went on, "Mind you, *I'm* not for the lads—don't get me wrong. Sure we all want to kick the Brits out to hell but they're going about it the wrong way. The Brits are a rare stubborn lot. And they don't give an eff about a few young slummy bastards being killed here. They'll never leave while the lads are playing it this way. They've been beaten into the ground all over the world but it'd be the last bloody straw if they let it look like a wee handful of Paddies had 'em beaten here."

"And what would happen to everybody's dole," I asked, "if the Brits were gone?"

My friend laughed. "Maybe a lot of people would have to earn their living, for a change! Though they tell me things are catching up that way now in the Free State—they say the gap is no way so big as it was."

That afternoon another driver aired similar views. "Why don't they stick to blowing up buildings and leave the Brits alone? So long as they keep on at the soldiers, the soldiers will keep on at us. Remember how cold it was there before Christmas? Well, one of the worst nights the Marines came along and lifted my eldest—nineteen he is, and does an honest day's work in a factory in Dundalk. And they stripped him to his underpants—shoes and socks and all came off—and then they stood him in the middle of the road for one and a half hours in freezing fog till our local curate came along to rescue him. They had to let him go—they had nothing on him. But that's all the good killing Brits does. They can't catch the lads who do the killing so along they come to take it out on the likes of us. And all we want is to get on with a quiet life."

Everywhere I went, people told me about the misdeeds of the Royal Marine Commandos who had been stationed in South Armagh for four months from mid-August. I had been hearing horror stories about them, at second or third hand, throughout the autumn, but I tend to take such stories not too literally. In an atmosphere as permanently tense as South Armagh's accuracy does not always flourish. Yet when I discussed those stories with people whose integrity was beyond question, I discovered that they were true. One charitable official, who had had considerable contact with the regiment, blamed the troops less than he blamed whatever military bureaucrat decides which regiment goes where. It would be impossible, he said, to imagine men less suited to the situation in South Armagh—"Those Marines made even the Paras seem effete". I had wondered, the day I crossed the border, what effect Provo graffiti has on the Brits. Apparently its effect on the Marines had been to release all their most violent instincts. They frequently broke street lamps with stones, slashed car-tyres, urinated on people's doorsteps, tied dead rats to knockers, beat up randomly selected passers-by on the streets and transported groups of local men to Bessbrook Barracks where for hours they were 'subjected to ill-treatment' before being released without charge. As one citizen dryly expressed it, "In South Armagh we knew nothing about terrorism and not much about vandalism till the Brits came."

After all that, I was cheered to find the townspeople so ready to acknowledge the good qualities of the Highland regiment that had recently replaced the Marines. Any glimmer of non-prejudice in Northern Ireland makes the heart bound hopefully. "They're quiet wee lads," was the general verdict. "The most polite we've ever had around here." Evidently somebody at Army Headquarters had judged it wise to make an effort to counteract the Marines.

I went one afternoon to inspect the football pitch at Cross-maglen, which was not as irrelevant an activity as it may sound. During the Marines era the army found that it needed a helicopter landing-pad on the pitch, which is directly over-looked by the army post. The post had recently been partially wrecked by a mortar-bomb attack which destroyed its water-supply; therefore water had to be lifted in by helicopter. Moreover, the army had to have access to their new pad from the main road, which meant heavy vehicles using the expanse of wasteland across which football crowds must walk to reach the pitch.

To the uninformed, none of this might seem very contentious. But in South Armagh—and indeed throughout Northern Ireland—Gaelic football is of more than athletic or recreational significance. It is one of the most sacred symbols of the Catholic minority's nationalism and determined non-Britishness. Consequently, to threaten the pitch, or even its access area, amounted to extreme provocation; in local eyes it was a deed scarcely less reprehensible than desecrating a Catholic church. Whether or not the army authorities were aware of this, they seem to have been genuinely unable to make alternative arrangements. When they began to use their new pad, a corner of the otherwise immaculately green and smooth pitch was badly churned up. Also, the access area was reduced to such muddy desolation that in normal Irish weather the pitch could be approached only by wellington-wearers.

The whole of South Armagh—and far beyond—seethed with fury; the Southern papers solemnly reported the outrage in detail; the President of the Gaelic Athletic Association travelled 200 miles from Cork to Crossmaglen to inspect the damage. (The GAA is an immensely wealthy and powerful organisation with clubs in almost every parish of the thirty-two counties. It was founded in the 1880s as part of the Gaelic Revival and at first it served a useful purpose in giving back to the dispirited countryfolk a sense of pride in their own traditions. But during the present century its narrow nationalism has contributed quite a lot to making a united Ireland impossible in the foreseeable future.) When the President made a formal complaint to the army authorities they promised to repair the damage and left the access area in a better state than they found it. But the sacrilege of landing British army helicopters on a Gaelic football pitch is unlikely ever to be forgiven.

As I was inspecting the pitch a four-man foot-patrol strolled through a gap in the hedge and crossed the field to inspect me.

They were indeed 'quiet wee lads', two of whom looked almost too wee to cope with their weaponry. The leader had an incomprehensible Scottish accent and they all looked rather wistful as though they were wishing they could be home for Hogmany. They asked no questions—very likely they already knew all about me—and when I wished them a happy and a safe New Year they smiled shyly and a little uncertainly. Possibly they thought I was being sarcastic.

Then a crackling order came over the walkie-talkie and one youth swiftly moved a few yards away, threw himself on his stomach on the grass and trained his rifle on a house in a terraced row beyond the pitch. At which point I departed with more speed than dignity having no wish to become another 'caught in cross-fire' case. But maybe that was a put-up job to give the visiting writer something to write about.

Later that day I called on an impeccably law-abiding elderly couple who live some miles from Crossmaglen. They complained eloquently about army harassment, not only during the Marines era but long before it; and then the wife—quite unaware of the implications of her story—described one search.

"Along these two came one morning to the front door, knocking and ringing the bell as if I was deaf. And there was crowds more of them up and down the village. Then this corporal says, 'Excuse me, m'am, I'm sorry to disturb you when you must be busy around the house, but I wonder could we please have a look inside, if you don't mind?' So I says to him, 'There's no good comin' to me with your "excuse mes" and your "pleases" and your "if you don't minds"! I know your sort and the way you treat decent people! A lot of hooligans is all you are with all your smarmy talk! And I'm not afraid to tell you so to your face! Sure you can have a look inside—I can't stop you, can I, when 'tis you has the guns! But you may be sure if I could stop you I would, and send you back wherefrom you came!' So in they clattered and sure enough they had the place turned upside down in ten minutes. Took me a week to get it straight again. And damage was done. A wardrobe door smashed and the chair covers all torn and ripped to bits—that's why the chairs look so shabby now. And they had my husband there stuck in a corner with his arms over his head for twenty minutes and a rifle in his ribs—and he a martyr to neuritis. Then when they were leaving one of 'em called out at the top of his voice from the street—'Thanks, m'am, for all that low-down on the Provos!' Vicious, they are! Downright vicious!''

Her husband told me that two days later, by a coincidence that might have proved unfortunate, their next door neighbour's nineteen-year-old son was lifted for being an active Provo. Most of the locals had not known that he was a 'volunteer'; people prefer to know as little as possible since they cannot then give information whatever methods may be used while questioning them.

Back in 'Cross', as the locals call their capital, I spent the evening in one of the village's several pubs. The owner played the accordion for hours while his customers sang patriotic ballads. Between songs the conversation was of memorable football matches, army misbehaviour, ways of fiddling social security benefits and the classic smuggling achievements of the past. Contemporary feats in that sphere were not discussed. Much cynicism was expressed about my ability or willingness to write anything accurate on South Armagh; clearly the locals have had their fill of media misinterpretations. Yet I was not allowed to buy one drink. As a stranger among people who still respect the ancient Gaelic code of hospitality, I had to be 'well looked after'.

In South Armagh, as in parts of Co Leitrim, one can still hear an echo of how people were in Ireland long, long ago before our Gaelic culture was obliterated. But one has to recognise, very sadly, that these isolated traditional pockets are too tiny to survive. Already the modern tide is eroding them through the ubiquitous Box. South Armagh will probably withstand that tide for longer than Leitrim because of the challenging British presence. However, if the unification of Ireland ever did come about it would probably be quickly followed by the Anglicisation of South Armagh.

Twice during the evening, routine army patrols came clattering in, their blackened faces looking half-sinister, half-comical. They stood around awkwardly, saying nothing and seeming almost apologetic, their meek demeanour contrasting oddly with their lavish armoury. The men at the bar ignored them but sang, extra loudly, the most belligerent ballads in their repertoire. It shocked me deeply—though unreasonably—that at the Christian season of goodwill nobody could or would offer these youngsters a drink before they went out to resume their patrolling through the savagely cold night. At last their leader asked fatuously, "Any problems? Any trouble going on?" Whereupon the very tall publican carefully put down his accordion, came out from behind the bar, strolled towards the slim little lieutenant and stood looking down at him in silence for a moment. Then he said, "We never have any trouble in this house and we never will have while I'm here—unless *you* make it." His tone was expressionless, neither threatening nor offensive. He was merely stating a fact. The patrol left then.

During the next ballad I meditated on the role of the army in South Armagh. For whose benefit are they there? The locals certainly do not need to be protected from the IRA and the army's inability to seal off the border has repeatedly been proved. If the troops were withdrawn from the area would Loyalist paramilitaries invade and the Provos retaliate? This is just possible. But even if it did happen could it be considered a greater evil than the atmosphere of ever-increasing tension, bitterness and misunderstanding generated by the presence of the Brits?

At 7.50 am on New Year's Eve I walked from the outskirts of Crossmaglen to the featureless wide square in the town centre; the Newry bus was due to start at eight o'clock. Not a mouse was stirring, not a light showed in any house. A mass of colourless cloud pressed down on the land and the air was raw and damp. Gradually the little town began to take shape around me in that strange, reluctant dawn-light of mid-winter—a light that seems no more than a weakening of darkness. Then across the square I saw grey shadows slipping around a corner from the Main Street and guns dully gleaming under a feeble street lamp. The last man of the foot-patrol was walking backwards, as usual, and suddenly I fell into a mood of despair. Unless one of the factions concerned can find the courage to lose face, this situation could go on for ever.

The bus started punctually and for the first half-hour I was the only passenger. We drove fast through vague grey light across bleak rough country. There was no traffic on the road but plenty in the air. I watched one helicopter landing in a nearby field; its doors did not open while the bus was in sight. Then we stopped frequently to pick up young factory-workers and it was nine o'clock by the time we got to Newry.

In the Belfast Express bus I found myself beside an elderly tweeded lady clutching *The Daily Telegraph* as though it were a talisman. She became very excited on hearing my accent and told me that for years she had lived in Co Cork where really the people were amazingly *nice*! "But now," she explained breathlessly, "all my Southern friends are afraid even to send me a Christmas card because you see my dear if the IRA caught them corresponding with Ulster Protestants they might be *shot*!" Myths do not circulate only among the uneducated.

11

The Turn of the Year in Belfast

Two hours and ten minutes after leaving Crossmaglen I was put down in Belfast carrying an air-line bag that could have contained a large bomb. Nobody had examined my luggage and from the bus depot I had access to many city centre buildings. When I remarked on this to local friends they explained that no bomber could be sure of getting through as there are frequent spot-checks on bus passengers. But I continue to be astonished that it is ever possible to travel straight from South Armagh into the heart of Belfast without let or hindrance. True, most stores, hotels, offices, pubs and banks now employ their own security officers. Yet when I went from the bus depot to a restaurant for a late breakfast the friendly woman security guard scarcely glanced at the contents of my bag. Possibly I give the impression of not being a bomber. But it is unsettling to think that I could have planted a dozen 'incendiary devices' in that building.

Leaving the restaurant, I wondered why I was so pleased to be back in Belfast. The ravaged city seemed the very epitome of dreariness on that dark grey morning of ice, sleet, mud and rain. Yet the people were as friendly, helpful and stoically cheerful as in the hot blue days of midsummer. I realised then that respect is at the root of my affection for this least popular city in the British Isles.

I missed Roz even more in Belfast than in South Armagh. For long years she has been providing me with moral support and, apart from that, one hears too often about buses being burnt, hijacked or getting in the way of snipers' bullets. The famous Black Taxis operate on the same convenient principle as the Istanbul *dolmus*, but they are either Green or Orange and it is not always easy for visitors to distinguish between the two fleets.

From the city centre I took a bus to one of the Catholic

ghettos. That cost me twenty-six pence, whereas a taxi would have taken me the same distance for ten pence. Behind me sat a shapeless, sandy-haired woman in a patched coat with a two-months-old baby under one arm and a thirteen-months-old baby under the other. "You're brave to take your friend's baby, too," said I obtusely. She laughed so heartily that the elder infant woke and howled. "They're *both* me own—an' on'y eleven months between 'em! The youngest of twelve, they are—an' all boys, too, an' I longin' all me life for a girl." She sighed. "Isn't it a tough world to be tryin' to raise twelve boys in? But T.G. so far they're good lads. Never been in no kinda trouble. The Daddy has no work so he's there to have an eye over them and a great difference it makes, towards them poor families with the man away all day an' the wains runnin' wild. But the eldest leaves school next year—that's when I'll worry. Bored, he'll be. I'd like to see him get over the water fast. But they say there's no work there either. Never mind—God is good!"

I asked her if the Peace Movement made her feel more hopeful and she looked at me in astonishment. "*That* lot! Sure what do they know about real livin', with their smart cars and fashionable clothes and colour tellies! They won't do no good to anybody 'cept the Brits. Catholics they may be, but they're not on our side"

Ten minutes later I was in the tidy living-room of a small flat talking to Tessie, a young woman who had recently been released from gaol. After a time I asked her if having been 'inside' for three years had in any way changed her ideas and attitudes. She looked at me silently for a moment, with cold, polite contempt. Then she said, "Republican attitudes don't change in three years—or in thirty, or in three hundred. Or in 800. We've been fighting the Brits now for 800 years. And if they're still around in another 800 we'll still be fighting them."

The despair which I had felt early that morning in Crossmaglen threatened to return. Any attempt to correct the Green version of Irish history would have led only to a breakdown in relations. So instead I suggested, "Don't you think things are changing all over the world? Can't you see some scope for compromise? Aren't young people becoming less nationalistic and more concerned about *human beings*, as such, regardless of race or religion? And don't you see that as a good thing?"

"You mean Communism?" Tessie's lip curled. "I'm not a Stickie! Whoever cared in Stormont or Westminster about *human beings*, if they were Irish Catholics? It's fine for you to preach in grand words about 'change'. What change have we ever seen in the past 800 years? No change—nothing but poverty and injustice and humiliation. And who owns the Six Counties? *We do*! Not the people who are kicking us around. *We own them*. And we're going to get them back no matter how many of us have to be tortured or killed or locked up for life. And when we have them back the others can stay if they behave themselves. We're not going to take it out on anyone once we have our rights. We've nothing against Prods or anyone else who calls himself an Irishman. But we're not going to stop fighting till we get our rights. And our rights are to rule over this country *which we own*. It doesn't belong to Britain and never has. We're not gangsters trying to rob anyone. We're soldiers fighting for our own country. You can put that in your book, and I hope people read it and think about it. And if the Brits say it's mean to blow up people in pubs tell them we think it's mean for a rich country of sixty millions to send in 14,000 troops to keep down half a million Irish patriots."

I said nothing. Anything I might have said—all I wanted to say—would have either made no impression or infuriated my companion. To have expressed my genuine sympathy with her feelings of deprivation and persecution would have sounded patronising when I could not support her method of correcting the situation. To have argued any particular point would have been impossible against a mind that regarded compromise as a betrayal and the exploration of new ideas as mere weakness.

Yet despite my silence something of my sympathy must have seeped through. Suddenly Tessie smiled and said, "You're not really against us, are you?"

"I'm not against anyone," I replied sadly. "I'm against a lot of the things people *do* up here, but I'm not against any of the *people*."

Tessie laughed. "That's real softie talk! If you were reared up here you'd know you have to be against a lot of people. And you have to do rough things. Stormont would be there still if we hadn't got rough. Violence pays and we know it and every government in the world knows it. We don't want to kill people but you can't have a war without killing. And in Occupied Ireland you'll never have justice without a war. It's not complicated. All you people coming along for a look make out it's a great big problem. But it's dead simple. It's a war for justice. And the war goes on till we get the justice. There was no problem in England forty years back. There was a war because the Brits didn't want Germans ruling their country so they got off their backsides and went out and killed millions of people all over the world—and they didn't only kill soldiers, either. Same thing here, only we don't have to kill so many. But we would if we had to. Maybe some day we'll have to kill thousands to protect ourselves. And if we have to we will. People talk about Catholics being massacred if the Brits go. But we're tough. We can deal with any lot that comes at us. We don't want to kill— remember that. But I'm sure the Brits didn't want to kill either when they bombed German cities into the ground. They just knew they had to."

"You may be tough," I said, "but are there enough of you?"

Tessie was confident. "One in defence is worth ten in attack. We'll be OK. Let the Brits get out and we'll do the rest. If we have to. We don't want a civil war. But if it comes we can take it."

When Tessie had gone into the little kitchenette to make tea I looked around me. The framed Proclamation of the Republic had already been pointed out to me; it hung over the settee and the Brits had smashed the glass during one of their frequent raids. Flanking it were a garish picture of the Holy Family and another of Our Lady of Lourdes. A crucifix hung over the door and on the telly stood a statue of the Infant of Prague. Opposite the settee hung three photographs: Tessie's parents on their wedding day, a Co Down Gaelic football team and a priest uncle who lives in America taken on a beach in California. Tessie's father had been 'killed in action' in 1972. Her siblings were all away—one didn't ask where, or what doing—and she shared this flat with her mother.

Mrs B— now came in, rather breathless, bearing a box of

small cakes covered with multi-coloured icing. The three of us
sat on the settee opposite a one-bar electric fire and drank tea
and ate the cakes and talked about inflation and the poor wee
lad in the flat below who got measles so bad he died. "On
Christmas Eve, it was," said Tessie, "and we were all that upset
we got no good out of the Christmas."

Mother had artificially ebony hair and a plump kind face
and a limp. Tessie scolded her for having gone out on the ice.
"With your hip you might have broke a leg. I could have gone
m'self only you were away before I noticed." Then she brought
out a slice of Christmas cake, specially for me. "It's only shop,"
she apologised. "We're not much good at the cooking in these
parts."

Again, as with Paddy in South Armagh, I had to make an
enormous effort to believe in the truth about these women. Part
of my mind seemed all the time to be struggling to reject the
outrageous fact that neither would have scrupled to bomb or
shoot innocent people if they reckoned that action might help
to get the Brits out. So often I had said—and listened to others
saying—'What sort of people can they be, who do these things?
How do their minds work? It's impossible to imagine the kind
of person who could do it. . . .' But we are unable to imagine
only because we are so determined that 'terrorists' must be 'different'. Not the sort of people we have ever met, not people
who lead ordinary lives with ordinary worries and concerns but
happen to have extraordinary convictions, desires, ideals or
obsessions.

The humdrumness of that scene made my conversation with
Tessie seem all the more macabre and frustrating. I felt that
in some way I must be at fault. I should be able to get through
to this ordinary young woman who was not unfriendly, not without humour, not apparently abnormal—and whose cultural
background I perfectly understood. Yet I could not. And my
preaching about the need to encourage communication
between the ghettos was made to look pretty silly by this failure.
What hope was there of direct Orange-Green communication
if I could not communicate with Tessie? One key to the non-
communication impasse is that small word 'war'. Green and
Orange paramilitaries alike—and their supporters—believe

that they are fighting a just war: the former to liberate their country from invaders, the latter to defend it from subversives. And one cannot communicate in the language of peace with people who speak only the language of war.

I walked away from Tessie's flat on an icy pavement that appeared to have been—and no doubt had been—hacked to bits with an axe. The road was littered with empty tins, sheets of newspaper, broken glass, large stones and chunks of brick. All around me were walls inscribed: PROVO RULE OK, FUCK THE BRITS, UP THE REPUBLIC, F.T.Q., REMEMBER 1916, FUCK ALL ORANGES, FUCK UVF, UFF, DUP, TO HELL WITH THE BRITS, 1916–1976 TOO LONG, JOIN THE IRA, GET YOURSELF A GUN. None of this graffiti was neat; the words had been hastily smeared and daubed and scrawled across almost every available blank space—the work of how many unemployed young men? Only the Irish tricolour had been carefully painted; that most naively ironic of symbols, in present-day Belfast, with its Green and Orange bands united by the White of peace. I resented seeing my country's flag thus depicted among the sordid slogans of a tribal world that seemed as remote as Central Africa from my own. And yet—it is not so. I had again caught myself in the act of self-deception. We would all like to think of Northern Ireland in the 1970s as remote from our own world. That would be more comfortable. But the mess is a part of every Irish citizen's responsibility, and ever English citizen's too. We have made it between us— encouraged by autocratic church leaders who have assisted the translation of irrelevant doctrinal differences into the language of frightened human hate.

By then I needed a drink but I had to walk over a mile to find a fortified pub. Its double barricade of thick steel wire extended from roof to street and I felt like a monkey in a cage as I walked to the locked door through a long narrow corridor between the inner and outer barricade. A burly, unsmiling security man in a torn boiler suit unlocked the door and looked at me very suspiciously. His expression softened slightly when he heard my accent but he thoroughly examined the contents of my brief-case, even opening a tin of throat lozenges. This conspicuous Catholic pub on a main road is one of the UVF's favourite targets. Just a few weeks before my visit two men had been shot dead as they left it.

The public bar was crowded, smoky and perceptibly unwelcoming. In the quiet but filthy lounge three youngish women were drinking vodka and beer—surely as nauseating a mixture as human ingenuity could devise. They gave me doubtful half-smiles as I went to the counter. I was now in territory where all strangers are suspect and the adolescent bartender was barely civil; he kept me waiting for my pint even longer than was necessary. From where I stood I could see the whole of the public bar and suddenly the security man appeared at the door and flicked his fingers above his head. For an instant everyone fell silent. Then six soldiers came slowly through the door, as every man at the bar—or so it sounded—began to sing a ballad about the Brave Men of Crossmaglen. At once the sergeant stamped on the floor, demanded silence and ordered everyone to empty his pockets onto the counter. It may be assumed that all those men were Provo-sympathisers. As they turned out their pockets, in silence, the vibrations of hatred, hostility and suppressed violence were more unnerving than any slanging-match or scuffle. It was almost a relief when one youth suddenly began to scream hysterical abuse at the soldier who was examining his possessions. He was slapped across the face four times, hard, and this provoked an oath-laden protest from his friends. But you don't sustain a protest if there are six loaded rifles in a gathering; you seek other opportunities for revenge. The sergeant again demanded silence and asked, "How come you chaps have hardly any money between you, when you're all drinking your heads off?" There was no reply. And when I later made the same enquiry, more diplomatically, I too failed to get an answer.

As the soldiers left one spotty private covered their retreat and then slipped out himself, wearing an agonised expression of tension. To me this had seemed an ugly incident. To the men at the bar it was a routine occurrence, just one more thread woven into the tapestry of violence that has become the backdrop to their lives.

The women in the lounge told me that they would have been identity-checked and insulted but for the presence of an obvious outsider. I do not know how accurate this information is but during the summer I had often got the impression that relations between the troops and the ghetto women are even worse than between the troops and the men.

Soon another woman joined us and at once I realised that she was a Provo. It is hard to explain how I knew. Partly it was to do with her reassuring and protective attitude towards her friends in relation to the army. And partly it was her general air of authority as she questioned me about my reasons for being in that pub.

I replied that for one thing I was thirsty and for another I wanted to meet the locals because I was writing about Northern Ireland. She frowned. "Who are you writing for?"

"For myself—and I hope for some readers, somewhere."

"Who's paying you?" The question had that characteristic Northern bluntness which I like though some Southerners think it rude. (They wouldn't mind the same information being sought if the seeker took half-an-hour to get to the point.)

"Nobody's paying me, as yet," I replied. "If it's worth publishing my publisher will pay me."

"Who's he?"

"John Murray."

"From Dublin?"

"No, from London."

"*London?* And what does he want to know about the Six Counties for, if he lives in London?"

"Well,"I explained, "it's not really that personal to him. It's *my* book and I'm writing it because I feel a lot of people need to know more about the situation here."

"But why do you think they'll be interested? Who cares about us?" She lit a fresh cigarette off her butt and got up to buy—or procure—drinks all round. Leaning on the little table, sticky with many layers of spilt drinks and overburdened ashtrays, she looked down at me. "Even the Americans are losing interest since those fuckin' Peace bitches started!"

"Losing interest in what?" I asked quickly.

"In Irish freedom and justice for Republicans. They think maybe we should settle for Peace instead and sink back into the gutters we started out from. Not bloody likely!"

When she was standing at the bar, out of earshot, one of the other women said, "Don't take no notice of Maire. She has to check on who's in here but she don't mean no harm. She's terrible goodhearted. Do anything for you, Maire would. Same as her grandfather, God rest him. Get the story off her about him and the wee babby—that'll be good for your book! And it's true. Me granny's still alive and she remembers every bit of it happenin' like Maire says."

So I got the story and here it is.

One summer evening many years ago Grandad found an abandoned baby girl on Cave Hill with a note pinned to her shawl asking the finder to bring her up a Presbyterian. He had eleven himself so he thought one more wouldn't make much difference. His wife agreed and they loved the little girl who was brought up a Presbyterian and sent to a state school and to the kirk every Sunday. When she was eighteen she married a Presbyterian lad who also loved her foster-parents, with whom the young couple spent every Saturday. Then one Saturday during a troubled time in the city an RUC sergeant was shot dead and Grandad was arrested and charged with the murder. His Presbyterian foster-daughter appeared in court and swore that he had been at home all day, which he had not. Because she was a non-Catholic her evidence was accepted and Grandad went free. And if that story isn't true it should be. Personally I think it sounds too improbable to have been invented.

It was now past two o'clock and at intervals, as Maire told her story—there were many embellishments—a few small children belonging to one or other of my companions would wander in, pursued by abuse from the security man, and ask if there was any dinner today or if they could have money for crisps. Usually they were shouted at impatiently but given some coins; then back they went to the cold streets. One father was 'in the Crum' (Crumlin Road Gaol); the others were in the public bar from which they occasionally emerged to 'lift a fag off the missus'. For some baffling reason the wives all seemed to be in control of cigarette supplies. Their children were, it seems reasonable to deduce, the next generation of bombers and snipers.

Eventually a few men—not husbands—brought their drinks out and joined us. Everybody had tales to tell of army harassment, by day and by night—the same houses and flats being searched over and over again, some as often as three times in one night though it was obvious that nothing would ever be found in those 'marked' homes. Several people remembered wistfully how wonderful it had been over the few days of Christmas, not having this persecution, never seeing a single soldier.

I asked then, "But what would happen if the Brits were gone? Have you forgotten '69? How things were before they came?"

An elderly man shook his head. "You don't have to worry. We had no Provos then. Now we'd be looked after." He glanced at Maire, half-nervously, half-defiantly. "I don't go along with all they do nowadays, but we need 'em."

"We do that," agreed a young man with a stiff knee. "We couldn't do without 'em, no way. For all we talk against them, there's none of us could lie easy in our beds if we'd nothing between us and the Oranges when we've got the Brits out—and they'll be gone any day now." He smiled amiably at me. "Bet you didn't know that, but it's true!"

Another young man tossed back his long black hair and asked me, "How much do you know about it all down there in the Free State? D'you know that we've been fighting Orangemen for 800 years? So they're not likely to put us down now, when we've better arms than we ever had before!"

"Quiet, Andy," warned Maire. "What d'you know about arms anyway?"

"Tell me, Andy," I said, "when do you think the Reformation happened? And the Plantation of Ulster? And when d'you think the Orange Order was founded?"

Andy shrugged. "Fuck dates! Maybe 800 years ago they weren't called Orangemen but they were the same kinda bastards and we were fightin' 'em for our rights!"

It was long after dark when a bony blonde named Josie asked me home to tea. Maire clearly disapproved of this gesture, no doubt for security reasons, but by then Josie was too full of vodka and beer to care. After five pints I was happy enough myself but still able to observe the truly appalling state of Josie's home. A newish house, it incorporated all the horrors of a traditional slum plus the modern convenience of a pile of very used disposable nappies which had not been disposed of. The eldest child—aged thirteen—was sent up the road for a cooked chicken and a sliced pan and Father brought out a bottle of poteen that had been sent from the Sperrins as a Christmas present. A neighbour came in with a bottle of supermarket port and half a Christmas cake from Canada and told us a long story about having been abducted by the UVF from a city centre pub the week before and taken for grilling to a pub on the Shankill and then raped by three men. Uncharitably, I had the impression that that last ordeal was not found altogether unpleasing.

I fell in the general estimation because I elected to drink only tea, despite the tempting alternatives. When Josie had thoroughly diluted her vodkas and beers with port, she rooted under the table among a pile of dirty clothes and broken toys and brought forth a photograph album. On the first page were two handsome young men in bathing trunks. "Both in England," said Josie tearfully. "They didn't want to join up so they had to go. Me dad was that mad at them. Now they're afraid to come home again. Their own father might put a bullet in them."

Her husband strode over to us. "Belt up, Josie! You're talkin' bloody drunken nonsense, so you are!" He took the album roughly and flung it behind the settee.

When I left, at 7.30, the baby had been given an aspirin to put it to sleep, Josie had passed out on the settee and everyone else was going back to the pub.

In the midst of all the politico-religious dissension, one tends to overlook the general social problems that make it so much more difficult to cope with Belfast's particular problem. Listening to the conversations in that pub and in Josie's home I was conscious of being in a shadowy semi-underworld where alcoholism, compulsive gambling, petty theft, amateur prostitution and random looting were features of everyday life. In such a milieu, as I have already said, an army of social workers might one day achieve something but an army of soldiers will never achieve anything. Except of course the hardening of anti-social

attitudes because persecution by the troops is seen as justification for every sort of law-breaking. If a Brit—representing Law
and Order—has smashed up your furniture in the small hours
you go out next day to get your own back, somehow, on society.
And when the Brits hear that the Taigs have been at it again
they feel justified in punishing the lawless bastards by smashing
up some more furniture—or faces. It is all so obvious; yet the
authorities, too, seem trapped inside this vicious circle of their
own creating. Some day, however, they will have to admit that
within communities already disposed to violence—as most slum
communities are—the brutalising presence of soldiers and guns
and threats can only lead to more and worse trouble.

As I stood in gusts of icy rain, on a battered, ill-lit street,
waiting for a Black Taxi, I was conscious of being a little tense
and very wary. But I felt none of the uncontrollable animal
fear I had experienced that midsummer night when Belfast
was still unfamiliar. Knowing the geography of a place gives
a certain sense of security, of being in control of one's own
destiny. And objectively there is no reason why one should
be jittery in Belfast. By international crime standards very few
people are killed in Northern Ireland. On New Year's Day the
newspapers announced that during 1976 295 people had been
killed in The Troubles and 296 on the roads of Northern
Ireland.

A taxi soon picked me up and though I was the only passenger the charge was just fifteen pence for a journey that would
have cost me at least £1.50 in London. When the driver put
me down in Castle Street he warned—"Don't take a taxi up
the Antrim Road, it'll knock you back pounds. No one likes
going up there after dark—they charge danger money rates.
Take a bus."

On the bus everyone was very helpful and there was a general
discussion about where *exactly* I should get off to avoid walking
further than necessary along Murder Mile. Belfast's permanent
state of emergency can draw people together in a heart-warm-
ing way and the driver offered to stop between the official halts
for my benefit. Then I eavesdropped on the two women behind
me, playing the grotesquely addictive Northern game of pick-
ing up clues to religion. When one woman remarked that Syd

would be starting at Inst next year all was revealed. Yet these Protestants had not been adversely affected by my accent and I remembered, with sorrow, how impossible it had been to convince my Catholic drinking companions of the afternoon that I was not only safe but welcome in most Protestant areas of the city.

As we passed the Lansdowne Court Hotel I noticed how badly it had been damaged by a recent bomb attack. During previous visits to Belfast I had often met nervous friends there because the security was reputed to be so good. When I mentioned this to the friendly women behind me they sighed and shrugged and one of them said, "If someone comes up and shoves a gun at your head what d'you do? You let him in with his bomb if you've any sense." Her companion nodded and recalled that a few days previously a public house security man who tried to thwart a bomber was shot dead.

I was going to stay with Protestant friends who were out for the evening so it had been arranged that I should pick up the key from their Catholic next-door neighbours with whom they have enjoyed half a lifetime of solid friendship. I had become very fond of this Catholic family during the summer and noticed then how taut their nerves were. Now I saw a FOR SALE notice at their front gate.

Mrs D— admitted me, having wisely shouted "Who's there?" before coming near the door. "I'm sorry," I said. "I see you have to move?" She nodded and led me into the sitting-room and silently showed me a letter, received on Christmas Eve, telling her that her eighteen-year-old son was on a Loyalist death list and would be removed from it only if the family had got out by 2 January.

I felt a sickening little shock of horror. One hears so much about this sort of thing that it becomes almost acceptable, in theory—just as one knows that certain races have to endure climates which we could scarcely survive. But to be abruptly confronted with it in action, in the home of a friend, brought the savagery of it into focus in a shattering way. "Where will you go?" I asked.

Mrs D— shook her head. "We don't know. To my mother-in-law, for the moment." Then suddenly she laughed. "Don't look so upset! We'll get by! Are you coming to our party tomorrow night?"

"Your *party*?" I said. "But you're moving house next day!" Again she laughed. "These days in Belfast, people don't put off parties because they have to move house!" And in that one sentence she explained why I believe the Northern Irish will come through this ordeal with their best qualities intact. When they do, they will have a lot to teach the rest of us.

Belfast city centre was a strange place to be at 11.30 pm on New Year's eve. The City Hall was floodlit and the Christmas trees were gay but there were no happy revellers; only the Peace People, gathering for their midnight rally, and the War People. Alert troops were patrolling on foot, or quickly driving to and fro in Land-Rovers or armoured vehicles, and at every corner and in almost every doorway stood a couple of RUC men. An icy north-east wind sneaked through the streets and the Peace People huddled together for warmth and sang jolly songs in a determined sort of way. There were scarcely 200 of us: not nearly enough, as one of the Peace Leaders pointed out, to replace those murdered during 1976. It was a much younger crowd than usual, no doubt because of the time and the weather, and there seemed to be as many men as women. There had been a lot of publicity in the local papers about the huge turn-out that was expected and a plan had been announced to light Peace candles at midnight and have the flame of Peace spreading from person to person throughout the vast throng. Perhaps this unwise build-up contributed to the sense of anticlimax. Certainly I, who had not been to a Rally since October, felt increasingly uneasy as the performance proceeded. For now it *was* a performance. The moving and exhilarating spontaneity of the early rallies had been replaced by an unattractively smooth professionalism on the platform. Unmistakably a show was being put on, partly for the media and partly for the loyal few who had turned out to sing with and cheer their three leaders.

To some observers the intense emotionalism of the Movement's origin was an ill omen. It started in the Catholic district of Andersonstown when a Provo, fleeing in a car from the Brits, was shot dead. His car then crashed into a family group killing three small children and seriously injuring their mother. At once an upsurge of 'anti-violence' feeling engulfed Andersonstown and was quickly harnessed and spread to other areas by the Peace People—an unmarried career woman, a housewife and a journalist who for years had been dedicated to pacifism. From the outset the Movement's critics asked, 'Why after this particular incident, which could be called an act of God? Why not after a young couple were shot dead in front of their two-year-old son and six-months-old daughter? Or after another young couple and their baby were burned to death by a petrol bomb thrown into their house? Or after any other deliberately-planned crime?' True, the killing of those children by a crashing car was an accident, though inevitably some people chose to talk about 'Three children killed by Provos' and others to talk about 'Three children killed by Brits'. (A futile argument like this can go on for ever in Northern Ireland.) But to me it seems unimportant which particular tragedy sparked off the Movement since it was so clearly a spontaneous cry from the weary hearts of thousands of ordinary people.

Cynicism increased when the Peace People, often under the sponsorship of media organisations, proceeded to fly hither and thither for months on end—to and from Britain, the US, France, Germany, Canada, New Zealand, Scandinavia, Australia. As a Catholic politician acidly pointed out, 'the problems of Belfast are not going to be solved in Buffalo, Berlin or Birmingham'. But the leaders are not to blame for their Movement's unsatisfactory change of direction. At the beginning they were adamant that they wished to collect no funds and would not become 'institutionalised'. The media, however, decided otherwise. And very quickly the Peace People lost their original image as authentic 'people of the people representing the people'.

It is hard to imagine anything more newsworthy, on the 'human interest' plane, than the women of the Catholic Falls and the Protestant Shankill marching together for peace despite their crippling inheritance of mutual distrust. Obviously it was desirable that this phenomenon, unique in the history of Belfast, should be given maximum publicity. And the world rejoiced to see that thousands of Northern Irish longed for peace so desperately that they were prepared to break with their most rigid traditions to express that longing. But the media were not content simply to serve a useful purpose. They took up the Movement, as eagerly and clumsily as a small child takes up a new toy, and very soon they had damaged it. The Peace People should have been left to get on quietly with the delicate task of using to best effect the flood of wholesome emotion released by their campaign. Instead they were transported, both physically and mentally, into a new world disastrously remote from that of their followers. Their chief strength as leaders had been that they were three ordinary Belfast folk—though not quite 'grass-roots', being far more articulate and financially secure than their average fellow citizen. But at least the two women were ordinary enough to be acceptable to those who scorn the leadership of 'middle-class intellectuals'. And the media took this strength from them.

The Northern Irish are much too level-headed to be impressed by flurries of sentimentality. Soon many were asking, 'But *why* are they being given Peace prizes and awards and medals and plaques and receptions? What have they done, so far, to earn them? Are we any nearer to Peace than we were a year ago? And what about all the other organisations that have been beavering away for years to promote peace? And all the community workers who have been slaving since The Troubles started to improve ghetto relations?' These questions did not come only from petty people, troubled by envy or jealously. To the Northern Irish a cart had been put before a horse and rewards given on the basis of nebulous hoped-for achievements.

This might not have mattered too much had the rewards merely taken the form of moral support and publicity for the Peace People. But by the end of 1976 hundreds of thousands of pounds had been given to a movement which naturally lacked the machinery to administer such funds. It is hard to credit the want of imagination behind the generosity which produced this sum. Nothing is less likely to foster peace than large amounts of money and these donations served only to distract the Peace People from their real task. If cash could solve Northern Ireland's problems Britain would long since have provided it.

Too much stress on the pacifist ideal is another of the Movement's handicaps, this one self-imposed. Personally, the older I get the more sympathetic I feel towards uncompromising pacifism. But at present it is very much a minority interest and to the average person has overtones of crankiness. And it is with the average ghetto person, who knows nothing and cares less about Tolstoy, Gandhi and Martin Luther King, that the Peace People should have been chiefly concerned. By constantly emphasising pacifist—as distinct from peaceful—thinking, they widened that gap opened by the media between themselves and their followers. Around Ballymurphy or Sandy Row pacifism seems an insipid swill of pious phrases and sentimental attitudes gleaned from books that no sensible person has ever heard of.

For a fervent pacifist, the temptation to use the Peace Movement to spread the gospel of non-violence must have been very strong. But it is unlikely that Northern Ireland can be transformed directly from a region where brute force prevails—under a relatively orderly surface—to a region where the pacifist philosophy is generally accepted. I do not like to mock such visions; they are good and beautiful and needed in the world and were I twenty-five years younger I might be able to believe that this miracle could be worked. But realism overtakes most of us in middle-age. First let the Peace People strive for that normal degree of stability and tolerance which now obtains elsewhere in Western Europe. If they then want to press on towards a completely pacifist state, good luck to them.*

I spent the first few days of the New Year in the Green ghettos amongst Provo supporters. Most Provos inherit a sort of fundamentalist Irish Republicanism as they inherit the colour of their skin. Unlike people who, as adults, have chosen to live by a certain ideology, they have never thought their way towards

---

* In July 1977 I visited the Peace People in their new headquarters, an ex-manse on the Lisburn Road for which they had recently paid £40,000. I then got the impression that within the previous six months the Movement had—after a period of great uncertainty and confusion—to some extent seen the error of its earlier ways. The more sensible of its representatives were prepared to acknowledge a massive loss of popular support and spoke with reassuring realism about its potential. Other leaders were still showing an unhealthy fondness for headline-catching 'gimmicky' activities. But one hopes that those who are working hard on sensible projects, and shunning publicity, will prevail in the end.

being Provos and this leaves them that much less likely to think their way out of it. It might seem that the reverse should apply; that if they could somehow be persuaded to stop and consider their position objectively they would the more easily abandon it because they had not initially reached it through any intellectual effort. But their Republicanism is an intensely emotional thing, a primitive religion on which devotees get 'high'. (The same of course applies to the Loyalists' political creed.)

Among the extremists to whom I talked were a few elderly men, respectable, educated and often quite affluent—the sort whom it has recently become fashionable to call 'the godfathers'. Others were young, active volunteers who are on duty for forty-eight hours, off for twenty-four, on again for forty-eight; these are paid £10 a week to supplement whatever their ingenuity can wring out of National Assistance. Their officers get £20 a week and lead a less boring but more dangerous life. During the volunteers' time on duty they hide in some safe (they hope) building and are irregularly supplied with meals—if they are lucky—by local sympathisers. If for any reason it becomes too risky to feed them they have to get by on iron rations. They are forbidden to drink while on duty and if they do are kneecapped. They know nothing about their next assignment, neither when they are going to be called upon 'to take action' nor what or where that action will be. Thus if they are 'lifted' they can give little useful information however much 'pressure' may be applied. As their average age has dropped, owing to the numbers now in prison, it has become increasingly important to withhold information from them; events have proved that seventeen- and eighteen-year-olds are much more likely to give in to 'pressure' than their elders. When the moment comes for action their officer arrives at the hideout, usually in a hijacked car, and on the way to their target they are told what they have to do. Frequently of course no action takes place during a duty-period and I asked two young men how they pass the time. "Cards and books," they replied laconically and nodded towards a stack of trashy paperbacks in one corner of the room.

As far as I know, I met no members of those criminal splinter groups who, having been armed by the Provos, are now doing their own thing. These outcasts are opposed not only by the conventional forces of law and order but by all 'orthodox' Provos who have, paradoxical as it may seem to us, very high standards of discipline and very firm principles about what is allowable under war conditions. If the wrong person is killed during an ill-planned bombing, as in the case of Professor Hamilton-Fairley, that is considered a tragedy and the Provos mean it when they say they are sorry. But such occasional accidents are seen as inevitable, however regrettable. On the other hand, the Brits—the detested enemy troops, the Army of Occupation—are to be attacked only when in uniform and armed. I listened, fascinated and astonished, to one argument between a seventeen-year-old recruit, who insisted that a Brit should be regarded as fair game always and everywhere, and three senior officers. These men were adamant that under no circumstances, however tempting a target he presented, must a Brit be shot when in civvies and unarmed. ('Not hurling, old boy!' as you might say.) I could scarcely believe my ears, so accustomed are we to thinking of Provos as gangs of thugs devoid of all moral sensibility. It was then that I fully appreciated the military nature of their thinking—or feeling. To them their campaign is, in a curious way, a conventional war, and they want to keep the party clean. The fact that most people regard them as an especially dirty bunch of urban guerrilla terrorists they find incomprehensible and very wounding to their collective *amour propre*. This aspect of the Provo character needs to be emphasised and dwelt upon. By virtue of their total dedication and sincerity, misdirected and perverted as it is, they deserve to have their viewpoint considered dispassionately. Or, to put the argument on a lower level, it is at least expedient to consider that viewpoint, when we remember that eight years of condemning, rejecting and despising it have achieved nothing.

By now one would expect the dividing line between the idealists and the criminals to be very blurred; and of course on some occasions it is—and then one gets particularly vile crimes, like the luring to death by 'mutinous' volunteers of three young soldiers on the pretext that they were being invited to a party. Generally, however, the line is quite clear, at least in the lower ranks. Towards the top there is much more blurring though obviously it is impossible to uncover hard facts. Maire Drumm, for instance, had bought a large pub in Dundalk, just south of the border, shortly before she was murdered in a Belfast hospital in December 1976. And it is not easy to see how a ghetto woman, whose husband had spent so much of his life in gaol, was able to raise the money to pay for such a property. Even the British government does not provide social security benefits on that scale. But none of the young volunteers with whom I spoke could possibly be mistaken for anything other than fanatical visionaries. Nowadays, however, most trained volunteers are in their teens and it seems probable that quite a number will eventually become criminals. It takes great strength of character to grow up in a world where the official representatives of law and order are despised, and to have access to guns and explosives, and yet to remain an idealist whose activities are strictly confined to the 'Fight for Irish Freedom'. Several of the older generation of Provos anxiously discussed this problem with me as parents elsewhere might discuss efforts to keep their youngsters off the drug scene. They were quite unaware of how odd their conversation sounded to someone who had been used to thinking of Provos *en masse* as vicious outlaws.

Only once while with the Provos did I feel fear and that was not in any rough pub or tough shebeen but in the comfortable sitting-room of a large villa overlooking a spacious garden. My hospitable, middle-aged host (Sean, let's say) had attended courteously to all my needs and we had been talking for about an hour. During that time I had tried to make it clear that I was not, despite my ancestry, a Provo supporter. But Sean seemed to have difficulty in accepting this. Evidently to him it was unimaginable that anybody whose grandfather had been out in '16 should not be a Republican at heart, even if they chose to deny it. And I preferred not to stress the point too vehemently. I was becoming rather exhausted by the need to steer an honourable course between downright hypocrisy and the angering of men who are capable of killing for all sorts of odd reasons. In Provoland my ancestry was a two-edged weapon. It gave me the entree to circles that would otherwise have remained closed but it also left me vulnerable to the charge of being a traitor. And some Provos hold strong views about traitors, disposal of. . . .

However, I temporarily forgot these inhibitions when Sean began to gloat over the assassination of the British Ambassador to the Republic in July 1976. He described this as the 'best event of the year' and I had to protest then; there comes a time when pussy-footing won't do. In a confused, pompous sort of way I felt that the honour of my country was at stake. Furiously I pointed out that by immemorial custom—a custom so ancient that its earliest acceptance can't be traced—an ambassador's inviolability is held sacred *even after war has broken out between the two countries concerned.* After days of cautiously not arguing against stupidities that had irritated or disgusted me, it was a relief to speak my mind. I said that in all the civilised world only the Ottoman government had ever disregarded this custom—and even they had not murdered ambassadors but merely imprisoned them in the Seven Towers for the duration of hostilities. Then the haze of rage cleared from before my eyes and I saw Sean's face. It was transformed. He seemed to be wearing a mask of hate. And his eyes were maniacal. Perhaps that word sounds too strong but none other will do; one cannot always describe extremists in moderate language. For a moment I wanted to run away. I did not imagine that the hate was directed against me but the evilness of it seemed impersonally threatening. After a moment I remembered where last I had felt a similar emotion: in Ian Paisley's 'church'.

Sean leaned forward and stared at me. "Maybe we could do even better than an ambassador this year—I wonder what you'd say to that? You know, you're not thinking straight. If Frenchmen had killed the Nazi C. in C. when the German army was occupying their country, would you have condemned them?"

My adrenalin had receded but I could not give in now. "An ambassador isn't a soldier," I said doggedly.

"No," agreed Sean, "but this fella was more dangerous than any soldier. The bloody bastard wasn't an ambassador—he was a *spy*! What are you on about? You're supposed to be a clever woman who writes books—how can they fool you so easily?"

This taunt reactivated my adrenelin. "Every ambassador is a spy, in one sense," I retorted. "And I don't care if he did belong to MI 4, 5, 6 or 7—he came to my country as an ambassador and you *can't* justify his murder!"

Sean sat back in his chair and suddenly was genial again. "Forget it!" he said. "You're just another dupe, fooled by the Brits like all that shower down in Dublin—Born-in-a-Garret and the Cruiser O'Brit and all the rest!" He lit another cigarette and shook his head. "I dunno what in hell we're going to do about the Free State. It'll be a lot tougher to crack, long-term-wise, than the Six Counties. It's gone corrupt. *You're* a good example, with all your fancy crap about ambassadors. Here the Brits are on the way out—no doubt about that. We have them on the run. And when they go there will be worse bloodshed for a while than we've ever seen yet. Then the Loyalists can be given autonomy and soon enough they'll settle down to being Irish. They *are* Irish now—matteradamn where they came from in the first place. Where did any of us come from? But that effing shower in Dublin—they'll be a hell of a lot harder to get rid of than the Brits up here." He threw his half-smoked cigarette into the fire and lit another. "Let me tell you one wee yarn. A few years back in Derry the Brits attacked the Rossville flats. Our lads had nothing at the time—not a gun between them. But the so-called Irish army was just a few miles away, over the border—hundreds of them, bristling with guns. So our O.C. nipped away across the border to beg a loan—just for forty-eight hours. Would the C.O. give them? The bastard said, 'No—no—no!' And from where he was standing at that minute he could hear the Brits shooting the shit out of his own countrymen!" Sean looked at me directly. "I suppose you'd say he was right?"

"Well, he didn't have much alternative," said I feebly, feeling that I had done my bit for the day and might be excused a relapse into semi-hypocrisy. Sean would not have been receptive had I reminded him that an Irish army officer takes an oath to defend the Republic and that the Provos have openly declared their hostility to our state.

I would never have admitted it to Sean, but I could not help feeling a twinge of sympathy for that army officer. Oath or no oath, it cannot have been an easy situation for him. Blood is thicker than constitutional arrangements.

Sean then suggested that we should go out for a drink. The area's most popular pub, which I had frequented during the summer, was now a burnt-out shell—"The UVF," explained Sean. There was another quite close but, "It's not my favourite," said Sean. "Too many windows. Still, we can sit in a corner."

As we walked down an ill-lit main road the headlights of passing cars revealed that all the parking meters had had their innards torn out for use as timing devices in bombs. "Waste not, want not," chuckled Sean. "Why make them when the city council gives them for free?" Then he remarked, "My youngest brother was shot dead a few months ago on that corner over there—by the Brits. But it was an accident, worse luck. Otherwise I could have arranged a revenge killing." At which point I felt it was time to give up trying to understand the ethics of Provoland.

When a car slowed beside us Sean impulsively spun around, putting himself between me and the vehicle, and his reaction stopped my heart for a moment. But the driver was only dropping off a passenger and as we continued Sean apologised for his jitters and I thanked him for his gallantry. "What does it feel like," I asked, "to be so recognisable and hated that any day, almost anywhere, you may be shot?"

He smiled. "Didn't you see for yourself just now? It doesn't do the nerves any good. But all the same you don't really worry. You can't afford to. You'd be no use to anybody if you did. It's harder on wives, I'd say. They're the ones do the worrying and live on tranquillisers. I just hope they do a proper job if they get me. I wouldn't want to be a cripple."

It was early enough for the pub not to be crowded. When Sean appeared the side door was bolted and chained and two youths joined the permanent security man at the main door. We sat in a corner from which every window was visible and I found all these precautions appealing to that childish love of drama which lingers on in many adults. Yet this was no game. If somebody took a pot-shot at Sean, as he and I sat close together, that shot might go a few inches in the wrong direction.

At the time one doesn't allow these realisations to bother one; as Sean had just said, 'You'd be no use to anybody if you did.' But on leaving Belfast a few days later I enjoyed a perceptible easing of tension.

It is a cruel irony that since 1970 the Provos have antagonised millions who were perfectly prepared, after the NICRA campaign of the late sixties, to admit that the ill-used Catholics of Northern Ireland needed help. They have put the Northern minority so far beyond the pale that many now refuse to think of them as people with real grievances and a normal quota of good qualities. Although they are not Northern Ireland's natural scapegoats the Provos have made them seem so. Nowadays almost everything that goes wrong can plausibly be blamed on them. Plausibly enough, that is, to convince the average British newspaper reader or television viewer that the whole 'Ulster problem' is merely a fight against IRA terrorism. When brave young British soldiers are being treacherously killed by cowardly snipers, how can the British public be expected to spare much sympathy for the community which has bred those snipers? If the British can be brought to the point of recognising injustice they will usually try to do something about it. But the general public in every country prefers not to have to think too hard and this leaves them easy prey to those media manipulators who favour black-and-white presentations of Northern Irish events. Such over-simplications are too often encouraged by spokesmen for the British and Irish governments and the British army; the Provos have given everyone an excuse for forgetting—or never discovering—how agonisingly complex is the background to the Northern tragedy. And the more strongly people feel about the 'fight against terrorism' being our primary consideration the less likely are they to contribute, by the force of public opinion, to the removal of some of the causes of that 'terrorism'.

The New Year got off to a bad start in Northern Ireland. Before the Peace Rally we heard a nearby car-bomb explosion which blew both legs off a forty-four-year-old Co Down woman up in Belfast to visit a friend. (It later transpired that the Provos had mistaken her car for that of an RUC man.) On 1 January a two-year-old girl was accidentally shot dead in her home while a gun was being cleaned, a fifteen-months-old baby was killed in his mother's arms when a huge car-bomb went off outside their house and a nineteen-year-old soldier was shot dead in Crossmaglen. When that last item of news came over the wireless I was lunching with an Alliance Party friend in the remains of an hotel that had recently been badly bombed following a managerial decision to pay no more protection money. The sense of shock I felt was a measure of our ineradicable egocentricity. Just because I had so recently been in South Armagh, and might have exchanged a greeting with the dead boy, and might have sat talking with his killer in a pub, I felt a degree of anger, sorrow and despair never normally provoked by reports of Northern disasters.

Soon after, as we were having coffee in the lounge, a young English journalist went to a nearby public telephone to ring London. Evidently his editor wished him to rush down to Crossmaglen but he sensibly pointed out that there would be nothing to see and nobody to talk to; he had already rung the army at Lisburn and Bessbrook and been refused an interview with the C.O. concerned. There followed a discussion about which 'story' should be used and in conclusion the young man said briskly—"OK. Let's forget the blown-up kid and stick to Crossmaglen." My companion caught my eye, read my thoughts and said, "But when will the kid's parents forget?"

12

Law and Disorder

On my way home I returned to South Armagh for a few days. As I got out of the bus in 'Cross', two hours after leaving Belfast, I felt rather as one does when getting out of a plane in Karachi or Delhi; I had moved too fast from one world to another. Cycling is by far the best way to travel around the North where regions only twenty miles apart can be so very unalike. On Roz I would have been aware of having travelled a long distance to Crossmaglen.

It was a relief that the soldier's death had not wrecked relations between the locals and the army. The Highlanders' C.O. had appeared on television a few hours after the shooting to promise that his men would not take it out on the South Armagh people and everybody I met confirmed that the regiment was keeping its word. But the troops, though no less polite than previously, looked very much more tense.

Near the bus stop I passed a foot-patrol as the strong gusty wind blew my sou'wester off my head and across the road. An adolescent soldier retrieved it and as he handed it back I said, "I'm sorry you lost a man." He looked at me blankly for a moment. Then suddenly his face puckered, just like a little child's. "He was my pal," he said. And he stood there, while his comrades waited for him, with tears streaking the black on his face.

Ever since the army was sent into Northern Ireland in August 1969, to defend the Catholics from the Protestants, there have been indignant comments on how unfair it is to expect a soldier to do a policeman's job and fight terrorism with his hands politically tied. Against this, many believe that the military authorities are quite pleased to have Northern Ireland as a training ground for new types of warfare. According to this view the army is contentedly planning to spend another eight years or so in the North 'perfecting anti-terrorist techniques', by the end of which time they reckon they will have 'just about cleaned the place up'. This attitude on the part of professional soldiers would be understandable. What alarms me much more is the tendency of British officers to see the IRA—and therefore the Catholic community—as their only enemy. (An exception was one officer of remarkable perception and humanity who had an unusual military role to play; he was among the few Englishmen I have ever met who appreciated every nuance of the Northern situation.) One senior officer told me cheerfully that he knew his men sometimes looked away when they saw Loyalist paramilitaries going about their business. Clearly it had never occurred to him that this bias, which is known to both Green and Orange paramilitaries, seriously diminishes the army's value as a 'Peace-Keeping Force'. Moreover, when the Irish army and police hear of instances of discrimination by the Brits they naturally feel less enthusiastic about helping them. The habit of 'looking away' can be catching.

It is often said that soldiers are not meant to think—only to act—and that they would be useless as soldiers if they ever paused for reflection. This of course is true and it sufficiently explains why some people feel that the army should be removed from the Northern scene. If ever a situation called for reflection, imagination, compassion and compromise this is it. I am not suggesting that the average soldier, as an individual, is devoid of these qualities; but the military life does not encourage him to cultivate them. To appreciate the extra degree of violence the troops inject into the atmosphere—just by being there, apart from particular actions—one needs to 'take the temperature' amongst those sections of the Catholic community most exposed to military influence. Then one realises that the interaction of troops and Catholic ghetto dwellers brings out the worst on both sides.

Many a teenage soldier must arrive in the North for the first time knowing nothing whatever about the conflict, having no bias for or against either side and feeling quite prepared, in the innocence of his heart, to befriend the entire population. But as soon as he is sent out on patrol he will become aware of his inheritance of hate. He will see it on the faces of many Catholics—and perhaps eventually suffer from it, if he is unlucky.

Then his mates will tell him about the sandwiches filled with powdered glass that were offered to one regiment and about innumerable other demonstrations of vengeful loathing. Thus he, too, will learn to hate.

One cause of bad relations between the army and the Catholic community is never mentioned though to me it seems of considerable significance. Over the years, countless opportunities to improve relations have been lost because of the deep cultural/social chasm that separates the officer (often an ex-public schoolboy) from the Catholic community leader (often an ex-ghetto lad or a small-farmer's son). Though the latter may have been to university and attained eminence in his own profession, his self-confidence often crumbles pathetically when he has to deal with a member of England's hereditary ruling caste. This is so even when the Englishman in question is aware of needing guidance and perfectly prepared to learn from the Irishman. On several occasions I heard prominent Catholics covering up their uncertainty about how to deal with this unfamiliar sort of human being by mimicking an officer's 'posh' accent, or making snide remarks about clueless and bloodless Old Etonians, or boasting of how they had scored off that half-wit who came along talking crap about 'co-operation'. Undoubtedly many officers are half-wits, in the Northern Irish context, but the Catholic leaders, if not so hamstrung by their social chip, could do a lot to help them to become less foolish. As it is, sheer class animosity too often makes it impossible for even the best-intentioned officers to receive guidance from Catholics. In a clumsy effort to overcome this difficulty the army sometimes publicises the fact that particular officers are themselves Catholics. But such gestures miss the point; the army authorities probably do not realise that for generations there has been considerable mutual dislike between Irish peasant Catholics and English upper-class Catholics. Four Catholic community leaders admitted to me that they find it easier to deal with Protestant officers who have risen from the ranks than with Catholic officers of the old school(s). Which of course is obliquely cheering; in the North one rejoices to find any situation in which religion is *not* the most important factor.

In every Catholic area, urban or rural, grim stories are told to illustrate the corruption and savagery of the Brits. It is easy to produce a long list of despicable crime committed over the past eight years by the licentious soldiery; theft, assault, robbery, manslaughter, planting of ammunition or incriminating documents on innocent civilians, looting, murder, rape—you name it, they've done it. But there have been huge numbers of soldiers stationed in Northern Ireland during that period—often living under appalling conditions—and though their behaviour while on duty is frequently deplorable their actual crime record is rather better than one would expect. When I commented on this to Ardoyne friends the remark was not well received and I can quite see why. It is easy for the outsider to be detached and fair-minded; my home is not repeatedly ransacked in the small hours and my child is in no danger of being killed in an 'incident' with the army.

The consequences of two teenage deaths, in the Turf Lodge area of West Belfast, show how effectively the Brits recruit for the Provos. In August 1975 Leo Norney, a seventeen-year-old post-office messenger who lived with his family, was shot dead when walking near his home by members of the Black Watch Regiment. (That same month five members of the same regiment were accused of planting bullets on young men from Turf Lodge and were subsequently gaoled for the offence.) At the time the army alleged that Norney was one of two men who fired on a foot-patrol. A year later an open verdict was returned at his inquest. Then, in April 1977, his parents were awarded £3,000 in the Northern Ireland High Court and the Ministry of Defence accepted that 'Leo Norney was a totally innocent party'.

Meanwhile, in September 1976, a thirteen-year-old boy, Brian Stewart, died in hospital having had his skull smashed by a plastic bullet. He had just left his home and was alone, innocently idling around a street corner where a few hours earlier a gang of older boys had stoned a foot-patrol, when he was deliberately fired on at close range by a soldier of the King's Own Borderers.

The Turf Lodge housing estate, built in the fifties, had for years been one of the least troubled districts of West Belfast. It was Stickie territory and the Provos' 'C' Company, 1st Battalion, which includes Turf Lodge in its area, got very little support. But after September 1976 came a swift change of mood. Apart from Brian Stewart's death there were many other instances of military brutality during the autumn and by November numerous Stickie and Irps supporters had gone over to the Provos. On 24 November a member of the Royal Welsh Fusiliers was shot in the neck as his patrol tried to escape from a furious mob; he was the first soldier to have been killed in Turf Lodge for six years. And at midnight on 31 December the Provos welcomed 1977 by attacking Fort Monagh barracks in Turf Lodge. A few days later they seriously wounded two members of a foot-patrol on the edge of the estate and further gun-battles and mortar attacks followed.

Considering the Norney and Stewart cases, one realises that in whichever direction the authorities jump, after tragedies of this sort, they must inevitably land in the soup. By failing to have the killer detected and tried they play the IRA's propaganda game; by charging him they undermine army morale— which is none too good at any time in Northern Ireland. What *should* be done? If the soldier involved is a thug who enjoys Paddy-bashing then in my opinion he should be charged with murder. If, however, he is some wretched dim-witted youngster who made a mistake because he was nervous, I personally would allow discretion to be the better part of justice and quietly send him home to Mum. But, looking at it from the Green point of view, why should any soldier be allowed to escape the consequences of killing an innocent citizen?

The army's ambiguous status in the North repeatedly produces this sort of mess. It describes itself as a 'Peace-Keeping Force', dedicated to restoring law and order, and is not officially at war with anyone. Yet its opponents describe themselves as the Irish Republican Army and do claim to be officially at war. So—is there a war on or isn't there? If there is, who, from the British point of view, is the enemy? Anyone carrying a gun? Anyone known to sympathise with those who carry guns? Or just anyone who happens to live in an area where guns are frequently found? Theoretically, armed men in the firing posture are the only legitimate targets. But there must be many occasions when a patrol recognises a paramilitary in another

posture and feels strongly tempted to take action. The fact that
the troops usually resist these temptations is a considerable tri-
bute to British military discipline.

Soon after my return home from Crossmaglen my own feelings about the security forces were precisely expressed in a newspaper article by the Most Reverend Dr Cahal Daly, Catholic
Bishop of Ardagh and Clonmacnois, who is himself from Co
Antrim and was for many years a professor at Queen's University, Belfast. Dr Daly wrote: 'I do not contest the legitimacy
and necessity of security operations. I contest the effectiveness
of current security operations to achieve their stated aim....
Armies are just not suited to civilian peace-keeping operations.
Surely military thinking has a very restricted relevance to
civilian subversion. Security in this situation has as much to
do with a battle for minds, for credibility and for confidence
as with military successes. From these aspects, present army
policies must be pronounced counter-productive.... What I
am saying is not anti-British prejudice. It is not said in anger.
It is said in great sadness. It is said with regret and with searching of conscience, for one is fully aware of the danger of being
misunderstood, of giving comfort to the IRA.'

'A battle for minds' is the key phrase in that quotation and
the first round has to be fought against the politicians of Belfast,
London and Dublin. Until these men have seen the futility of
merely exchanging blows with the paramilitaries—or have
been replaced by others able to see it—there is no hope of a
constructive reassessment of security methods.

After the London bombings of January 1977 Roy Mason,
Secretary of State for Northern Ireland, told foreign journalists
in London that the Provos were attempting to stage 'spectacu-
lars' to prove they were still in business but that the security
forces 'would take more slices off the terrorist hide'. Strangely,
these words shocked me, when I read them in my *Irish Times*,
no less than the murder of the Englishman, Jeffrey Agate, which
was reported on the same page. Yet perhaps not strangely, since
the two reports were simply different aspects of a single
horror—the brutalising effect of war.

In Dublin, during the same period, Mr Mason had his
counterpart in the then Minister for Justice, Patrick Cooney,

who lost his seat in the general election of June 1977. On 14 January Mr Cooney said, "The people of this island can solve the problem of violence in one way only—by turning against the paramilitaries and handing them over to the police.... Every citizen must feel duty bound to report to the gardai any knowledge he or she has of actual or intended crimes. To do so is a basic civic duty. The subversives and those associated with supporting them must be made to feel the cold breath of the people's scorn for their aims and abhorrence for their methods. Thus, with the help of the security forces, the law-abiding people of Ireland will finally remove the baneful influence of the men of violence from our presence.... Do we want to share the fate of the German people whereby a whole race and innocent generations have to bear the obloquy of the actions of a small number? For seven years now small groups of evil men have been committing unspeakable atrocities in our name. If mere exhortation could have ended that situation, it should have ended long ago, because for the past seven years violence has been condemned from platform and pulpit, but apparently without any result whatever. It is quite clear that mere condemnation is not enough."

To me all this seems grossly misleading—and therefore dangerous. For centuries the Northern Irish problem has been fertilised by over-simplifications. 'All Protestants are bigots, all Catholics are traitors, all Orangemen/Nationalists have guns, all RUC men are thugs, all Catholic priests are subversives, all Unionists are bullies, all Taigs are dishonest'—and so on and on and on, seemingly forever. It cannot help to add to this dismal catalogue by saying, 'Do we want to share the fate of the German people whereby a whole race and innocent generations have to bear the obloquy of the actions of a small number? For seven years now small groups of evil men have been committing unspeakable atrocities in our name. ...' This particular over-simplification has become very popular in the Republic where we seem to use it as a sort of tranquilliser. It is less disturbing to think of 'small groups of evil men' than to accept the existence of a million and a half fellow-Irishmen who have been pitchforked, by historical events for which no one now living can be blamed, into a situation of such profound mutual distrust and antipathy that some of them have gone right round the bend. I am not suggesting that the majority in either community is behind the extremists. But I am suggesting that the extremists are just that—*extreme* representatives of their respective communities. They are not another sort of human being—'evil men' existing in isolation from the 'law-abiding people of Ireland' and radiating a 'baneful influence' throughout their neighbourhoods. Most Northerners do indeed deplore their 'unspeakable atrocities', yet the mere existence of those two communities, each laden with prejudice against and ignorance of the other, powerfully reinforces the extremists even while they are being reproached or rejected by their political or religious leaders.

The majority of Northern Irish abhor paramilitary methods but do not scorn paramilitary aims. How could Mr Cooney expect all Northern Protestants to scorn the aims of men who want to defend them from the wiles of the Romish Republic? And how could he expect all Northern Catholics to scorn the aims of men who want the Brits out? For half a century the Dublin government encouraged the Northern minority to dream of a united Ireland and on one celebrated occasion some of its ministers actually encouraged them to fight for it. Yet a few years later our Minister for Justice expected the same minority to wake up from its dream and meekly toe the new line that had been marked out for it by Dublin.

In fact many Northern Catholics awoke from their dream long before Dublin began to prod them but it does not help to condemn those who are still asleep. The Northern extremists and their supporters, whether Orange or Green, are never going to be guided onto the path of virtue by condemnation for the very good reason that they believe they are already on it. So their contempt and hatred for those who oppose them are merely strengthened by each fresh proof that their aims are scorned.

Mr Cooney thought it quite clear that 'mere condemnation is not enough' and I would argue that at this stage any condemnation—*of people*—is too much. Condemning the 'men of violence' is essentially a negative attitude which compounds the aggression in the Irish atmosphere. For every paramilitary picked up there may well be two recruits if we continue to look upon extremists as unworthy of our understanding. Lord Melchett was once severely criticised for opening a new UDA club in Belfast and settling down afterwards to have a few jars with Andy Tyrie and the lads. He was probably unaware of the club's provenance when he agreed to open it (Andy Tyrie has a nice sense of humour) but in my opinion he was perfectly right to stand his ground when the penny did drop. It would be no bad thing if our cabinet ministers took it in turns publicly to go on the tiles around Dublin with members of the two Sinn Feins. And I am not joking. The more communication the better, however much it may scandalise conservative (or Conservative) citizens.

For millenia most civilisations have conditioned people to fight back and when our society seems threatened we instinctively assume that extremists can be dealt with only by matching their own ruthlessness. During the past few years I have heard many laments, in both Britain and the Republic, about 'the mistake at the beginning'. This mistake, according to large numbers of otherwise balanced and kindly people, lay in not 'sending the troops in to shoot—mopping them up when they started—imprisoning the lot and hanging the leaders from lamp-posts'. In this respect I, too, had a closed mind not very long ago. At times of despair and anger, when yet another 'terrorist atrocity' had been committed, I often felt that the security forces should be much tougher and that for certain offences the death penalty should be brought back in Britain and used in Ireland. I am not by temperament squeamish about inflicting deserved punishments. I do not believe that criminals should be provided with interior spring mattresses, colour television, heated swimming pools and first class tuition to enable them to get university degrees. But neither do I now believe that it makes sense to treat the Northern Irish paramilitaries as common criminals.

The only way in which the battle for the extremists' minds can be won is by overcoming one's repugnance for their ideas and actions and communicating with them simply as other human beings. Instead of opposing violence to violence, tolerance must be opposed to intolerance and reflection to hysteria. But to achieve anything worthwhile this communication must be based on sincere efforts to understand. Condescending media interviews, with the Orange or Green extremist being kept emotionally at arm's length, have for years been a common feature of the Northern scene. One has to struggle to remember that the extremists *do* have a point of view which to them is valid, however absurd or debased it may seem to us. It is hard to be convincing, in the abstract, about such matters. Yet when one is actually talking to 'the men of violence' it is surprisingly easy to understand the workings of their hearts, if not of their minds. And once some understanding has been gained, it becomes possible to differ from them without despising them. I have made valued friends among both Orange and Green paramilitaries; few are so extreme that they refuse to respond to the concern of a non-extremist.

We all need to change gear mentally, as it were, and to approach the Northern problem at a different pace. Instead of compulsively and impulsively abusing the paramilitaries as gangs of thugs labelled IRA, UVF—and so on—we must focus on the fact that each group is made up of individuals most of whom have been born into the spiritual and intellectual equivalent of a Calcutta slum. Many paramilitary deeds are revolting crimes but the paramilitaries themselves are not, usually, revolting criminals. I have made this point before but I am not apologising for repeating it. We *must* peel off the terrorist labels and look at the individuals underneath and try to understand why they are what they are—and ask ourselves what we would be had fate arranged for us to be born into an extremist family down a backstreet off the Falls or the Shankill.

Whatever Dr Daly or anyone else may think or write, Direct Rule, with 14,000 troops in Northern Ireland, can and probably will go on indefinitely. But meanwhile the Northern disease will be worsening. Mr Mason was of the opinion in January 1977 that 'the security situation continues to improve'. Yet three months later, on 21 April, the British Attorney-General, Mr Sam Silkin, told the European Human Rights Court in Strasbourg that 'terrorist activities were increasing in intensity and seriousness despite the measures taken by the authorities to deal with them'. True, the RUC Chief

Constable's Report for 1976, published in June 1977, showed that that year the Northern Ireland detection rate had almost reached the level of other metropolitan areas in Britain. In 1976 1,278 people were brought before the courts on terrorist offences and 963 were convicted. Some of this success is due to the restructuring of the RUC and the establishment of Regional Crime Squads whose members have been specially trained in Britain. The RUC are also aided by a seven-day detention period during which all but the toughest men can be 'persuaded' to sign statements, and by the increasing willingness of the courts to regard such statements as admissable evidence. These figures perhaps prove to Mr Mason that violence is now at an 'acceptable' level and that the forces of law and order are being 'effective'. But what is happening to people's minds and souls as they learn to live (or die) with this 'acceptable' level of violence? And how 'effective', in the long term, are police methods which arouse widespread public contempt and hostility? What problems are now ripening in the prisons of Northern Ireland as men who have been forced to confess to crimes they never committed plot their revenge on society? By abandoning British standards of justice, under pressure from paramilitary groups of every sort, the Northern Ireland Office is conceding ultimate victory to those who wish to destroy Northern Ireland as a recognisable part of the United Kingdom.

13

July Journal

Belfast. 11 July 1977

Last evening at Victoria Coach Station in London I caught myself doing it again—scanning people's faces to determine their religion. The Northern Irish way of life had already reclaimed me.

Three motor coaches were leaving for Belfast, via Stranraer-Larne, and Protestants were herding into the front two leaving the last for an English family going to Carlisle, half-a-dozen homing Taigs and myself. A plump granny from Newry sat in front of me and turned round to observe, "Thanks be to God we've our own bus! They'd ate you, so they would, when they've drink taken comin' up to the Twalfth!" The raven-haired young man beside me was from Strabane where unemployment figures often reach 20 per cent. He had been in London for a week, unsuccessfully hunting a job that would enable him to house his wife and four children in Britain.

I slept fitfully on the floor and at 2.45 sat up to watch the dawn. The crescent moon and the morning star were close together, luminously defying the midsummer sun. A Belfast mother travelling with four small children remarked that she'd sooner die than do the journey again. She had been to visit a sister who was ailing in Birmingham and took the wains to let them see a bit of normal life. The baby and the two eldest had been left back home in Andersonstown with the Daddy. That's why she had to get home before the Twelfth; the Daddy mightn't be able to hold them back from seeing the march. "Not that *I'd* mind them watchin'," she emphasised, "but there's others wouldn't hold with it." She glanced around swiftly and lowered her voice. "It's terrible hard to explain to the wains that they'd be got if they watched nowadays. And not by the Oranges, either." Her expression, as she spoke, was familiar to me. Belfast women's faces wear a certain indescribable

look—made up of fear, contempt, furtiveness and sulkiness—
when they are alluding to intimidation by the respective paramilitaries.

On Stranraer pier at 5.30 the sun was already warm and brilliant. Beyond the glassy, duck-egg blue harbour-water the little
town straggled along its promontary to merge with woodlands
near the tip. Oddly, there was not even an attempt at a security
check as we boarded. The half-empty boat had no holiday feeling and few children or tourists were visible.

Watching the shadowy Antrim Hills appearing along the
horizon I felt confused. This was my first approach to Northern
Ireland from Britain and of course I felt that I was going back
to my own island. Yet I was not going *home*. . . . All rather disconcerting. As the coastline of Ireland's most industrialised
corner became clearer I remembered Macaulay's reference to
William III's rendezvous with Schomberg at Belfast: 'The
meeting took place close to a white house, the only human
dwelling then visible, in the space of many miles, on the dreary
strand of the estuary of the Lagan.' Absurd and inconvenient
as it may seem, there *are* two distinct Irish traditions within
this minute island inhabited by scarcely four and a half million
people. And the creation of Belfast, on the dreary estuary of
the Lagan, is the work of only one of them.

At 9.30 we docked and at 10.00 sweat was dripping off me
as the bus sped along a new stretch of motorway. Past Ballylum-
ford—across the bay—with its so-politically-important power-
station; past Kilroot where Jonathan Swift had his first living;
through Northern Ireland's oldest town, Carrickfergus, where
William landed in 1690 and Ireland's last witchcraft trial took
place in 1771; past hideous, huge factories; past Cave Hill
which looks like a giant's profile and is said locally to have inspired Gulliver—and then I could see those other, man-made
Belfast landmarks, Samson and Goliath. I felt a rush of delight
and affection. Strange that two cranes, of all things, have come
to seem friendly objects, symbolic of Belfast's more admirable
characteristics. When first constructed Samson and Goliath
were the biggest cranes in the world and for all I know they
may still be.

Belfast was very quiet today. The annual holidays have

begun and most of those not wishing to participate in the Twelfth, and with enough money to get away, have departed—the majority, it seems, to Donegal. In Protestant districts countless men and women were out painting hall-doors, window-frames, garden gates. Round almost every corner gay arches—this year usually incorporating the Queen and Prince Philip as well as King Billy—span narrow streets of terraced brick houses. And Union Jacks, Ulster flags, and red, white and blue bunting are everywhere aflutter. I counted nine gable-walls on which murals of King Billy had been skilfully painted from eaves to ground. The Orangeman is so *industriously* loyal. It's impossible to imagine even the most fervent Irish Republican going to such lengths every year to celebrate 1916. Not only because he is lazier than the Orangeman; he is also less adolescent.

On scores of streets enormous bonfires, fifteen or even twenty feet high, had been carefully constructed for tonight's ritual. As I passed one I was proudly told that it contained over 200 old tyres. These edifices are of great significance to their builders. For the past few nights, in certain areas, youths have been sleeping out to guard them from the depredations of Taigs or rival Oranges. An amateur social historian met on the boat this morning told me that he has traced the Eleventh bonfires back to London's seventeenth-century Apprentice Boys who at the Restoration dragged effigies of Popes and Cardinals through the City to the stakes at Smithfield. I myself have heard none of the notorious chanting that accompanies Orange bonfire building and burning but I am assured the tradition is being maintained with such variations as "Yippy, yippy, yippy, the Pope's a bloody hippy". In 1977 the outsider tends to be amused rather than shocked on hearing this sort of thing. It's hard for us to realise how provocative such chanting can still be within earshot of conventionally devout Northern Catholics. Tonight I can appreciate the value, at this season, of a British Peace-Keeping Force. Whatever disquiet may be felt about the Brits' everyday role, they almost certainly save lives during the month of July. For the past eighty years or more, ferocious anti-Catholic rioting has frequently accompanied the Orange celebrations. Indeed, the Orange Order has been involved,

directly or indirectly, in almost every major riot in Northern
Ireland since 1830.

At 8.0 pm I began my bonfire walkabout—along the Ballysil-
lan Road, then down the Crumlin Road into the heart of the
Shankill. Crowds of men and youths had collected around
every waiting pyramid of wood, rubber and old clothes. In
places empty beer cans and broken wine bottles were ankle-
deep while anti-Papish ballads were being indistinctly sung to
the music of flutes, pipes and accordions. It was a windless,
cloudless, very hot evening. A gloomy RUC man on duty at
the top of the Woodvale Road told me that all day he'd been
praying for rain; I was soon to see why. Half-way down the
Shankill Road I turned off into a narrow street of dingy terraced houses, several of which had been bombed or burned and
then bricked-up. Here a massive mountain of planks, crates,
roof-beams, doors, tyres, carpets and old mattresses had been
created at the junction of four little streets; its base extended
from kerb to kerb and its summit was directly below and almost
touching a line of telegraph wires. Groups of women stood on
the pavements, leaning against door-jambs or window-sills and
looking apprehensive rather than festive. I joined three at a
corner house, near the pyramid, and on opening my Southern
mouth was greeted with much astonishment but no hostility.
When I commented on the perilous location of the bonfire one
woman smiled sourly. "That's what they want—to do as much
damage as they can. More vandalism is all it is now. It used
to be a happy night out for the kids but these times it's plain
destruction."

Her neighbour nudged her then and muttered, "Here they
come!" Together we stared towards the Shankill Road and saw
about thirty youngsters in their early teens turning off the main
road and strolling up the centre of our street. Four other women
moved along the pavement to join us and exclamations of
horror came from every tongue. At first I was puzzled. The
youngsters were quietly eating chips out of sheets of greasy
paper and doing no harm to anyone. When I saw them swaying
and heard them mumbling I assumed they were having a
game—pretending to be drunk. Most of them were fourteen
or fifteen; two of them were twelve. Then as they passed us

one girl staggered, flung away her chips, grabbed her boy friend's arm to steady herself and vomited a great deal of red wine all over his flared jeans. And so it went on. A few others also vomited; some passed out and lay still; several collapsed in pairs on the pavement and fumbled ineffectually with each other's zips. Two couples embraced lingeringly and then disappeared round a corner to an old bomb-site overgrown with long grass. One girl stumbled, fell into the gutter onto a broken bottle and became hysterical at the sight of her own blood.

I felt then the blackest despair I have known in Northern Ireland. The scales are weighted so heavily against these children—and against their children, and their children's children. Those self-righteous, self-centred politicians who wrecked the Northern Ireland Executive and have allowed Northern Irish society to fall apart should have been down the Shankill tonight.

"I'm ashamed any stranger should see it!" said the elderly woman on my right. Her hands were twisting in powerless rage and she was crying. "One o' them wee girls is me own grand-daughter—what good to deny it? Doesn't the whole street know? Sixty-five years I'm living on this street and never thought to have such humiliation. Look at her—me own flesh and blood—lying there in a stupor. And if I went near her the boy friend'd hit me. Fifteen she is. But the neighbours know there's no blame on me. Her father was reared decent and sober and God-fearing and away to St Andrew's twice every Sunday. And so he stayed till this curse of easy money and drinking-clubs came in on us."

"It's only these few days," said I, feebly attempting to console her. "They'll be OK again next week."

She blew her nose and shook her head. "Don't you believe it! We see this carry-on every week-end regular, Twalfth or no Twalfth."

"But where do all these children get the money?" I asked. "Even in the clubs alcohol isn't free."

"They earns it, some of 'em, working behind the scenes after hours in supermarkets and suchlike. More of 'em steals. A few of 'em helps the paras and gets good pay. And it don't take too much to make wains drunk."

At that moment a neatly-dressed small boy with well-brushed hair came up the street and disappeared round the corner to where the pyramid-builders were having their pre-fire carousal. My friend nodded after him. "See that wee lad? Eleven, he is, and the smartest shop-lifter in Belfast. His mother taught him. He could lift the coat off your back and you wouldn't ever be the wiser."

I lowered my voice. "What would happen if you told the police about him?"

My friend looked away. "You can't do things like that in Belfast nowadays. We all mind our own business, so we do."

Two of the four corner houses near the pyramid were bricked-up ruins but clearly the other two needed protection. I had just remarked on this when three surprisingly good-humoured policemen came up the street on foot carrying a long ladder, a saw, lengths of chipboard and several sacks. They spent twenty minutes boarding up all the endangered windows before draping wet sacks over the boards. The elderly, flustered householders were advised to keep on pouring water over the sacking while the bonfire raged. Then, still looking good-humoured, the police departed. I couldn't help wondering how they would have reacted to a similarily placed bonfire in a Catholic area.

A frail, lame woman, leaning on a walking-stick, had meanwhile joined us. Her face was very lined and her mouth thin-lipped. "Wouldn't you think them poor peelers have enough to do, without all this commotion," she observed to no one in particular.

"But why on earth do they allow such huge bonfires to be built here in the first place?" I asked in genuine bewilderment.

The frail woman stared at me expressionlessly for a moment but said nothing. Then a youngish red-head to whom I'd been talking earlier lent forward and whispered in my ear, "Tis a UDA bonfire we have here."

By then it was 10.15. As the light began to fade huge columns of smoke, soon turning golden-pink and glittering with swift sparks, rose above the roofs in every Protestant direction. But somehow—though I have always loved bonfires—I couldn't see this orgy of burning as entertainment. I have watched too many columns of smoke rising over Belfast in the past twelve months. Here fires are no longer fun-things.

For some reason our own bonfire had not yet been lit so I peered round the corner to see what was happening. Another mountain of supplementary fuel lay in the middle of the street and a score of young men were sprawling against walls, still drinking and singing. Nearby groups of very small children— girls and boys, none of whom could have been more than eight—were fighting and playing and cursing as they waited for the fun to start. "Tis a scandal!" muttered the frail woman. "These wains shoulda been asleep two hours ago. There's some there won't be in bed at all tonight. I could show them to you. Their mothers and fathers will be too drunk to shove a key in the door."

A few minutes later three men suddenly appeared with burning brands and thrust them into the heart of the pyramid. Kerosene or petrol must have been involved; the whole thing took off with a roar. Then a shaven-headed youth came racing towards us out of the dusk. He climbed the pyre as the flames flared faster and higher and around me the women gasped with fear. Reaching the summit he clung to the topmost tyre for a moment, waving a clenched fist, his head thrown back as he shouted a message of hate. On the far side flames were already rising above the summit and on our side they were shooting up between planks to touch the youth's trouser-legs. Briefly he was silhouetted against the blaze—reckless, fanatical, primitive—calling on all his tribe to destroy their Papish enemy; thus he exposed the evil at the core of Orangeism. Consolingly, however, his melodramatic belligerence aroused no enthusiasm amongst any section of the small crowd. And it angered the local UDA leader, a burly man of about forty. When the youth had nimbly leaped through the flames to the ground he was seized by the shoulders, thrown against a wall and punched hard in the face. With blood streaming from his nose he slunk away.

Everybody was retreating further and further from the increasing heat, backing down the street and looking anxiously at their little homes. The telegraph wires had long since caught fire and soon the telegraph pole nearest the pyre was ablaze.

It looked very beautiful—a giant torch sparking and flaring—but also slightly frightening. Fire out of control scares us at a very deep level. Clouds of steam were billowing from those windows where unfortunate householders were trying to keep sacks wet. Their task had a distinctly mythological flavour: puny humans desperately defying Xiuheuctli the Fire-God. And of course it was a hopeless task. Soon the window-frames and doors of all the corner houses were burning and the fire-brigade arrived. "At least they're lettin' 'em up the street this year," said the sad grandmother. "Last year they stoned 'em so hard they couldn't use the hoses and them three houses below there was burnt out."

As I walked home up the Shankill and Crumlin Roads fire-engines were racing and wailing all over the city like demented monsters. And now, as I write, I can see the many columns of smoke merging into one gigantic cloud above Belfast. It seems, appropriately, to have an orange tinge.

12th July.

At 9.10 am I was introduced to the Loyal Orange Lodge that had adopted me for the day. It was a Primary—as distinct from District, County and Grand—Lodge in rather a 'deprived' area. Around the Orange Hall little tables were laden with beer bottles and whiskey glasses, and scrubbed-looking Orangemen, in their Sabbath suits, were drinking and smoking and quietly chatting. Each had his sash to hand, carefully wrapped in brown paper or a plastic bag, and at the back of the Hall the first relay of banner-bearers were adjusting their leather harness and fixing bouquets of Sweet William and orange gladioli to the banner poles. I had scarcely crossed the threshold when I was being offered 'a wee one'. At the risk of seeming effete I chose beer. It was, as I have said, 9.10 am.

A year ago I would have felt a little uneasy at this gathering but by now I have reached a certain understanding of the Orange psyche. However much the Orange leaders may rave and rant against Papists and Southern Irish knaves, your average Orangeman is prepared to be a good host to everybody. If the Pope himself had appeared on the Field today I do believe he would at once have been offered 'a wee one' by men who last evening were kicking his effigy down Sandy Row. The Orangeman's ferocity is in the main a herd thing; given the wrong sort of leadership (which he always has been given) he can be very dangerous indeed. Left to himself he is as friendly and generous as any other Irishman.

Tony Gray tells a splendid story to illustrate the Orangeman's defective historical sense. A bewildered Englishman, finding himself caught up in Belfast's Boyne Anniversary celebrations, asked the spectator beside him, "What's going on?" "It's the Twalfth," he was told curtly. "Yes I know it is," said the Englishman, "but what's all this about?" With a gesture of impatient disgust the Belfastman dismissed him: "Och away home and read your Bible, man!" Even Mr Paisley's bible fails to describe King William's victory over King James at the Battle of the Boyne on July 1 (O.S.) 1690. But it is true that many Orangemen have transposed the origins of their Order to biblical times, though they are vividly aware that the Twelfth festivities commemorate the victory at the Boyne of some 40,000 Protestants (mostly Dutch, Danes, Germans, Scots and English) over some 30,000 Catholics (mostly French).

There are two ways of approaching the Twelfth. It can be taken either as a super-de-luxe, hyper-Bank-Holiday-cum-Folk Festival or as a militant demonstration of Northern Irish Protestant power and the Orange Order's determination to retain that power at the expense of the democratic rights of one-third of the population. I thoroughly enjoyed myself today because I resolved to take it on the entertainment level, as many Northern Catholics used to do in the fifties and sixties when community relations were gradually mellowing. This of course is the more superficial level—though it is perfectly genuine—and inevitably I also caught a few ugly glimpses of the deeper level. Yet it cannot be said that Belfast's mood today was anything but good-humoured, happy and relaxed. Astonishingly relaxed, considering Northern Ireland's present state. It did one good to see laughing teenage boys, and fat beaming ladies wearing Union Jack overalls and carrying Union Jack parasols, dancing together in the streets of their devastated city. And to see wide-eyed young soldiers laying down their weapons for long enough to take photographs of the banners and the bands.

At 10.00 am our Lodge moved off from the Hall having had some trouble awakening two young men who had fallen asleep where they sat; no doubt they were up all night with their bonfire. Since nine o'clock the air had been full of music and marching as Lodges from all over the city made their way to Carlisle Circus, the starting point for the procession of 299 Lodges and innumerable bands—including thirty from Scotland. At this stage I temporarily left 'my' Lodge, whose appointed place was near the end of the parade; I wanted to hurry ahead to reach a vantage point from which I could see the whole procession passing. For over an hour I walked fast through city centre streets lined with thousands upon thousands of cheerful citizens; and I found that even on pavements it is oddly untiring to walk to the beating of drums. Then the intense noon heat slowed up the proceedings and at a few points halts were called for ten minutes or so to give musicians and banner-bearers— not to mention all the aged stalwarts involved—a chance to refresh themselves with fizzy drinks or beer, depending on their devotion to Temperance. (Apart from the banners of many Temperance Lodges, I saw very little evidence at any time in Northern Ireland of leanings towards temperance.) These halts gave me a chance to overtake the leaders and by 1.30 I was sitting on a not too-crowded pavement on the Upper Malone Road next to a four-man UDR patrol who were lounging against their Land-Rover looking as though they wished that they too were marching.

Only then did I notice that the honour of leading the parade had been granted to the Dublin and Wicklow Loyal Orange Lodge. And so confused have all my emotional reactions become by now that I felt quite proud to see my fellow-Southerners in this position—though I know very well their Orangeism may mean a somewhat luke-warm loyalty to the country of their residence. Most of the Dublin and Wicklow Orangemen were elderly if not downright ancient and their attire was impeccably traditional. They wore dark city suits, white shirts, bowler hats, Orange Order cuffs, white gloves and orange collarettes (The Sash) decorated with war medals and esoteric badges denoting the wearer's precise status within this semi-secret society. Many carried tightly-rolled umbrellas as though they were bearing ceremonial swords and a few were solemnly shouldering silver-tipped pikes—perhaps in memory of the good old days before the Brits stood between them and the Papists. For the next hour and a half I watched hundreds of Loyal Orange Lodges passing; few were as correctly dressed as the Republic's representatives. (There were Lodges too from Leitrim, Donegal, Monaghan and Cavan, some with a surprising number of young members.) Nowadays the Belfast working-classes have little time for formal dressing-up and within the past ten or fifteen years quite a number of professional men and businessmen, to whom dark suits and bowlers would come naturally, have quietly dropped out of the Order. Certainly since Direct Rule was imposed there have been fewer practical reasons for joining. When it comes to appointments and promotions the British Government is not impressed (possibly even the reverse) by Orange membership cards.

Each Lodge is ritually preceded by its banner and sometimes four strong men and a few small boys are required to cope with one banner—the boys holding its tasselled 'stays' lest the wind might take control. The gaily-coloured hand-painted pictures are often, I gather, of immense significance, yet many Loyal Orangemen are unable to explain why their particular banner depicts this or that. The most startling banner today showed a map of Ireland (unpartitioned) with the main cities marked. The map was surmounted by an inscription in Irish which I'm ashamed to say I couldn't translate; underneath were the words 'Ireland's Heritage' and a quotation from St Luke: 'Occupy till I come.' Possibly this Lodge is dominated by the illegal Tara paramilitaries who are rumoured to advocate the conquest of the Republic by Orangemen as the only sensible solution to Ireland's problems. My favourite banner, however, depicted Queen Victoria and Prince Albert graciously receiving homage—and an overflowing casket of jewels—from a dark-skinned gentleman wearing a turban. The inscription read: 'The Secret of England's Greatness'—an accurate indication of the place in the groove where Orangeism has stuck. Many inscriptions, on both banners and drums, betrayed the Northern Protestant's much-discussed 'siege-mentality': 'Whiterock—Save the Covenant!', 'Ulster Defenders' Temperance', 'Naval Lodge—No Surrender!', 'Donegall Pass Defenders', 'Sandy Row Defenders', 'UVF Flute—For the Throne is Established by Right!', 'Ravenhill Road Volunteers', 'Cootes' Defenders', 'Banbridge Bible and Crown Defenders', 'Victory Total Abstinence', 'Templemore True Blues—If God be with us who can be against us?', 'Co Cavan Defenders', 'Duke of Manchester Invincibles', 'Woodvale Park Church Defenders', 'Shankill Heroes', 'Young Men Faith Defenders', 'Glenavy Chosen Few', 'Armagh True Blues—Trust in God and Keep Your Powder Dry!', 'Falls Road Methodist Church Defenders', 'Sons of Conquerors', 'Christian Crusaders', 'Rising Sons of Portadown'—and so on and on. That last Portadown Lodge had the only openly provocative banner; it depicted Catholics drowning Protestants in the Bann in 1641. Which indeed they did do—and as many as possible—but to call attention to that fact in Northern Ireland 336 years later seems unhelpful.

The North supports more bands per head of the population than anywhere else in the UK (perhaps than anywhere else, period). On the Twelfth they are all out vying with one another in putting up the best performance but they have recently had to narrow their repertoire. Such popular tunes as 'Croppies [Catholics] Lie Down' and 'Kick the Pope' are no longer publicly played. And the fearsome Lambeg drums are not now carried in the Belfast parade because their enormous weight slowed up the proceedings too much. At least, this is the official explanation for their absence. A plausible rumour has it that the organisers of the March were advised to confine them to rural areas for the future because of their power to arouse aggression.

Even without the Lambegs, there are hundreds of bass drums, kettledrums, pipes, flutes, accordions, fifes, cymbals, trumpets—and the musicians are as varied as the instruments. I saw every type, age and size of person playing, from 8-year-old girls in thick blue woollen cardigans, white shirts and red skirts to 75-year-old veterans in gorgeous scarlet uniforms with gold braiding. Incidentally, the only unnerving touch today was provided by the Sandy Row Girls' Band; these musicians were scarcely in their teens but a tougher-looking group of human beings I have never seen. I would far prefer to meet an Orange Volunteer unit armed with machine guns than just one of those maidens wielding a feather-broom.

To give a full description of this extraordinary spectacle would take up more pages than I have left at my disposal. It has often been called Europe's greatest folk-festival and today I could see why. I could also understand the grudging admiration and veiled pride with which many Northern Catholics refer to this essentially anti-Catholic demonstration. It is a magnificent event, unique to Northern Ireland, and they would hate to see it suppressed.

Every Orange march goes to a suitable field where most of the marchers collapse forthwith on the grass. The local leaders of the Order then make inflammatory speeches, which reassuringly few listen to, and after an interval for rest, refreshment and relaxation the Lodges and bands reconstitute themselves and march back to their Orange Halls. Nowadays, for security reasons, the Belfast Lodges all have to march back together at about 6.00 pm and this has marred the Twelfth, according to three old-timers to whom I spoke on the Field. Previously the festivities used to continue for many hours and as dusk fell neither Temperance nor Chastity remained the prevailing ideal.

Also for security reasons, the location of Belfast's Field has recently been changed from Finaghy to Edenderry and by the time we felt the blessed grass beneath our feet most of us had walked at least eight miles. Edenderry is aptly named—an enormous, sloping field surrounded by well-wooded rolling countryside. The atmosphere was very Bank Holiday this afternoon with litter knee-deep and the smell of deep-fried chips wafting from mobile cafés inscribed EEZI SNAX. An RUC inspector told me that the army reckoned there were some 40,000 on the Field—about 25,000 marchers and the rest enthusiastic followers like myself. In one wired-off corner the Brits had set up a discreet observation post but this was a mere formality; over today's proceedings there was no shadow of even the possibility of Trouble.

To end my account of the Twelfth on this note would be agreeable but not, alas! realistic. One can't all the time overlook the deeper implications of the Orangemen's festival because what is said from the platforms on the various Fields can be of crucial importance for Northern Ireland. True, I counted only 118 people out of some 40,000 listening to the speeches at Edenderry today. But the thousands who were not listening are, by the mere fact of being Orangemen, more or less amenable to the influence of their leaders when political crises arise. And today's speakers had the sort of minds that make even the Roman Curia seem progressive.

The guest speaker was Mr Thomas Orr, the Scottish Grand Master, who made predictable noises about a recent rumour that Prince Charles was contemplating marriage with a Roman Catholic. Should any such unlikely thing happen, said Mr Orr, the Prince would have to abdicate. There could be no question of constitutional changes to allow a Roman Catholic to sit on the throne of England. The Orange Order would not permit it. But Mr Orr added that he didn't think it likely the Queen would ever agree to such a marriage; the whole thing was probably no more than sly kite-flying on the part of the Vatican.

Mr Thomas Passmore, County Grand Master for Belfast, stood up next. He reminded us of the Orangeman's Christian duties, and his obligation to uphold civil and religious liberty for all, and then we were told that the Order is just as determined as in 1912 not to have anything to do with Home Rule. "British we are!" cried Mr Passmore. "And British we stay!" He added that without Ulster the UK would cease to exist and the Union Jack would become 'a useless rag'.

Mr Passmore was followed by Sir George Clark, Past Grand Master of the Grand Orange Lodge of Ireland and once a powerful member of the Unionist Party Standing Committee. His cultivated voice contrasted sharply with the previous speakers' tones but his sentiments were True Blue. He began by referring to 'another country' (guess where!) which is organising a campaign to destroy Ulster and which only a few days ago claimed jurisdiction over Northern Ireland because its constitution claims ownership of the whole island. Then he warned us about the present administration's dangerous ten-

dency to placate enemies of the state by giving them the opportunity to pursue their objectives freely in other, 'more civilian'
ways. (A curious turn of phrase.) He emphasised that it is not
enough to defeat the IRA. Their supporters (i.e., Catholics)
must be prevented from gaining any foothold in administrative
bodies, in housing, in hospitals, in building contracts, in planning, in grasping and monopolising jobs and fringe benefits and
positions of influence and power. I can quote the exact words
with which Sir George concluded this typical Orange oration:
"We want to see the enemies of Britain defeated, not only in
a military sense but in all their efforts to forward their greedy,
destructive and immoral policies." In brief, however many
Offices of Fair Employment the misguided British may set up
there must be 'No Surrender!' on the point of job discrimination.

Eighteen years ago, in 1959, the Young Unionists organised
a political school at Portstewart. Sir Clarence Graham, chairman of the Standing Committee, then said that he would like
to see Roman Catholics not only joining the Unionist Party but
being selected as candidates for Parliament. He was vigorously
supported by the Attorney-General, Mr Brian Maginess, but
within a week Sir George Clark had made it very clear that
the Orange Order would never agree to Roman Catholics being
accepted as members of the Unionist Party much less as parliamentary candidates. He was backed by Lord Brookeborough
and many other Unionist/Orange leaders; none of them could
see the wisdom of drawing into the Unionist Party that new
generation of educated, moderate young Catholics who were
no longer dreaming of a United Ireland. Nor could the Order
see—they still can't—how hypocritical they look in the eyes of
the world when they demand 'democratic' rule for Ulster, and
claim to be 'British', while excluding, on religious grounds,
more than one-third of the population from membership of the
only political party that could ever win an election in Northern
Ireland.

The North might be a much happier place today had
Clarence Graham and Brian Maginess been victorious in 1959.
And the Unionist Party, too, might be in a healthier state. Now
it has split into five parties, each of which deeply distrusts the

others, and it seems unlikely ever to be reunited. But this is probably a good thing. John Harbinson, one of the North's most astute political commentators, has remarked that it may only be through the destruction of the Unionist Party that the Ulster problem can be permanently solved. He might have added— 'and the Orange Order'. But in fact the Party and the Order have been so closely intertwined for so long that the disintegration of the former must inevitably—and perhaps quite soon— bring about the collapse of the latter as a political force. But not, I hope, as a folk-tradition. No one could wish for the Orange drums to be silenced and the banners forever folded. Our world has little enough left of colour and pageantry. We can't afford to lose the Twelfth.

13th July

Last night, while having supper (and several not-so-wee-ones) with 'my' Lodge, I mentioned that I was going to Scarva today. "Nobody bothers with *that*", was the immediate reaction. "It'll seem terrible dull after the Twalfth." I had been told the same thing by several on the Edenderry Field; no one I met yesterday had ever been to Scarva, or wished to go, and I sensed an undercurrent of rivalry. To the Belfast Orangeman there is only one March and he argues that to draw the crowds Scarva's 'imitation' has to be reinforced by a sham fight. This, however, is not true. Scarva is an Event in its own right and musically much more impressive than the Twelfth. But it is also far less pleasant. The sham fight sets the tone and the sectarian basis of the festivities is not so easy to ignore. Perhaps The Troubles have accentuated this; Scarva village is on the edge of the Murder Triangle where so many members of the security forces have been killed by Provos and so many Catholics have been killed by Protestants.

The Twelfth is the Orangemen's day but the Thirteenth is the Blackmen's. For an analysis of the Blackmen's position within the Orange Order see Tony Gray's *The Orange Order*; the Order is such a curious and complex institution that my readers could only be further confused were I to try to disentangle Black from Orange in a paragraph. So I shall confine myself to saying that between 50 per cent and 60 per cent of

Orangemen belong to the Imperial Grand Black Chapter of the British Commonwealth. (This does not mean that they originated south of the Sahara, though in fact the Orange Order does have fifteen Loyal Orange Lodges in Ghana with not a white man among them. These were founded by nineteenth century Ulster missionaries and there is something very piquant about the notion of innocent Ghanaians having been drawn into this weirdly primitive white man's cult.) You can't become Black unless you are already Orange and when Tony Gray asked a prominent Blackman why 13 July is the Blackmen's day he was told, "Well, in the streets of Belfast there's a saying that on the Twalfth the Orangemen goes out and kills the Papishes and on the Thirteenth the Blacks ates them." A funny joke—unless you happen to be a Northern Catholic when the humour of it somehow eludes you.

Beside me in the bus from Belfast sat a middle-aged County Cavan Orangeman who has been working in Belfast for the past twenty years and never misses Scarva because "The bands are so good". They are, too. The cream of Northern Ireland's musicians go to Scarva because there they do not have to compete with brash bands from every corner of every Protestant ghetto in Belfast.

Scarva village—population 240—practically disappears on 13 July. Today an estimated 30,000 men, women and children swarmed all over it as they made their way to and from the Field in front of Scarva House; and all around, in recently cut hay meadows, thousands of parked cars glinted in the sun. King Billy is said to have camped under an old oak tree in the grounds of Scarva House, on his way from Carrickfergus to the Boyne, and in the courtyard the famous Sham Fight takes place. Uncertainty surrounds its origins. The official Orange historian insists that it commemorates a faction fight which took place in 1672; many Scarva people believe it commemorates a skirmish at nearby Lisnagade in 1783 between Protestant Peep o' Day Boys and Catholic Hearts of Steel; others say it commemorates a fight between Protestants who were celebrating the victory of the Boyne on its first anniversay in 1691 and Catholics who attacked them. All that really matters, however, is that it commemorates another victory of Orange over Green. During the nineteenth century similar annual sham fights were staged in several Northern towns and villages; there was even one in Bandon, Co Cork, which then had an exceptionally numerous Protestant population.

For thirty years Charles Whitten, a publican (King James), and Charles Dillon, a motor mechanic (King William), have been acting in the pageant. Both are Scarva born and bred and the four horses come from the stable of a Scarva farmer. Almost everybody involved belongs to the local Sir Alfred Buller Memorial Royal Black Preceptory No. 1000 (including perhaps the horses: by now nothing would surprise me about the Orange Order) and this RBP is responsible for many of the Thirteenth arrangements—which annually become more complicated as the Scarva festival grows in popularity. The bands are the real attraction; although the Sham Fight is given so much publicity it is not in fact great entertainment.

Today the throngs crowding around the courtyard made it hard to see exactly what went on but I glimpsed enough of the half-heartedly scuffling 'armies', brandishing wooden 'swords', to realise that this ritual, marking the humiliation of Catholics, is a dying tradition—and one for which there will be few mourners outside the Orange Order. William and Schomberg, wearing orange-red uniforms, and James and Sarsfield, wearing emerald green, duelled on horseback while their infantry fired at the flags taking care never to damage Williams's. After some forty-five boring minutes the Jacobean flag was shot to bits and James was led from the courtyard, his head hanging with shame, by the proudly triumphant William.

The Blackmen seem to be even better organisers than the Orangemen. On the Field today numerous marquees had been set up by various Preceptories and sit-down luncheons or light refreshments were being served at non-profit-making prices. Many tents, stalls and side-shows added to the carnival air while evangelical literature and impassioned open-air preaching were freely available every hundred yards. Some picnicking families had crates of beer beside them; when I enviously enquired about its source I was offered a bottle and told that outside Scarva House grounds several marquees were selling every sort of booze.

Officially the Blackmen disapprove of alcohol but the first pub-marquee I entered was jam-packed with dehydrated marchers all looking frightfully respectable in dark suits, bowler-hats, black cuffs, black collarettes decorated with elaborate silver emblems and Masonic aprons suitably embellished. The Blackmen who march at Scarva seem much more middle-class than the average Belfast Orangeman and the majority still dress very formally.

While fighting my way towards the bar I got into conversation with a member of one of the RBPs and outside the 'pub' we sat on the grass together to put the world to rights over our beer. Sam was about my own age, with three teenage children, and we discussed Child Rearing in the Mordern World and found ourselves in perfect agreement on the subject. Then we considered the not unrelated topic of security in Northern Ireland and Sam said, "I'd bring back hanging; it's the only way to get rid of terrorists. D'you know it costs £80 a week to keep a prisoner? Why should we spend that on murderers and bombers and thugs when there's good folk going hungry in Ulster? If I knew for certain sure a man was a murderer I'd go out myself with my own gun and shoot him dead—because I know we haven't a decent God-fearing government with enough guts to string him up. And the Lord wouldn't blame me for doing the right thing. When two soldiers was murdered and the RUC couldn't *prove* cases against certain chaps they told the UVF who those chaps were and that got them looked after. When you've a rotten weak government like them fellas at Westminster you have to defend your own community."

Sam was not afraid to speak out thus to a stranger because he believed he was right. He had a kindly, honest, strong face; clearly he was not a vicious man but an affectionate, responsible husband and father; a solid citizen who would always pay his bills, tell the truth, be kind to his neighbours and never injure an innocent person. Yet I can easily believe that in certain circumstances he would indeed go out and kill a Provo who had himself killed. And the papers would report the deed as 'another sectarian murder' though Sam would see it as 'doing his duty'. I looked at him in silence—and for a wild moment wondered if he was right. Have we become too soft, too swayed by sentimental considerations of people's exonerating motives, too concerned with the letter rather than the spirit of the law? Certainly I can feel more respect for Sam's attitude than for the attitude of policemen who reckon it's a good idea to keep the conviction figures up by forcing people to confess to crimes they never committed.

This conversation was yet another example of how temperamentally akin are Northern Ireland's Protestants and Catholics on certain fundamental points. Both have a marked tendency to make their own rules when the Powers That Be seem to them unjust or inadequate. Dissatisfied Catholics maintain that they must fight the Brits because the Northern minority is being oppressed—even though it is being oppressed not by Britain but by the Northern majority. And dissatisfied Protestants argue themselves into believing it right to assist the inept security forces by personally eliminating individuals known to be a threat to law and order. The longer I spend in Northern Ireland the more topsy-turvy it seems.

14

Not Without Hope

During the past year I have often protested that this book is not about politics—that I don't understand political manœuvrings—that I detest the hypocrisy that seems to infect even the most admirable politicians. Yet meanwhile I have been discovering that one cannot feel deeply about the North without spontaneously arriving at quasi-political conclusions or at least having quasi-political emotions.

More than ten years ago M. W. Heslinga discerned within both Northern tribes 'a sense of regional fellowship, a sense of difference from Southerners, that mixture of contempt and defensiveness that is typical of the strongly-marked provincial character'. Since then this sense of regional fellowship has been strengthened by the horrors the Northerners have been sharing even while they have been inflicting them on each other's communities. My own conviction now is that Northern Ireland has already become as 'separate' from both the UK and the rest of Ireland as England and Scotland are from the Republic. These historical processes do not always wait on the decisions of politicians; they sometimes go their own way at their own pace, leaving the politicians to catch up with them as best they may. Frequently a new consciousness of their 'Northern Irish identity' has to struggle in Northern minds and hearts against inherited hardline Orange or Green attitudes—like a rose trying to grow through a tangle of nettles and thistles. But we can take comfort from the fact that this consciousness does exist and is slowly becoming more widespread.

Yet an increasingly provincial outlook can provoke only modified rapture; while useful as an antidote to sectarianism it is scarcely the healthiest or most normal collective attitude for any European society in the 1970s. Luckily, however, there are tiny signs that it is beginning to be counterbalanced in Northern Ireland by the European Idea, which to outsiders has already made both the partition of Ireland and the complete separation of the Republic from the UK seem rather ridiculous. That same European Idea is no doubt partly responsible for the fact that we in the South are now far less 'trying to be Gaelic' than we were during my childhood. Many of us have implicitly accepted the fact that an 800-year-old relationship—however unhappy during some of its phases—cannot be ignored and that Britain can never realistically be regarded by Irish people as a 'foreign country'.

The only alternative to deep and drastic re-thinking about Northern Ireland—in both Britain and the Republic, by politicians and ordinary folk alike—is a continuation of the present conflict into the twenty-first century. While everybody holds fast to their traditional ideas, and reacts in traditional ways to the stimulus of violence, there can be no solution. Here a variation on *Noblesse Oblige* comes into the picture. Those of us who have been privileged to grow up in societies free of the peculiar tensions which afflict Northern Ireland have a responsibility to try to help the Northern Irish to find peace—for instance, by encouraging them to think about their problems in new ways.

It is not my intention to sound patronising; by now I feel a great respect as well as a deep affection for the Northern Irish. But we are all in this muddle together, like it or not, and we must help each other to get out of it. The Northern Problem is—one hopes—the last act in that Anglo-Irish tragedy which we have been enacting for centuries past on the stage of our two islands. Now the British and the Southern Irish are bored and impatient. They want the play to end—and who can blame them? It has gone on too long, the plot has become too confusing, it is very expensive to produce and the critics are not impressed. Nevertheless, the British Government is the only authority now constitutionally entitled to rule Northern Ireland and so the British members of the cast have no alternative but to remain on stage. That being so, it is in their own interest to try to follow the plot and thus put themselves in a position to influence its future development.

The role the Dublin Government should now play is obvious to many outside observers. But it is not yet obvious to those of our politicians whose minds are still befogged by traditional prejudices which they prefer to call 'national aspirations'. In the Republic there is at present a fairly general and often relieved acceptance of the fact that events since 1969 have made a United Ireland impossible. Yet to take the honest next step, by holding a referendum to delete Articles 2 and 3 from the Constitution, seemingly overtaxes our leaders' moral courage. Such a momentous decision would inevitably cause a frisson of shock throughout the whole Northern Catholic community and the older moderate Nationalists would feel even more bitterness and disillusion, in relation to the South, than they now do. But shock treatment can be therapeutic when used to wean people off their self-deceptions. Nobody stands to gain, in any way, from any section of the Northern community continuing to dream about a United Ireland. Moreover, the Unionist leaders see no reason why they should ever seriously settle down to negotiate with a government which has nasty expansionist designs on their territory. So from the point of view of soothing the greatest number, and improving the chances of rational discussion and agreement, there is everything to be said for scrapping those Articles.

It is perfectly true, as 'no-change' Southern politicians are wont to point out triumphantly, that many Northern Protestants have never heard of Articles 2 and 3 despite the best efforts of their political and religious leaders. Our Constitution is quite often discussed among writers, academics and crusading liberals but it is not a favourite topic among the farmers of Tyrone, the shopkeepers of Down or the shipyard-workers of East Belfast. Their fears of Southern/Romish domination antedate it by many years and would no doubt survive its changing by many more. But this is no reason for retaining those offensive Articles. As archaic components of the Green Myth, they wonderfully reinforce the Orange Myth—and so prolong the North's agony.

To abandon our territorial claim to the whole island of Ireland may look like caving in, backing down, losing face and all the rest of it. But does that matter? Does it matter if the Unionists/Loyalists/Orangemen seem to have won a round? What is so disgraceful about changing one's aspirations? We do not live in an unchanging world and if a change of aspirations becomes the best way to help people we profess to be so interested in—well then, let's change them. Or is it the land we are chiefly interested in? If we care more about the ownership of the North than about the well-being of its inhabitants, then I suppose it is logical of us to retain Articles 2 and 3. But in that case let's admit that we want more territory and not pretend that we are being loyal to an ideal. Humbug of the most shameless sort, on everybody's part, has done Ireland enough harm already, North and South.

Only one sure prediction can be made about the present Irish Troubles: they will not go away tomorrow, or the day after. No political initiatives or emended legislation or constitutional juggling can bring true peace to Northern Ireland until its people have changed within themselves. Some experts like to tell us that the problem is mainly, or entirely, an economic one. But when talking with the Northern Irish—in their farmyards or shops or pubs or rectories or slum kitchens or country-house drawing-rooms—it seemed to me primarily emotional/ethical/psychological. Therefore the outlook is depressing if one thinks exclusively within the time-scale of individual lives; only the passing of generations can bring about the profound changes that are needed. Yet depression is curiously inappropriate to Northern Ireland today; although it should be a gloomy place it is not. (Often it can be heart-breaking but that is something different.) Amidst all the physical destruction and mental distress there is an enormous amount of creative energy at work. The essential changes are unmistakably under way and there are exciting vibrations of hope in the atmosphere. Increasingly I tend to view The Troubles as a painful purge that had to be endured by a diseased society as a prelude to a happier era than the North has ever known before.

Not nearly enough attention is paid to the progress that has been made within the past decade. Since 1969 we have seen the collapse of an undemocratic system of government, the disintegration of a blatantly sectarian political party, the weakening of the Orange Order, the abolition of the B Specials, the extraordinary proliferation of small community groups which are involving more and more people in the improvement of

their own living conditions, the birth of the Alliance Party and
the Social Democratic and Labour Party—neither of which is
hung up on traditional prejudice—and the recognition by
many in both tribes of the fact that they belong together as
neither belongs to Britain or the Republic. We have even seen
a public expression of this budding unity during the brief glory
of the early Peace Marches. The effect of the Peace People's
thinking and feeling against violence must not be overlooked
however little confidence is now generally felt in the Movement
as an organisation. Thought and emotion have their own force.

Last week a friend called to see me and said anxiously,
"Aren't you almost finished your book? You won't have to go
up there any more, will you?" To which I replied, "I won't
have to go up there any more, but I'll *want* to—and often."
The Northern Irish may not be comprehensible but they are
very addictive.

AUTHOR'S NOTE

It gives me great pleasure to acknowledge the generosity of the American Irish Foundation, from whom I received their Literary Award in 1975.

AUTHOR'S NOTE

Bibliography

Discover Northern Ireland: Ernest Sandford, N.I. Tourist Board (1976).
The Making of Modern Ireland: 1603–1923: J. C. Beckett, Faber (1966).
The Shaping of Modern Ireland: edited Conor Cruise O'Brien, Routledge (1960).
Prejudice and Tolerance in Ulster: Rosemary Harris, Manchester University Press (1972).
The Ulster Crisis: A. T. Q. Stewart, Faber (1967).
The Ulster Debate: Various, Bodley Head (1972).
The Ulster Question: T. W. Moody, Mercier Press (1974).
Divided Ulster: Liam de Paor, Pelican (1970).
Peace in Ulster: David Bleakley, Mowbrays (1970).
The Great Fraud of Ulster: T. M. Healy, Anvil Books (1971).
The Protestants of Ulster: Geoffrey Bell, Pluto Press (1976).
Orangeism: M. W. Dewar, John Brown, S. E. Long, Grand Orange Lodge of Ireland (1967).
The Orange Order: Tony Gray, Bodley Head (1972).
The Ulster Unionist Party: 1882–1973: John F. Harbinson, Blackstaff Press (1974).
The People's Democracy: 1968–73: Paul Arthur, Blackstaff Press (1973).
From the Jungles of Belfast: Denis Ireland, Blackstaff Press (1973).
Yours Till Ireland Explodes, Mr Mooney: Harry Barton, Blackstaff Press (1973).
Yours Again, Mr Mooney: Harry Barton, Blackstaff Press (1974).
Law and State: Kevin Boyle, Tom Hadden, Paddy Hillyard. Martin Robertson (1975).
Faulkner: David Bleakley, Mowbrays (1974).
Paisley: Man of Wrath: Patrick Marrinan, Anvil Books (1973).
The UVF: 1966–73: David Boulton, Torc Books (1973).
The Secret Army: J. Bowyer Bell, Sphere Books (1970).
How Stormont Fell: Henry Kelly, Gill and Macmillan (1972).
The Fall of the N.I. Executive: Paddy Devlin, Kerryman (1975).
The Guinea Pigs: John McGuffin, Penguin (1974).
Towards a New Ireland: Garret Fitzgerald, Torc Books (1972).
States of Ireland: Conor Cruise O'Brien, Panther (1974).
The Northern Ireland Problem: Denis Barritt and Charles Carter, OUP (1972).
Children in Conflict: Morris Fraser, Pelican (1974).
Corrymeela: The Search for Peace: Alf McCreary, Christian Journals (1975).
Violence in Ireland: Various, Veritas and Christian Journals (1976).
Conflict in Northern Ireland: John Darby, Gill and Macmillan (1976).

Minority Report: Jack White, Gill and Macmillan (1975).
Tudor and Stuart Ireland: Margaret MacCurtain, Gill and Macmillan (1972).
Ireland in the Twentieth Century: John A. Murphy, Gill and Macmillan (1975).
No Surrender!: Tony Gray, Macdonald & Janes (1975).
Governing Without Consensus: Richard Rose, Faber (1971).
Northern Ireland: A Time of Choice: Richard Rose, Macmillan (1976).